Vocational Education and Professional Training

Vocational Education and Professional Training

Elena Norris

Larsen & Keller
www.larsen-keller.com

Vocational Education and Professional Training
Elena Norris
ISBN: 978-1-64172-650-4 (Hardback)

Larsen & Keller
Published by Larsen and Keller Education,
5 Penn Plaza,
19th Floor,
New York, NY 10001, USA

Cataloging-in-Publication Data

Vocational education and professional training / Elena Norris.
p. cm.
Includes bibliographical references and index.
ISBN: 978-1-64172-650-4
1. Vocational education. 2. Vocational guidance. 3. Vocational teachers--Training of.
4. Career development. 5. Profession, Choice of. I. Norris, Elena.
LC1043 .V63 2021
370.113--dc23

For more information regarding Larsen and Keller Education and its products, please visit the publisher's website www.larsen-keller.com

Table of Contents

Preface

This book has been written, keeping in view that students want more practical information. Thus, my aim has been to make it as comprehensive as possible for the readers. I would like to extend my thanks to my family and co-workers for their knowledge, support and encouragement all along.

The form of technical education which aims at preparing people for various roles related to a specific occupation, trade or vocation, is known as vocational education. Training under vocational education provides career training for jobs which are based upon practical fields or manuals. This type of education is non-academic. They are mostly provided at post-secondary, higher education and further education level. Under apprenticeship, new generation of practitioners of a profession with on-job training are trained with some classroom work and study. Vocational schools are educational institutions, which are especially designed to provide vocational education and technical skills. Online vocational education is an emerging field, providing education about various trade skills from professionals to those living far. This book provides comprehensive insights into the field of vocational education and training. Such selected concepts that redefine this field have been presented in herein. This textbook aims to serve as a resource guide for students and experts alike and contribute to the growth of the discipline.

A brief description of the chapters is provided below for further understanding:

Chapter - What is Vocational Education?

Vocational education is referred to as career and technical education that prepares individuals to work as a technician, tradesman, artisan, etc. Market driven education, state driven education and occupation driven governance are the three major types of vocational education. This chapter has been carefully written to provide an easy understanding of vocational education.

Chapter - Diverse Aspects of Vocational Education

Some of the diverse aspects of vocational education are open learning education, cooperative education, dual education system, distance education, virtual learning environment, problem-based learning education, etc. This chapter delves into these aspects of vocational education to provide an in-depth understanding of the subject.

Chapter - Learning Styles

There are different learning styles that are used in vocational education such as visual learning, auditory learning, competency-based learning, work-based learning, experiential learning, etc. This chapter closely examines these learning styles of vocational education for a thorough understanding of the subject.

Chapter - Apprenticeship

Apprenticeship is the system of vocational training for preparing a new generation of tradesmen, artisans, technicians, etc. Cognitive apprenticeship, engineering apprenticeship, seaman apprenticeship, degree apprenticeship, higher apprenticeship, etc. fall under its domain. All the concepts related to apprenticeship have been carefully analyzed in this chapter.

Chapter - Types of Vocational School

Vocational school is an educational institution that provides vocational education and technical skills required by the apprentices. Vocational-technical school, music school, drama school, journalism school, etc. are some of its types. All these types of vocational school have been carefully analyzed in this chapter.

Chapter - Various Professions under Vocational Education

Various professions that fall under vocational education are dental laboratory technician, carpentry, technical trainer, electrician, fashion design, photographer, wiremen, welding, embroidery, etc. This chapter has been carefully written to provide an easy understanding of these professions of vocational education.

Elena Norris

1
What is Vocational Education?

Vocational education is referred to as career and technical education that prepares individuals to work as a technician, tradesman, artisan, etc. Market driven education, state driven education and occupation driven governance are the three major types of vocational education. This chapter has been carefully written to provide an easy understanding of vocational education.

Tertiary Education

Tertiary or third level education is referred to as the educational level which lies after post-secondary education. Tertiary education commences after post-secondary or school level education is completed by an individual. These days, the concept of tertiary education isn't rare and is rather considered as a mandatory requirement for anyone who wants to take up a respectable job.

Tertiary education or qualification makes job seekers employable, even though it may not always guarantee success. As soon as a person steps out of school or secondary education, he/she has to choose a tertiary education path which is not just to his/her liking and interests but also guarantees a career ahead. The following is a detailed tertiary education hierarchy to help you understand the various education levels present after schooling:

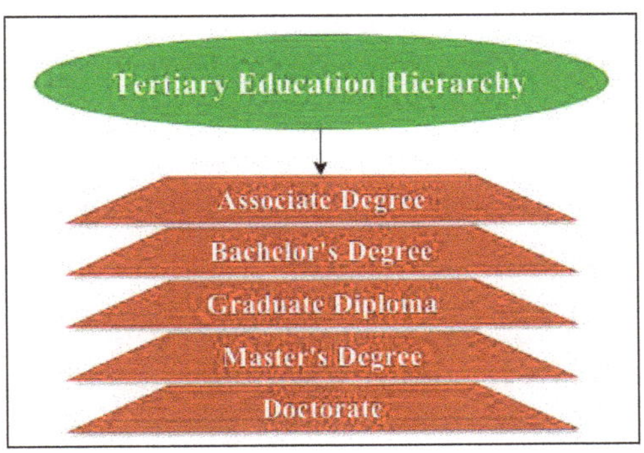

Tertiary education contributes to social and economic development through four major missions:

- The formation of human capital (primarily through teaching).
- The building of knowledge bases (primarily through research and knowledge development).
- The dissemination and use of knowledge (primarily through interactions with knowledge users).
- The maintenance of knowledge (inter-generational storage and transmission of knowledge).

The scope and importance of tertiary education have changed significantly. Over 40 years ago tertiary education, which was more commonly referred to as higher education, was what happened in universities. This largely covered teaching and learning requiring high level conceptual and intellectual skills in the humanities, sciences and social sciences, the preparation of students for entry to a limited number of professions such as medicine, engineering and law and disinterested advanced research and scholarship. These days, tertiary education is much more diversified and encompasses new types of institutions such as polytechnics, university colleges, or technological institutes. These have been created for a number of reasons: to develop a closer relationship between tertiary education and the external world, including greater responsiveness to labour market needs; to enhance social and geographical access to tertiary education; to provide high-level occupational preparation in a more applied and less theoretical way; and to accommodate the growing diversity of qualifications and expectations of school graduates.

As participation in tertiary education has expanded, tertiary education institutions (TEIs) have assumed responsibility for a far wider range of occupational preparation than in the past. As the result of a combination of the increased knowledge base of many occupations and individual's aspirations, not only doctors, engineers and lawyers but also nurses, accountants, computer programmers, teachers, pharmacists, speech therapists and business managers now receive their principal occupational qualifications from a TEI. Furthermore, TEIs are now involved in a wider range of teaching than their traditional degree-level courses. While the extent of such teaching is not large, many examples can be found of TEIs that offer adult education and leisure courses, upper secondary courses to prepare students for tertiary-level study and short specific occupational preparation at sub-degree level. In addition, it has become more common for TEIs not only to engage in teaching and research, but also to provide consultancy services to industry and government and to contribute to national and regional economic and social development.

Substantial reforms are taking place in tertiary education systems mainly aimed at encouraging institutions to be more responsive to the needs of society and the economy. This has involved a reappraisal of the purposes of tertiary education and the setting by governments of new strategies for the future. It has also involved more room of manoeuvre for institutions but with clearer accountability for the institutions to society. The tertiary sector is expected to contribute to equity, ensure quality and operate efficiently.

Main Trends within Tertiary Education

Although not all countries are in the same position, a number of trends within tertiary education emerge.

- Expansion of tertiary education systems: The expansion of tertiary education has been remarkable in recent decades. Globally, in 2004, 132 million students enrolled in tertiary education, up from 68 million in 1991. Average annual growth in tertiary enrolment over the period 1991-2004 stood at 5.1% worldwide.
- Diversification of provision: Expansion of tertiary education was accompanied by a diversification of provision. New institution types emerged, educational offerings within institutions multiplied, private provision expanded and new modes of delivery were introduced.
- More heterogeneous student bodies: The rise of female participation has been the most noteworthy trend affecting the composition of student bodies in tertiary education. A second prominent development is the growing participation of more mature students leading to a rise in the average age of student bodies. In addition, in most countries, tertiary student bodies are increasingly heterogeneous in terms of socio-economic background, ethnicity and previous education.
- New funding arrangements: A number of trends are also discernible in funding arrangements for tertiary education. First, there has been a diversification of funding sources. Second, the allocation of public funding for tertiary education is increasingly characterised by greater targeting of resources, performance-based funding and competitive procedures. Third, a number of countries are expanding their student support systems.
- Increasing focus on accountability and performance: The development of formal quality assurance systems is one of the most significant trends that have affected tertiary education systems during the past few decades. Starting in the early 1980s quality became a key topic in tertiary education policy. The expansion of tertiary education has raised questions about the amount and direction of public expenditure for tertiary education. In addition to fiscal constraints, increased market pressures have also fostered the growing focus on accountability in tertiary education.
- New forms of institutional governance: Over the past few decades important changes have occurred in the leadership of tertiary education institutions, including the emergence of new perspectives on academic leadership and

new ways of organising the decision-making structure. Academic leaders are increasingly seen as managers, coalition-builders or entrepreneurs.

- Global networking, mobility and collaboration: Tertiary education is becoming more internationalised and increasingly involves intensive networking among institutions, scholars, students and with other actors such as industry. International collaborative research has been strengthened by the dense networking between institutions and cross-border funding of research activities.

Main Policy Challenges

In the governance of tertiary education, the ultimate objective of educational authorities as the guardians of public interest is to ensure that public resources are efficiently spent by TEIs to societal purposes. There is the expectation that institutions are to contribute to the economic and social goals of countries. This is a mixture of many demands, such as: quality of teaching and learning defined in new ways including greater relevance to learner and labour market needs; research and development feeding into business and community development; contributing to internationalisation and international competitiveness.

There is a tension between the pursuit of knowledge generation as a self-determined institutional objective and the statement of national priority as defined in the aims and goals of the tertiary system. The objective, from a governance point of view, is then to reconcile the priorities of the individual institutions and the broader social and economic objectives of countries. This entails determining how far the former contributes to the latter as well as clarifying the degree of latitude the institution has in pursuing its own self-established objectives. The main policy challenges are listed in table. Most countries face the challenge of simultaneously raising tertiary education participation rates, improving quality and achieving a sustainable level of financial support. Many countries are also now in a transition from a focus on quantity to a greater emphasis on the quality, coherence and equity of tertiary education.

Table: Main challenges in tertiary education.

Domain Main challenges	Main challenges
Steering tertiary education	Articulating clearly the nation's expectations of the tertiary education system Aligning priorities of individual institutions with the nation's economic and social goals Creating coherent systems of tertiary education Finding the proper balance between governmental steering and institutional autonomy Developing institutional governance arrangements to respond to external expectations
Funding tertiary education	Ensuring the long-term financial sustainability of tertiary education Devising a funding strategy consistent with the goals of the tertiary education system Using public funds efficiently

Quality of tertiary education	Developing quality assurance mechanisms for accountability and improvement Generating a culture of quality and transparency Adapting quality assurance to diversity of offerings
Equity in tertiary education	Ensuring equality of opportunities Devising cost-sharing arrangements which do not harm equity of access Improving the participation of the least represented groups
The role of tertiary education in research and innovation	Fostering research excellence and its relevance Building links with other research organisations, the private sector and industry Improving the ability of tertiary education to disseminate the knowledge it creates
The academic career	Ensuring an adequate supply of academics Increasing flexibility in the management of human resources Helping academics to cope with the new demands
Links with the labour market	Including labour market perspectives and actors in tertiary education policy Ensuring the responsiveness of institutions to graduate labour market outcomes Providing study opportunities for flexible, work-oriented study
Internationalisation of tertiary education	Designing a comprehensive internationalization strategy in accordance with country's needs Ensuring quality across borders Enhancing the international comparability of tertiary education

Main Policy Directions

To meet the challenges outlined above, a number of policy options are suggested across the many facets of tertiary education policy – governance, funding, quality assurance, equity, research and innovation, academic career, links to the labour market and internationalisation. Table summarises the main policy directions. Not all of the policy directions apply equally to all 24 countries participating. In a number of cases many, or most, of the policy suggestions are already in place, while for other countries they may have less relevance because of different social, economic and educational structures and traditions. This is a challenging agenda, but tackling one area without appropriate policy attention to inter-related aspects will lead to only partial results. Nevertheless, it is difficult to address all areas simultaneously and resource constraints mean that trade-offs are inevitable.

Steering Tertiary Education: Setting the Right Course

- Develop a coherent strategic vision for tertiary education.
- Establish sound instruments for steering tertiary education.
- Ensure the coherence of the tertiary education system with extensive diversification.

- Build system linkages.
- Strengthen the ability of institutions to align with the national tertiary education strategy.
- Build consensus over tertiary education policy.

Matching Funding Strategies with National Priorities

- Develop a funding strategy that facilitates the contribution of the tertiary system to society and the economy.
- Use cost-sharing between the State and students as the principle to shape the funding of tertiary education.
- Publicly subsidise tertiary programmes in relation to the benefits they bring to society.
- Make institutional funding for instruction formula-driven, related to both input and output indicators and including strategically targeted components.
- Improve cost-effectiveness.
- Back the overall funding approach with a comprehensive student support system.

Assuring and Improving Quality

- Design a quality assurance framework consistent with the goals of tertiary education.
- Develop a strong quality culture in the system and put more stress on internal quality assurance mechanisms.
- Commit external quality assurance to an advisory role as the system gains maturity but retain strong external components in certain contexts.
- Align quality assurance processes to the particular profile of TEIs.
- Avoid fragmentation of the quality assurance organisational structure.

Achieving Equity

- Assess extent and origin of equity issues.
- Strengthen the integration of planning between secondary and tertiary education systems.
- Consider positive discrimination policies for particular groups whose prior educational disadvantage is well identified.

- Provide incentives for TEIs to widen participation and provide extra support for students from disadvantaged backgrounds.

Enhancing the Role of Tertiary Education in Research and Innovation

- Improve knowledge diffusion rather than strengthening commercialisation via stronger IPRs.
- Improve and widen channels of interaction and encourage inter-institutional collaboration.
- Use the tertiary education sector to foster the internationalisation of R&D.
- Broaden the criteria used in research assessments.
- Ensure the shift towards project-based funding is monitored and provide a mix of funding mechanisms.

Academic Career: Adapting to Change

- Give institutions ample autonomy over the management of human resources.
- Reconcile academic freedom with institutions' contributions to society.
- Improve the entrance conditions of young academics.
- Develop mechanisms to support the work of academics.

Strengthening Ties with the Labour Market

- Coordinate labour market and education policies.
- Improve data and analysis about graduate labour market outcomes.
- Strengthen career services at secondary and tertiary educational levels.
- Enhance provision with a labour market orientation.
- Include labour market perspectives and actors in policy development and institutional governance.

Shaping Internationalization Strategies in the National Context

- Develop a national strategy and comprehensive policy framework for internationalization.
- Improve national policy coordination.

- Encourage TEIs to become proactive actors of internationalization.
- Create structures to promote the national tertiary education system.
- Develop on-campus internationalization.

Implementing Tertiary Education Policy

- Establish ad-hoc independent committees to initiate tertiary education reforms and involve stakeholders.
- Allow for bottom-up policy initiatives to be developed into proposals by independent committees.
- Recognise the different views of stakeholders through iterative policy development.
- Favour incremental reforms over comprehensive overhauls unless there is wide public support for change.

Common Policy Themes

Despite the major differences and traditions across countries, they share some common policy priorities.

Establishing a Grand Vision for Tertiary Education

A first priority for countries should be to develop a comprehensive and coherent vision for the future of tertiary education, to guide future policy development over the medium and long term in harmony with national social and economic objectives. Ideally, it should result from a systematic national strategic review of tertiary education and entail a clear statement of the strategic aims. It would also require reflection, debate and consensus-building. A representative body could help reconcile the diverging interests of different stakeholders – government, institutions, students, teaching staff and scientific community, private sector and civil society – by having them work together towards recommendations for the medium and long term strategy for tertiary education.

The success of tertiary education also depends on policies across a range of governmental areas. Inter-ministerial bodies that link education officials to public authorities with responsibility for complementary lines of policy such as immigration, science and technology and labour market policies can play an important role in widening and regularising policy consultation within government.

Extensive and flexible diversification may provide countries with a wider capacity to address varied national needs – in terms of research and innovation, the development of a skilled workforce, social inclusion and regional development – than a system of limited and fixed diversification. Thus, countries might want to assess how much diversification, of what sort and in which regions is best-suited to meet the strategic goals of the system. The mission and profile of individual institutions would need to be clearly defined in accordance with this diversification strategy. There is no single model or best approach to devising a system of tertiary education with extensive levels of diversification. In particular, a diverse system of tertiary education can be conceived either with distinct institutional sectors or within a single institutional type.

Ensuring that the Capabilities of Tertiary Education Contribute to Countries' Economic and Social Objectives

In all of the sets of policy suggestions strong emphasis is placed on the need to ensure an outward focus of tertiary systems and TEIs. This entails strong educational links to employers, regions and labour markets; effective university-industry links for research and innovation; participation of external stakeholders in system and institutional governance and in quality assurance; a significant share of external funds in institutional budgets; and a broad internationalisation policy portfolio.

One simple way to encourage institutions to more deliberately contribute to the goals of the tertiary system would be for the tertiary education authorities to require all institutions in receipt of public funding to prepare and regularly update, meaningful strategic plans aligned with the national tertiary education strategy. It would also be important to review options to widen the scope of institutional autonomy so as to allow for greater responsiveness (to students, stakeholders, regions) and efficiency in operations. At the same time, the national policy towards institutional governance needs to allow institutions to make the most of their autonomy and new responsibilities. It would be important to establish a legal framework that provides them with the opportunity to establish a local governing body which would operate at a strategic (as opposed to scientific) level, would comprise internal and external stakeholders and would be supported by a senior management group.

Despite the policy attention on the commercialisation of university R&D results in recent years, methods and instruments to support the diffusion capabilities and interactive support activities of tertiary institutions deserve closer policy consideration. Linkages and collaboration between the tertiary education sector and other actors in the research and innovation system need to be further developed, with the aim of improving knowledge diffusion. The tertiary education sector should be flexible and responsive to industry needs in terms of co-operative projects and policy needs to ensure that small and medium-sized enterprises (SMEs) and firms from all technological sectors are considered when programmes are designed.

Academic freedom has been, according to some groups, under threat as a result of a number of trends within tertiary education. At the same time, institutions are under pressure to use public funds to the benefit of society as a whole. This calls, in most countries, for a re-conceptualisation of what comprises academic work. In this context, academic freedom needs to be framed within institutions' obligation to society, e.g. with academics pursuing their objectives while accounting for institutional goals, being provided with support and conditions to meet these goals. Academics also ought to have autonomy in the design of the courses they teach and freedom to select research topics and approaches to research – possibly within priorities defined at the institution or system level. They should not be constrained in their interpretation of research results or prevented from publicising them; this greater freedom ought to go together with greater accountability for the outcomes of their academic activities.

Devising Sound Instruments for Steering Tertiary Education

As tertiary education authorities divest some responsibilities such as the direct administration of academic institutions and take on others in terms of policy steering and performance evaluation, they need to change their competencies and organisation. An evaluation of their staff expertise and current skill needs may be useful to identify potential mismatches and to develop professional development and training programmes to keep pace with changing demands. Instruments could be developed for steering that achieve accountability and also permit wide scope for institutional autonomy. Possible ways of meeting these two goals and optimise outcomes in the areas of quality, efficiency and system responsiveness include, for example, instruments such as performance contracts or performance-related funding and the collection and dissemination of more and better information, for system monitoring, policy development and information to stakeholders.

Government control and oversight is not the only means to steer the behaviour of educational institutions – and in some instances may not be the best. Depending upon national circumstances, governments may wish to evaluate how they may strategically use institutional competition and student choice as a means to achieve stronger performance from their tertiary system. This may be achieved by recognising new types of institutions, allowing the portability of institutional subsidies and student support, strengthening credit transfer and articulation arrangements to foster mobility between institutions and improving the availability of information about quality to prospective students.

Developing a Funding Strategy that Facilitates the Contribution of the Tertiary Education System to Society and the Economy

The overarching foundation for any funding strategy is that public funds steer the tertiary education system in a way that facilitates its contribution to society and the economy. A guiding basis is to design a funding approach to meet the policy goals sought for the tertiary education system – e.g. expansion, quality, cost effectiveness, equity, institutional or system capacity – which differ across countries at a given point in time.

A number of principles should govern the funding of tertiary education. To begin with, there are good arguments to support cost-sharing between the State and students (and their families). In light of the evidence of the private benefits of a tertiary degree, graduates could bear some of the cost of the services offered by tertiary institutions. The case is stronger when limitations in the public funding of tertiary education lead to either the rationing of the number of students, the decline of instructional quality (as a result of declining expenditure per student), or the limited availability of funds for supporting disadvantaged groups.

Another basis for funding tertiary education is the principle of allocating public funds in relation to the relevance to society at large. In ideal terms this would translate into the public funding of activities which generate educational externalities to the benefit of society as whole – irrespective of the nature of the provider – and levels of public funding which reflect the magnitude of educational externalities relative to private benefits.

Another fundamental pillar is a comprehensive student support system. It facilitates access by reducing liquidity constraints faced by students. A mixed system of grants and loans would assist students in covering tuition fees and living costs, alleviating excessive hours spent on part-time work, or disproportionate reliance on family support. In many countries student support systems need to be expanded, diversified and to place extra emphasis on the financial need of students.

Finally, the criteria for the distribution of funds to institutions need to be clear to all. This is best achieved through a transparent formula which shields allocation decisions from political pressures and tailors incentives to shape institutional plans in harmony with national goals. The basis for allocating "core" funding to institutions – in particular that related to instruction – should to some extent be output-oriented to support excellence in teaching and learning. However, performance-based funding mechanisms should be carefully implemented to avoid undesired effects.

Emphasizing Quality and Relevance

It is important, in order to build a national commitment to quality, that the aim of the quality assurance system be clear and expectations be formulated in alignment with the tertiary education strategy. A well co-ordinated quality assurance system might be expected to ensure that: each student is provided with quality and relevant education; the overall system is contributing to the social and economic development of the country; TEIs' activities foster equity of access and outcomes; quality assurance contributes to the improvement of co-ordination within and integration of the overall tertiary system. There is also a balance to be struck between accountability and quality improvement. From an accountability point of view, it is important that quality assurance systems provide information to various stakeholders but quality assurance also needs to be/ become a mechanism to enhance quality rather than simply force compliance with bureaucratic requirements.

A strong quality culture in TEIs – shared by the academic leadership, staff and students – helps to reinforce the quality assurance system. To a large extent, this attention to maintaining and improving academic standards builds up over-time. However, evidence suggests that a strong quality culture may also develop as a result of public intervention, e.g. through the creation of internal quality assurance systems by TEIs or in response to appropriate incentives such as publishing student evaluations of their learning experience.

The development of the quality assurance system needs to be seen as an ongoing process. Whilst there is a clear need and rationale for external quality monitoring during the early stages of development to fulfil the need for accountability and ensure that baseline standards of quality are met throughout the system, this rationale is likely to fade over time. It would therefore be important – once baseline standards are met – that external quality assurance evolves towards an advisory role to enhance improvement.

The approach to ensuring relevance to society should also be closely interconnected with quality assurance mechanisms, since low-quality programmes are, for example, unlikely to be relevant to the labour market. Thus for an approach based on relevance to be successful, a robust system of quality assurance needs to be in place.

Raising the Profile of Equity within National Tertiary Policy Agendas

Clearly, issues of equity in tertiary education in many countries need to become more prominent in national debates and policy making. A coherent and systematic approach to equity would, in the first instance, assess where equity problems arise: whether they are related to income constraints faced by families and insufficient student support, inequity of opportunities at the school level, admissions issues, or other barriers such as the lack of knowledge about the benefits of tertiary education. This requires the systematic collection of data to inform the development of appropriate policies to reduce inequalities in tertiary education, e.g. the socioeconomic background of the tertiary student population, completion rates by family background, regional flow of students, student's part-time work, or the social and economic conditions of student life.

Key ingredients in an equity agenda include career guidance and counselling services at the school level, the integration of planning between secondary and tertiary education systems, opportunities for tertiary education study from any track in upper secondary school, a varied supply of tertiary education to accommodate a more diverse set of learners, alternative types of provision to account for the cultural diversity of the population, the expansion of distance learning and regional learning centres, positive discrimination policies for particular groups whose prior educational disadvantage is well identified and incentives for TEIs to widen participation and provide extra support for students from disadvantaged backgrounds.

Positioning National Systems in the International Arena

The background for internationalisation varies considerably across countries according to their economic and political power, size and geographic location, dominant culture, the quality and typical features of their tertiary education system, the role their language plays internationally, as well as their previous internationalisation policies. In this context, it is important for countries to develop a national strategy or master plan for internationalisation in light of their country-specific goals in the tertiary education sector, but also beyond education (human resources development, research and innovation etc.).

Obviously, this strategy needs to adapt to country-specific circumstances, building upon natural advantages and acknowledging constraints and there is no ideal internationalisation strategy other than maximising the benefits of internationalisation in the national context.

While the national/sector level has an important influence on the international dimension of tertiary education through policy steering, funding, programmes, regulatory frameworks and cross-departmental policy coordination, internationalisation activities are pursued at the institutional level and within TEIs at the discipline level. Given the diversity of TEIs, the principal potentials for national policy lie more in creating the framework conditions for them to become proactive actors of internationalisation, through interventions designed to remove blockages, by granting more autonomy to TEIs to make them more responsive to their external environment, or by including a special internationalisation strategy in the annual negotiations between the tertiary education authorities and TEIs as a way to promote their engagement in international cooperation and exchange. Government authorities also have a role to play to steer institutional strategies in directions that are sustainable over time in order to protect the sector and achieve the goals set in the national strategy. Greater sustainability of internationalization strategies can be achieved by promoting the diversification of international activities.

Policy initiatives and institutions' efforts should also be targeted at the development of on-campus internationalisation, in recognition that only a small proportion of students take part in international mobility. This can be done by allowing and encouraging institutions to deliver part of their programmes in foreign languages and to intensify international enrolments in order to widen the scope for intercultural exchanges oncampus.

Implementing Policy Successfully

The process of policy design involves a number of challenges to yield sound results. Ideally, policy would need to be based upon informed policy diagnosis, drawn on best practice, backed up by adequate research evidence and consistent – both intrinsically and with policies in other areas of public action. Of equal importance is consensus-building among the various stakeholders involved – or with an interest – in tertiary education.

In order to build consensus, it is important that all stakeholders see proposed tertiary education policies within the broader policy framework and strategy. Indeed, individuals and groups are more likely to accept changes that are not necessarily in their own best interests if they understand the reasons for these changes and can see the role they should play within the broad national strategy. There is therefore much scope for government authorities to foster the chances of successful policy implementation, by improving communication on the long-term vision of what is to be accomplished for tertiary education as the rationale for proposed reform packages.

Other possible approaches for successful policy implementation include the use of pilots and policy experimentation when needed, favouring incremental reforms over comprehensive overhauls unless there is wide public support for change, avoiding reforms with concentrated costs and diffused benefits, identifying potential losers from tertiary education reform and building in compensatory mechanisms and improving communication on the benefits of reforms and the costs of inaction.

General Education

General Education is the program of education that typically developing children should receive, based on state standards and evaluated by the annual state educational standards test. It is the preferred way of describing its synonym, "regular education." It is preferred because the term "regular" connotes that children receiving special education services are somehow "irregular."

General Education is now the default position since the passage of the reauthorization of IDEA, now called IDEIA (The Individuals with Disabilities Education Improvement Act). All children should spend a significant amount of time in a general education classroom, unless it is in the best interest of the child, or because the child is a danger to him/herself or others. The amount of time a child spends in the general education program is part of his or her Placement.

Once again, General Education is the curriculum designed for all children which is meant to meet state standards, or if adopted, the Common Core State Standards. The General Education program is also the program which the state's annual test, required by NCLB (No Child Left Behind,) is designed to evaluate.

IEP's and "Regular" Education

In order to provide FAPE for special education students, IEP goals should be "aligned" with the Common Core State Standards. In other words, they should show that a student is being taught to the standards. In some cases, with children whose disabilities are severe, IEP's will reflect a more "functional" program, which will be very loosely aligned with the Common Core State Standards, rather than directly linked to specific grade level standards. These students are most often in self-contained programs. They are also the most likely to be part of the three percent of students allowed to take an alternate test.

Unless students are in the most restrictive environments, they will spend some time in the regular education environment. Often, children in self-contained programs will participate in "specials" such as physical education, art and music with students in the "regular" or "general" education programs. When assessing the amount of time spent in regular education (part of the IEP report) time spent with typical students in the lunchroom and on the playground for recess is also credited as time in the "general education" environment.

Testing

Until more states eliminate testing, participation in high stakes state tests aligned to the standards is required of special education students. This is meant to reflect how the student performs alongside their regular education peers. States are also permitted to require that students with severe disabilities are offered an alternate assessment, which should address the state standards. These are required by Federal Law, in the ESEA (Elementary and Secondary education act) and in IDEIA. Only 1 percent of all students are allowed to take an alternate test and this should represent 3 percent of all students receiving special education services.

Vocational Education

Vocational education is the instruction intended to equip persons for industrial or commercial occupations. It may be obtained either formally in trade schools, technical secondary schools, or in on-the-job training programs or, more informally, by picking up the necessary skills on the job.

Vocational education in schools is a relatively modern development. Until the 19th century such education, except for the professions, was provided only by apprenticeship. This situation was partly due to the low social status associated with such instruction as opposed to a classical curriculum, which was considered "necessary for a gentleman." With the growth of industrialization during the 19th century, however, several European countries, notably Germany, began introducing vocational education in elementary and secondary schools. In Great Britain, however, opposition to vocational education persisted into the 20th century, although a few trade and junior technical schools were established by local authorities before World War II. By the late 19th century public (common) school vocational education in the United States consisted of manual training and practical arts. These programs were gradually expanded until 1917 when federal aid was provided to public schools for trade and industrial, agricultural and homemaking courses.

After World War II the demand for trained paraprofessionals in the relatively new fields of computer science, electronics and medical services led to an increased interest in short-term postsecondary specialized training programs in these areas as an alternative to a traditional college education.

Features of Vocational Education and Training

VET from an Epistemological and Pedagogical Didactical Perspective

Vocational education's identity is rooted in distinctive knowledge production, representation, use and transfer, which can be associated with distinctive ways of teaching and learning. There is a certain canon among VET researchers in this respect, starting with referring to the distinction Aristotle made in the Nichomachean Ethics between episteme (pure science), techne (art or applied science) and phronesis (prudence or practical wisdom), the latter two forming the backbone of a theoretical foundation of VET. From an epistemological point of view, Researchers could summarise these accounts as 'tacit knowing view' as opposed to a 'cognitive view'. A cognitive view would understand knowledge as information and emphasise that it is mainly explicit (know-that), abstract, standardised and impersonal. Such a view would argue that knowledge is mainly produced by scientific disciplines and applied in practice. For such knowledge, teacher-centred learning would be most efficient, as teaching is seen as an offer of structured information to be processed by students. The learning result is also explicit knowledge (rules, theories), which can be tested by paper and pencil. In contrast the tacit knowing view understands knowledge as experience and emphasises that knowledge is mainly practical (know-how, skills), implicit, personal and situational. Learning means making practical experience (learning by doing) and is seen as a social process that happens through socialisation in communities of practice. Teaching mainly means to create the learning environment in which students can gain experience.

Although often referred to as a particular feature of VET, Researchers can find tacit knowing views in some contexts traditionally not associated with it this may be problem-based and case-study learning in practice-oriented higher education programmes or learning in a Montessori school or in organisational learning. In the European policy discussion increasing attention has been given to the term 'work-based learning' in recent years. This is related to the fact that formal systems of vocational education and training that integrate extended phases of practical learning within the company seem successful in integrating young people into the labour market. However, here it is important to point out that work-based learning is primarily a specific way of organizing learning, which can be realised in either of the two views. The tacit knowing view would assume that certain dispositions could not be learned in any other context than practice itself. In any case, learning in practice or work-based learning is an essential feature of a modern understanding of VET.

The distinction between the tacit knowing view and the cognitive view is also important with regards to a concept often used in close alliance with VET: technical education. This is often associated with sub-baccalaureate level education programmes, for example in technical colleges that lead to respective intermediate level technical occupations. What is important here is that the knowledge that technical education would usually refer to, as the object of educational delivery processes, would be derived from the body of relevant scientific disciplines. The body of knowledge would not be the practical knowledge of the occupation or profession itself but parts of the available scientific knowledge that can be applied to work contexts (applied knowledge). This goes along with connotations of appropriate forms of delivery and the way this knowledge can be used in work contexts. In an ideal typical view, the notion would be that the respective 'applied' scientific knowledge can be transferred by the learner from the (school-based) learning situation to the real work situation, in which the knowledge can then be applied. This view has been strongly challenged by proponents of the tacit knowing view and the concept of 'boundary crossing' that puts emphasis on the equivalence of both forms of knowledge for education.

These distinctive and conflicting views on VET can also be explained by its different historical origins. One (practical knowledge) is rooted in the tradition of master craftsmen supervised by craft guilds of the Middle Ages, who were entitled to employ young people (apprentices) as an inexpensive form of labour in exchange for formal training in the craft. The other (applied knowledge) can be dated back to early military academies of the 17th and 18th century at which separation between engineering (and training for engineers) and the workshops (such as producing artillery) manifested itself.

Corresponding to these epistemological viewpoints Researchers can also identify distinct pedagogical-didactical perspectives, for instance by contrasting the master-apprentice principle with the teacher-classroom setting. However, the pedagogical principle of master-apprentice has developed over the years more and more into a dual principle, combining learning at work and in school and is currently being discussed under the concept of crossing boundaries. Within the tradition of apprenticeship is a development which started with only work-based learning, to which some schooling (in terms of further education) was added mainly in the 19th century; this was followed by reforms of the 20th century which manifested the school as an equally important learning site. Since the beginning of this century there has also been a rise in a third learning site for apprenticeships, such as learning in inter-enterprise training centres in addition to learning at the school and the workplace). Formal VET programmes that are exclusively work-based are rare, but for continuing VET and vocational learning in informal contexts (such as informal apprenticeships) this is still the dominant form. These 'educationalised' forms of traditional VET need to be distinguished from 'vocationalised' forms of schooling. The latter also form part of VET, but are rooted in the traditional classroom setting while also integrating work-based elements.

Both the principle of duality and the master-apprentice principle can be identified in all kinds of learning and educational settings: examples are universities for art or music in the form of 'master classes' or dual higher education studies. This perspective draws our attention to educational areas and learning situations that need to be considered in a broader understanding of VET.

VET from an Education System Perspective

Two distinct forms and traditions of VET (apprenticeships and technical schools) which continue to have an effect on contemporary conceptions of VET. In the second half of the 20th century researchers saw the emergence of new VET sectors. The massification of higher education and (a new) vocationalism resulted in increasing provision of VET at higher levels, while the economic crises of the 1970s and the recessions of the early 1980s and 1990s resulted in new vocational programmes addressing youth unemployment and programmes for retraining (often forming part of active labour market policy). There was a general increase in the variety of forms of VET, types of providers, levels and funding sources and mechanisms. The perspective which mainly looks at these aspects as an education system perspective, which is also the approach taken by international statistics. Researchers first discuss how the definition of VET in international statistics evolved and then consider further characteristics usually emphasised from this perspective.

An education system perspective would look at the way VET as an institution has evolved and continues to evolve over time. However, there are various ways in which VET can be conceptualised as an institution, applying different concepts such as VET as a sector, VET as a system, VET as organisational field, VET as a community, or VET as a culture. Recent literature on cross-country comparative institutional research allows the synthesis of these approaches, taking as a common starting point the organisational population, which makes up VET and the relations between its elements. Institutional approaches look at those organisations or units that, as a whole, constitute a recognised area of institutional life: providers, 'customers' and regulatory authorities, organisations running public (co) funding VET providers, types of programmes, target groups and governance structures. VET as defined in statistics also forms part of this institutional perspective. However, a synchronic analysis of VET, as defined in statistics and frequently taken as a starting point, would not shed much light on the phenomenon that interests us. In contrast, a diachronic study or analysis, concerned with the evolution and change of international definitions of VET in statistics over time, could provide a first reference point, before then addressing national definitions (which is the main focus of this assignment).

Changing approaches in statistics in classifying VET are likely to reflect changes in the overall education landscape. In turn, classifications determine the statistical visibility of VET and vocational qualifications in the labour market and thus are likely to have an impact on the shared visions of VET and its relevance for the world of work. The international standard classification of education (ISCED) has, since 1976, provided the key instrument for cross country comparison of education and it is worth analysing how VET has been conceptualised in this classification. The first version of ISCED contained neither a definition of VET nor of VET programmes. Programmes were classified only according to the level of education (for example upper secondary) and field of education (for example agriculture). Only by combining these two dimensions could a proxy for VET programmes be realised.

Only in 1997 was a definition for VET introduced and the programme orientation (general, pre-vocational, vocational) implemented. However, for many studies the programme destination (direct entry into the labour market or access to higher education) was more important in distinguishing VET from general education. While the definition of VET has not really changed through the most recent release of 2011, programme orientation and destination have been complemented by type of qualification (full/partial). There is also the explicit intention to implement on levels 6 to 8 a distinction between academic and professional.

These changes in the global statistical definition and classification of VET are remarkable. From an initial situation in which the distinction between VET and general education was apparently less important, Researchers arrive by the mid-1990s at a conception which essentially understood VET as being terminal. At the beginning of this decade the international classification began to acknowledge both a trend towards modularisation of education (distinguishing between full and partial qualification) and the vocational drift in higher education (distinguishing between academic and professional).

From this brief digression into international statistics Researchers can learn at least three distinct features of VET, of which the first two are in decline:

- VET as terminal programmes not providing access to higher education.
- VET focused on the middle level of education.
- VET programmes oriented towards technical or occupation-related content.

In Table researchers aim to specify these aspects and to discuss further important dimensions from an education system perspective.

Table: Changes in the definition and classification of vocational programmes in ISCED 1977, 1997 and 2011.

Year	Definition: Vocational education.	Classification approach
2011	Is designed for learners to acquire the knowledge, skills and competences specific to a particular occupation, trade, or class of occupations or trades. Vocational education may have work-based components. Successful completion of such programmes leads to labour market-relevant vocational qualifications acknowledged as occupationally oriented by the relevant national authorities and the labour market.	Programme orientation (vocational or general) and programme destination (access to higher education) is complemented by type of qualification (full/partial). On level 6-8, a distinction between 'academic' and 'professional' is intended, but not yet implemented.
1997	Is mainly designed to lead participants to acquire the practical skills, know-how and understanding necessary for employment in a particular occupation or trade or class of occupations or trades. Successful completion of such programmes leads to a labour-marketrelevant vocational qualification recognised by the competent authorities in the country in which it is obtained (e.g. Ministry of Education, employers' associations).	Programme orientation (vocational or general) and programme destination (labour market, access to higher education, etc.) is introduced by which VET be identified.
1977	No definition of VET or vocational programme provided.	Only by combining the 'level of education' and 'field of education' could VET be represented

The simple original formula of VET as 'middle level education not leading to higher education' no longer holds true. Although most designated VET programmes and VET learners can be found at the middle level of education (ISCED 11 levels 3 and 4), there are programmes at all levels. Many basic education programmes, such as for migrants, with clear vocational components have emerged in the past decade in Europe and are (would be) classified as lower level (ISCED 11 level 2). Many of them are not (yet) formal programmes and their orientation and purpose may also depend on the source of funding (for example labour, immigration or education budgets). The idea of classifying the increasing number of vocationally oriented programmes at higher levels (ISCED 11 levels 5 to 7 as 'professional') does not really improve transparency. It would be more relevant to distinguish between:

- Programmes of advanced further training which, in terms of the main providers (companies and further education providers), the mode of governance (high level of coordination) and the source of funding (companies), come close to the type of company-based training at upper secondary level best illustrated by apprenticeships (for example master craftsmen programmes).
- Specialised vocational schools or vocational colleges (some of which were transformed into universities).
- Vocationally oriented university programmes.

The last of these usually identify themselves as higher education as opposed to vocational education, irrespective of their clientele or orientation. For our analysis of the conception of VET, Researchers are less interested in which VET programmes exist at which levels than in the dominant national picture. Is VET, as suggested by its national definitions and mission statements, mainly associated with lower levels of education, middle levels of education, middle levels plus some higher VET, or mainly higher levels?

Researchers will probably find some sort of VET, in terms of professional education, at the higher end of an educational and occupational hierarchy in all countries. This may be through academic studies for liberal occupations such as lawyers, notaries, engineers, architects, doctors, or accountants, or through more workbased programmes such as for aircraft or sea captains. However, the former are rarely associated with VET and the latter form a minority with little influence on the overall conception.

Directly linked to level is the age of learners and student identity. We can assume that VET which is mainly associated with higher levels will be targeted at young adults, while VET which is restricted to upper secondary education may mainly target adolescents. A dispersed aged structure within VET could be an indicator for a more pronounced lifelong learning perspective. A strong indicator for a particular conception of VET is also the legal status of VET learners: are they predominately students/pupils, workers or do they have a special status, for instance as apprentices? If there is no predominant status and the diversity of VET learner identities is the particular characteristic of VET in a certain country, this might also be an indicator of a differentiated system.

For workers or novice workers to be the dominant group can only be expected if companies are among the key providers, in which case it is also likely that companies are an important source of funding. If schools and higher education, mainly financed by the State, are the main providers of VET we could also assume a predominately State-led governance mode. Due to their flexibility, further education providers are usually better suited to attracting money from different sources including spending on active labour market measures. However, some countries finance their VET systems exclusively from employment/labour market budgets; this suggests that the main focus of VET is addressing youth unemployment as well as lower attractiveness of VET compared to general/academic education.

The question of parity of esteem between vocational and general education probably forms part of any conception of VET, although it is rarely explicitly referred to in official definitions. It is associated with the sort of deeper beliefs and assumptions about VET that seem to be obvious to every citizen in the country, but difficult to understand for outsiders. As such, 'measured' attractiveness is only a weak indicator of parity of esteem, as there is no common international ground for measuring national cultures. Parity of esteem between vocational and general education is mainly determined by the dominant provisions of VET and the occupations or professions they prepare for, rather than the various minority provisions, such as the liberal occupations mentioned above. Although difficult to explain to outsiders, the question of parity of esteem is a very good starting point for diagnosing national conceptions of VET. We can start by scrutinising a simple judgement like 'VET is lower (or equal) to general education', asking: 'Why? And which part of VET do you have in mind, when making such a judgement?' The response also depends on the person asked.

VET from a Socioeconomic and Labour Market Perspective

VET contributes to social stratification by providing access to particular career pathways, also backing the social reproduction of fields of economic activity. It contributes skills, competences and attitudes required by companies and their work systems, allowing workers to cover the requirements of their given workplace, while workplaces allow the acquisition of skills. Companies represent both the demand and the supply sides in a market for skills. VET provides benefits for employer organisations and individual workers alike, giving centre stage to the questions such as who contributes how much to the costs of VET and how are benefits distributed across the 'industrial divide'. These questions are mainly discussed by education economists, yet, also by sociologists working on employment systems and industrial relations.

Cross-country comparative research has shown that national approaches to VET differ greatly when it comes to the role of VET in social stratification, work organisation and matching on the labour market. These differences could be – yet are not necessarily – mirrored in differences in national conceptions of VET across countries. The role of VET and the range of approaches covered by the term differ in the transition from education to the workplace and the socioeconomic stratification as a whole. Individuals engaged in VET of a particular type – and at a particular point of time during their life course – might experience poor or bright career opportunities compared to individuals with a similar number of years in general education. They might or might not be better off as individuals lacking any education beyond compulsory schooling.

VET prepares for different levels of jobs and career pathways within the occupations hierarchy. National employment systems differ with regard to the role and timing of initial and continuing vocational education; initial vocational education prepares for different sets of job roles. Cross-country comparative research on work and employment systems provides typologies for contrasting the most usual combinations of work organisations and related occupational structures and IVET systems. Following the analysis of Maurice and colleagues and related studies, national work systems could be understood as dominated either by the so-called organisational space or occupational space.

When organisational space dominates, firms tend to organise work processes in what they perceive their best interest and in an idiosyncratic way, with large differences in work organisation and job demands between firms. Workplaces are shaped in accordance with the chosen way to organise the work process, with little consideration paid to the qualification and skills of the job holders. Most jobs do not require initial vocational education, yet jobs for unskilled workers are organised in chains, starting with jobs involving only elementary skill demands and leading to jobs with more advanced skill demands. Most learning takes place on the job or in short spells of off-the-job training. Workers move on from job to job, with the speed of movement determined by their demonstrated skills and their ability to acquire required skills on the move. Typically, workers deal only with routine tasks, while any exceptions from the rule are addressed by technicians or managers. For workers on the blue-collar job ladder, there is typically no opportunity to join the ranks of managers or professionals. Beyond a large group of vocationally unskilled workers, firms employ groups of technicians and professionals in management and research. These groups are qualified in forms of VET on post-secondary or tertiary level and hired directly after graduation. Organisational space is thought to fit well with simple and Tayloristic forms of work organisation, yet, not so well with lean models of production. In countries where organisational space dominates, large groups of workers may be without formal vocational qualifications, having acquired nearly all of their vocational skills on the job; there may also be small groups of vocationally trained technicians and comparatively larger groups of management professionals with training in the higher education sector. Initial vocational education and training (IVET) at secondary level is typically marginalised, often more remedial in nature and poorly rewarded in the workplace.

The exceptions are post-secondary technical schools, preparing for technical roles. The proportion of professionals of all kinds – including managers – who have acquired professional skills within higher education is generally quite high. Wage differences between unskilled and skilled workers on the one side and professional groups (technicians, managers) on the other are marked. Given the restricted opportunities for everyone without postsecondary or higher education, the prestige of IVET at upper secondary level is poor and there is a strong preference for completing at least a more selective, academic upper secondary education before entering the workplace. IVET at secondary level mainly prepares students with weak school performance or former dropouts for entering any first job. Examples for countries with work systems dominated by organisational space include France, Japan, the United Kingdom and the United States, although countries within the group differ considerably.

When occupational space dominates, firms organise work processes by exploiting broad and standardised vocational qualifications, which allow graduates to perform a multitude of job roles. Workers are less attached to (chains of) workplaces; they function as parts of multiply skilled, self-organising teams, built out of more novice and experienced workers, which can deal with both routine and extraordinary workplace requirements. Typical workplaces and skill demands are much more similar across firms belonging to one economic sector. Demands in more standardised workplaces and the content of standardised vocational qualifications are continuously adjusted to each other. Workers holding a vocational qualification could change between firms, without seeing much of their skills becoming obsolete. Firms can draw on a large stock of vocationally qualified workers, as young people are motivated to enter vocational education pathways and little learning is devoted to skills required for a particular firm only.

Most workers in manufacturing and service alike hold vocational qualifications, supported by a small fraction of unskilled workers and a comparable small fraction of managers and engineers from higher education. When occupational space dominates, discretionary as well as lean modes of work organisation are the most likely to be applied, while simple or Tayloristic modes of work organisation seem less appropriate. Starting from vocational education at upper secondary level, it is possible to move on to the ranks of technicians and mid-level managers, although acquiring a formal degree in further education might be requested.

Wage differentials between vocationally skilled workers and employees with post-secondary and tertiary education are comparatively low, as pay for vocational skills are comparatively high. Beyond traditional pathways for moving up the blue-collar career ladder (for example the craft master qualification), various forms of continuous higher VET at post-secondary and tertiary level grow in importance. IVET at upper secondary level is a key part of the education system, enjoys its own legitimacy and high prestige. It may allow for smooth entry into the labour market, particularly where IVET is organised in a German-type apprenticeship approach. IVET grants membership to an occupational group and – comparable to traditional professions – novice workers are expected to develop with and contribute to the development of, the particular occupational group over the whole life span of their careers. Examples of countries where occupational space dominates include Austria, Denmark, Germany, the Netherlands and Switzerland.

Table: Key dimensions of occupational versus organizational space.

	Dominance of organisational space	Dominance of occupational space
Occupational structure/hierarchy	High number of low skilled, low number of vocationally skilled at medium level, high number of skilled employees with qualifications at post-secondary or tertiary level. Vocationally skilled workers are mainly: semi-skilled workers; technicians.	Low number of unskilled, high number of vocationally skilled workers at medium level, low number of employees with post-secondary or tertiary degrees. Vocationally skilled workers are mainly: skilled workers with a qualification at upper secondary level.
IVET prepares for	entry-level jobs	membership in an occupation/(para) profession

The dichotomy of occupational versus organisational space as summarized in table can guide reflection on a country's specific conception of VET from a labour market perspective, just as the one on cognitive and tacit knowing views could do from an epistemological perspective. These are used here as contrasted ideal types, which can only be found for parts of the labour market; usually diverse hybrid spaces exist. Further, the institutional changes (for example in terms of liberalisation) that countries have experienced in the past two decades may be profound, so that initial attributions may not be fully adequate anymore.

There are various other typologies and approaches from the sociology of labour markets literature (internal versus external/occupational labour markets; primary and secondary labour markets) and life-course research on the transitions from school to work (organisation, occupational, Mediterranean, professional and transitional labour markets) which could be considered to guide our thinking on VET conceptions. Economic research in human capital theory has also made significant contributions relevant for understanding IVET and CVET.

Approaches taking a socioeconomic or labour market perspective as their starting point share a functional perspective on VET. It is understood mainly by its broad range of functions within social and economic processes, summarized by Billett as follows:

- Cultural reproduction, remaking and transformation of occupational practices: for example the continuity, maintenance and transformation of culturally derived occupational practices that are essential to countries, communities and individuals.
- Economic efficiency: for example meeting particular occupational requirements.
- Societal continuity: for example reproducing societal norms and values.
- Individuals' fitness for particular occupations and readiness to engage in work life: for example meeting students' needs and readiness to work and learn.
- Individual progression and continuity: for example supporting development throughout working life.

VET definitions provided by international organisations typically also adopt a functional view of VET, yet emphasise only one or a smaller number of the dimensions outlined. Compare the following examples: 'a means of preparing for occupational fields and for effective participation in the world of work' (UNESCO/ILO); 'a method of facilitating poverty alleviation' (UNESCO/ILO); 'to equip people with knowledge, know-how, skills and competences required in particular occupations or more broadly on the labour market'. The socioeconomic, transitions-related perspective (preparing youth for the labour market) has emerged as dominant in the functional view of VET, followed by the importance of VET for economic efficiency. However, it has been stressed by different approaches, from pedagogy to the sociology of innovation, that workers' skill profiles do not only have to match workplaces, but that skilful, knowledgeable workers can and do contribute to change, knowledge creation and innovation in the workplace. Vocational education and training contributes to workers' capabilities to promote continuing innovation and improvement in the workplace; it may be the backbone of a country's innovation system. For some countries, vocational education and training and skilled work requiring skills at intermediate, nontertiary level, is perceived as being integral to the respective national innovation system. The fact that workers not only adapt to the organisations they work in, but also exert an influence on the way the organisation changes, is captured through many transnational surveys, such as the European company survey or the European survey on working conditions. In Germany, belief in VET as a fundamental driver of innovation has found its way into vocational education and training curricula through the idea of Gestaltung (in the sense of shaping skillfully a meaningful total), reflecting an ability to be acquired by vocational qualifications, from level three of the German qualifications framework upwards. This also shows that, at a discursive level, there can be a close connection between humanitarian goals and economic functionalities.

Towards a Multi-perspective Conceptual Framework of VET

The way vocational education and training might be conceived from a pedagogical point of view differs from a theory of knowledge point of view; economists and labour market sociologists would point at different characteristics and so do people in education administration.

From an education system perspective the scope of courses would be interesting, since the range includes both programmes with very specific purpose (for example for licensed roles such as workplace safety, lifting, welding) and multi-year courses with high-level qualifications associated with paraprofessional occupations or degree programmes leading to prestigious occupations such as law and medicine. Another relevant dimension for this perspective is the extent of articulation between VET and higher education programmes. Researchers could have also been more specific on target groups, such as young school leavers, women returning to working life, or the long-term unemployed or on selectivity of access. It makes a difference whether programmes are selective according to prior educational performance or if there is no selection at all and also if companies are in charge of selection. Related to this is the question of whether VET is free of charge for the learners, if they have to pay fees or if they receive remuneration during their programme, as in the case with many apprenticeships. It would be interesting to see how varied are providers and whether key providers also extensively provide continuing education and training, or if such provision is limited. From a labour market perspective, the dominating forms of work organisation, such as whether organisational, occupational or professional, would be interesting. We could have made a reference to the degree of regulation, such as VET leading to regulated occupations or those that are less/not regulated.

This list of features of VET could be easily extended and be developed into an even more comprehensive system for characterising VET programmes and subsystems. However, as our aim is to get a broad overview on the dominant national conceptions of VET we have limited ourselves to such aspects that are recurrent in definitions of VET. We reduced a more comprehensive list of features to the one shown in Annex 2 and summarised in figure. After piloting the work in five countries we reduced the list and shaped the concepts further. Researchers intended to use this list of descriptors both for the analysis of current conceptions of VET and changes in conceptions in the past two decades. However, at this stage we deliberately decided not to propose any direction of change (as for example in the conceptual framework of Rojewski), but put the variants of VET side by side. The ultimate goal remains to identify both current patterns of VET in Europe and patterns of change.

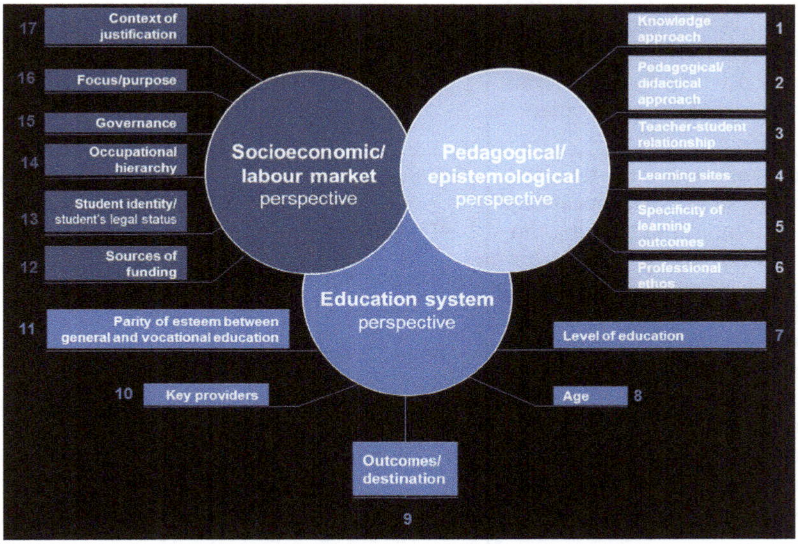

A conceptual framework to characterise VET.

In its most simple application, this framework should allow us quickly to identify and classify aspects referred to in definitions or explanations of VET at a certain time. For example, we can argue that Cedefop's definition of VET is very broad as it only refers to occupation-related skills and the transitional and matching aspect of VET. The UOE (UNESCO, OECD, Eurostat) definition of VET, in contrast, is narrower as it adds to these features the workbased component (though optional) and restricts VET to formal education. In place of limited definitions (in terms of aspects mentioned), the German definition of VET (as provided in the German Vocational Training Act) also refers to occupational hierarchy (qualified occupation/work), learning sites ('allow for job/work experience'), the kind of knowledge and the changing requirements across working life. However, these examples also demonstrate that an analysis that is restricted to formal definitions of VET falls short of providing a distinct picture of VET in the respective country. For this reason, we need to shift the focus from definitions to conceptions of VET as suggested in the introduction.

Table: Examples of VET definitions and features of the conceptual framework they refer to.

Definition	Dimensions referred to:	Variants emphasised:
Education and training which aims to equip people with knowledge, know-how, skills and competences required in particular occupations or more broadly on the labour market (Cedefop).	Specificity of learning outcomes Main focus	Occupation-specific or broader vocational-field related Supply of skilled labour
VET is designed for learners to acquire the knowledge, skills and competences specific to a particular occupation, trade, or class of occupations or trades. Vocational education may have work-based components. Successful completion of such programmes leads to labour market-relevant vocational qualifications acknowledged as occupationally oriented by the relevant national authorities and the labour market (UOE).	Specificity of learning outcomes Learning sites Main focus Outcomes/destination	Occupation-specific or broader vocational-field related Some work-based learning (optional) Supply of skilled labour Occupational qualifications or rights
'For the purposes of this act, the term "vocational training" shall mean vocational training preparation, initial training, further training and retraining. Initial training shall, through a systematic training programme, impart the vocational skills, knowledge and qualifications (vocational competence) necessary to engage in a form of skilled occupational activity in a changing working world. Initial training shall also enable trainees to acquire the necessary occupational experience' (extract from the German Vocational Training Act).	Knowledge base Learning sites Specificity of learning outcomes Outcomes/destination Socialisation Occupational hierarchy Focus of content	Practical knowledge/experience-based Multiple learning sites Occupational qualifications or rights Occupation-specific Distinct occupational or professional ethos Skilled worker Becoming a member of an occupation Broad preparation for changing requirements across working life

The example of Austria demonstrates, using the framework, how the conception of company-based VET has changed over time and how changes in the understanding of VET become manifested in law. The Austrian Vocational Training Act, which regulates the company-based part of the apprenticeship system, came into force in 1969 (the same year as the German Vocational Training Act). It primarily regulated the duties of apprentices and their masters and so is more a labour law than an education law: it only detailed the master apprenticeship relation, without reference to other features of VET. However, in 2015 it was amended by a general paragraph on the objectives of vocational training which now refers to a skilled labour force, the matching and transition aspect as well as VET's contribution to economic growth.

This tentative application of the analytical framework already shows some strengths and weaknesses. As table shows, the framework allows a quick and systematic analysis of the characteristics of VET referred to in national policy definitions. The Austrian example in Box shows how the change of definitions over time could be studied. For instance, 'economic growth and competitiveness' appears as a new (explicit) feature to 'justify' Austria's apprenticeship systems. In this way, we should be able to analyse both changes in definitions and conceptions of VET over time at country level and eventually summarise them by identifying particular change patterns in Europe. However, the examples also show the limits of any standardised instrument, in that they conceal interesting nuances between alleged similar conceptions. With the German example the language barrier also becomes evident.

Importance of Vocational Education

Vocational Education is traditionally non-academic in nature and is totally related to a specific trade, occupation or vocation. Because it is Vocation based, it is called Vocational Education. Until recently i.e until the end of the twentieth century, the aim of vocational education was to focus on specific trades such as automobile mechanic or welder and was therefore associated with the activities of lower social classes. Because of this, it attracted a level of stigma. Vocational education, in fact, is closely related to the age-old apprenticeship system of learning.

But with the development of economies worldwide, the labour market became more specialized. The demand for higher levels of skill both in government and business sector started increasing. This lead to the further development of vocational education through publicly funded training organizations and subsidized apprenticeship or traineeship initiatives for businesses. At the post-secondary level vocational education is typically provided by an institute of technology, or by a local community college. Vocational education has also diversified over the 20th century. Demand for Vocational Professionals is required more than ever in various industries such as retail, tourism, information technology, funeral services and cosmetics, as well as in the traditional crafts and cottage industries.

Vocational education prepares an individual for a job and not college. While most colleges will accept vocational education students, they tend to be limited because most colleges lack proper courses. Vocational education is a multifaceted one as it tends to focus around several careers which include auto repair, woodworking, carpentry, blacksmith, cosmetology and other fields. There are many vocational schools across the country which provide the students to gain valuable hands-on experience.

How is Vocational Education Beneficial?

- Vocational education helps people in the better performance of their jobs as they acquire a great learning experience. Working professionals get a chance to hone their skills while making money.

- Vocational education and training is a sort of introduction as it gets employees ready for the workplace which comes in handy while performing various tasks.
- Due to the nature of the skills it imparts, a student doesn't consider it a futility as compared to academic education.
- Vocational Education as the term itself denotes the students are specialised and therefore they have more chances of employment as compared to others.
- Many students who are in a dilemma whether they should attend college or not, Vocational education really opens a completely new door.
- It makes an individual a responsible and independent whereas those who study regular courses lack in this sphere.
- The career of one's own choice is one of the major benefits of this education. A vast majority of people are caught in the wrong jobs because they were in it for the sake of job, money, lack of alternative and professional compromise whereas an individual pursuing Vocational Education is already pursuing his dream job.
- This type of education is a great asset to the economy. Our government need not import foreign technicians on higher wages as our own can do the required work.
- Certain vocational skills acquired from Vocational Education teaches students the importance of manual work. The physical labour done under certain jobs makes them strong, healthy, active. Majority of Vocational Skills are applicable all over the world and these create employment opportunities in foreign countries.
- Technical programs develop the economy by bridging the demand and supply gap with highly skilled workers. It also gives students the opportunity to take marketable skills from the classroom directly into the working world.
- Better Vocational Education also attracts foreign investment and foreign exchange in form of foreign conglomerate and foreign students.
- School drop-outs and adults can also receive this type of education as it provides an opportunity to learn a skill or trade. There are many well-paid career fields in which a college degree is not required.
- Another benefit is that Hands-on work activities allow direct application of acquired knowledge.
- This education provides stable jobs as these are the jobs whose demand is never fulfilled.

Models in Vocational Education

In vocational education and training three ideal types of regulation and governance are usually distinguished on the dominant either from the state, the market or professional group's initiatives. The prevalent typology in policy research distinguishes three models of governance, which can be termed market-driven, state-controlled and occupation-driven or corporatist VET governance). In the following the three models are explained in terms of their regulative momentum and their rational of agency.

The market-driven model of VET governance is characterised by the immediate control of vocational qualification by the employment system and the demand on the labour market. Vocational qualification is oriented towards the requirements of employers and takes place on the job and in a private sector of training providers offering job-related learning modules. The responsibility for the training process rests with the learners, who are expected to acquire the qualifications required by employers on their own. Typical examples of this model are the United States and Japan, where the relative absence of a regulated VET system is associated with a large number of students attending upper secondary schools and higher education. In this system the access to VET is controlled by employers as "customers", whose needs and demands determine the contents of training so that the transfer of qualifications from one company to another is difficult. On the one hand this system is regarded as quite flexible and adapted to the needs of the employment system, on the other hand the dependence on the private supply of training opportunities and the risk of underinvestment in vocational education are seen as serious flaws of this model.

The state-controlled model of VET is characterised by a dominance of school-based vocational education, which is subject to a relatively tight regulation by state authorities. In this model, which is prevalent, for instance, in France or China, the regulation is based on the school's logic of action and includes a focus on civic education. Enterprises do not have an institutionalised role in this system, but serve as suppliers of internships while all regulatory functions – planning, management and control – are concentrated in the public sector. The contents of vocational education are typically based on theoretical and academic types of education. Due to the integration into the state-controlled education system there is a relatively close connection to general education. Moreover, the supply of training opportunities is independent of the provision of training places by private companies. The major difficulty of this system is the weak linkage to the labour market.

Table: Three main VET systems and their rationality.

Type of VET system	Rationale of agency
Market driven	Employers as customers; individual training company needs determine VE curriculum and company training, transfer of skills to other companies rather difficult because many different certificates; VET example countries: UK, US, Ireland and Japan.

State driven	Merely school based, schools logic of action, more theory driven, less work process driven; little real work orders, rather costly model while training labs need constant modernization; more simulated instead of real work task completion, example VET countries: France, China, Spain, Portugal, Poland.
Occupation driven and corporatist VET governance	Mixed system regulation; employers' associations great influence, in some countries also the unions, based collective bargaining for defining occupations and their constant modernization; Variations of systems in countries like Germany, Austria, Denmark, Netherlands, Norway, Northern regions of Italy and Switzerland.

The third model is referred to as occupation-based or corporatist regulation. This model is derived from the apprenticeship tradition in the craft trades. It is characterized by a strong influence of the training companies and the chambers and or professional associations, the corporate bodies that represent the business and trade community. This concerns the entry conditions to training as well as the definition of training contents and the ways the training and teaching processes are examined. Today occupation-based regulation is part of "mixed" systems of cooperative governance in which the regulation of vocational education takes place in a plural network of state bodies, enterprises or employers' associations as well as trade unions or professional associations. Variations of these mixed models of regulations can be found in systems of cooperative (dual or alternating) VET as they exist in Austria, Denmark, Germany Norway and Switzerland.

References

- Tertiary-education-hierarchy: hierarchystructure.com, Retrieved 02 June, 2019
- Skills-beyond-school, education-41303688: oecd.org, Retrieved 28 April, 2019
- General-education-glossary-term-3110863: thoughtco.com, Retrieved 25 March, 2019
- Vocational-education, topic: britannica.com, Retrieved 16 May, 2019
- Conceptions-of-vocational-education-and-training-an-analytical-framework- 321184380: researchgate.net, Retrieved 15 March, 2019
- Importance-of-vocational-education: targetstudy.com, Retrieved 14 January, 2019
- Vocational-education-and-training-three-types-of-governance-models: jobmarketmonitor.com, Retrieved 26 August, 2019

2

Diverse Aspects of Vocational Education

Some of the diverse aspects of vocational education are open learning education, cooperative education, dual education system, distance education, virtual learning environment, problem-based learning education, etc. This chapter delves into these aspects of vocational education to provide an in-depth understanding of the subject.

Open Learning Education

Open education is a philosophy about the way people should produce, share and build on knowledge.

Proponents of open education believe everyone in the world should have access to high-quality educational experiences and resources and they work to eliminate barriers to this goal. Such barriers might include high monetary costs, outdated or obsolete materials and legal mechanisms that prevent collaboration among scholars and educators.

Sharing is probably the most basic characteristic of education: education is sharing knowledge, insights and information with others, upon which new knowledge, skills, ideas and understanding can be built.

What are Open Educational Resources?

Open educational resources (OERs) are learning materials that can be modified and enhanced because their creators have given others permission to do so. The individuals or organizations that create OERs—which can include materials like presentation slides, podcasts, syllabi, images, lesson plans, lecture videos, maps, worksheets and even entire textbooks—waive some (if not all) of the copyright associated with their works, typically via legal tools like Creative Commons licenses, so others can freely access, reuse, translate and modify them.

Why are Open Educational Resources Beneficial?

Applying open licenses to educational materials allows educators to collaborate when building materials specifically differentiated for their students. For example, a mathematics teacher might acquire openly-licensed word problems for her students, but re-write the exercises to include language that is more geographically specific or demographically relevant. In turn, she can share her modified problems with others who may wish to use them.

At the same time, collaborating on OERs allows educators to work together when ensuring consistency among their materials. Public school teachers in the United States, for instance, may wish to share resources they've developed in order to adhere to government-mandated educational standards, like the Common Core State Standards.

Some educators suggest that OERs might help reduce costs associated with producing and distributing course materials in both primary and secondary educational institutions. Teachers can download these materials—often at low costs—for use in their classrooms, but they can also update these materials and share their contributions with others, keeping content timely, relevant and accurate. In this way, they needn't wait for textbook companies to issue entirely new editions of their (traditionally copyrighted) learning materials.

Students also benefit from open educational resources when they access these materials to supplement the education they might receive in a classroom. Some students do not have access to a high-quality education, but using OERs affords them opportunities to enhance their knowledge independently—in spite of the barriers preventing them from acquiring the knowledge and skills they seek.

Open educational resources are most useful when educators distribute them in open formats, so teachers and students can use those resources regardless of the particular technical platforms their schools have adopted.

Open education can take a number of forms:

- Education for all: Free or very low cost school, college or university education available to everyone within a particular jurisdiction, usually funded primarily through the state.
- Open access to programs that lead to full, recognised qualifications. These are offered by national open universities or more recently by the oeru.
- Open access to courses or programs that are not for formal credit, although it may be possible to acquire badges or certificates for successful completion. Moocs are a good example.
- Open educational resources that instructors or learners can use for free. Mit's opencourseware, which provides free online downloads of mit's video recorded lectures and support material, is one example.

- Open textbooks, online textbooks that are free for students to use.
- Open research, whereby research papers are made available online for free downloading.
- Open data, that is, data open to anyone to use, reuse and redistribute, subject only, at most, to the requirement to attribute and share.

Education for all – Except Higher Education

Open education is primarily a goal, or an educational policy. An essential characteristic of open education is the removal of barriers to learning. This means no prior qualifications to study, no discrimination by gender, age or religion, affordability for everyone and for students with disabilities, a determined effort to provide education in a suitable form that overcomes the disability (for example, audio recordings for students who are visually impaired). Ideally, no-one should be denied access to an open educational program. Thus open learning must be scalable as well as flexible.

State-funded public education is the most extensive and widespread form of open education. For example, the British government passed the 1870 Education Act that set the framework for schooling of all children between the ages of 5 and 13 in England and Wales. Although there were some fees to be paid by parents, the Act established the principle that education would be paid for mainly through taxes and no child would be excluded for financial reasons. Schools would be administered by elected local school boards. Over time, access to publicly funded education in most economically developed countries has been widened to include all children up to the age of 18. UNESCO's Education for All (EFA) movement is a global commitment to provide quality basic education for all children, youth and adults, supported, at least in principle, by 164 national governments. Nevertheless today there are still many millions of 'out-of-school' children worldwide.

Access to post-secondary or higher education though has been more limited, partly on financial grounds, but also in terms of 'merit'. Universities have required those applying for university to meet academic standards determined by prior success in school examinations or institutional entry exams. This has enabled elite universities in particular to be highly selective. However, after the Second World War, the demand for an educated population, both for social and economic reasons, in most economically advanced countries resulted in the gradual expansion of universities and post-secondary education in general. In most OECD countries, roughly 35-60 percent of an age cohort will go on to some form of post-secondary education. Especially in a digital age, there is an increasing demand for highly qualified workers and post-secondary education is a necessary gateway to most of the best jobs. Therefore there is increasing pressure for full and free open access to post-secondary, higher or tertiary education.

The cost of widening access to ever increasing numbers results in increased financial pressure on governments and taxpayers. Following the financial crisis of 2008, many states in the USA found themselves in severe financial difficulties, which resulted in substantial cuts to the U.S. higher education system. Thus solutions that enable increased access without a proportionate increase in funding are almost desperately being sought by governments and institutions. It is against this background that the recent interest in open education should be framed.

As a result, open is increasingly (and perhaps misleadingly) being associated with 'free'. While the use of open materials may be free to the end user (learners), there are real costs in creating and distributing open education and supporting learners, which has to be covered in some way. Thus a sustainable and adequate system of publicly funded education is still the best way to ensure access to quality education for all. Other forms of open education are steps towards achieving fully open access to higher education.

Open Access in Higher Education

In the 1970s and 1980s, there was a rapid growth in the number of open universities that required no or minimal prior qualifications for entry. In the United Kingdom, for instance, in 1969, less than 10 percent of students leaving secondary education went on to university. This was when the British government established the Open University, a distance teaching university open to all, using a combination of specially designed printed texts and broadcast television and radio, with one week residential summer schools on traditional university campuses for the foundation courses. The Open University started in 1971 with 25,000 students in the initial entry intake and now has over 200,000 registered students. It has been consistently ranked by government quality assurance agencies in the top ten U.K. universities for teaching and in the top 30 for research and number one for student satisfaction (out of over 180). It currently has over 200,000 registered students. However, it can no longer cover the full cost of its operation from government grants and there is now a range of different fees to be paid.

It should be noted however that there is no publicly funded open university in the USA, which is one reason why MOOCs have received so much attention there. The Western Governors' University is the most similar to an open university and private, for-profit universities such as the University of Phoenix fill a similar niche in the market.

As well as the national open universities, which usually offer their own degrees, there is also the OERu, which is basically an international consortium of mainly British Commonwealth and U.S. universities and colleges offering open access courses that enable learners either to acquire full credit for transfer into one of the partner universities or to build towards a full degree, offered by the university from which most credits have been acquired. Students pay a fee for assessment.

Open, distance, flexible and online learning are rarely found in their 'purest' forms. No teaching system is completely open (minimum levels of literacy are required, for instance). Thus there are always degrees of open-ness. Open-ness has particular implications for the use of technology. If no-one is to be denied access, then technologies that are available to everyone need to be used. If an institution is deliberately selective in its students, it has more flexibility with regard to choice of technology for distance education. It can for instance require all students who wish to take an online or blended course to have their own computer and Internet access. It cannot do that if its mandate is to be open to all students. Truly open universities then will always be behind the leading edge of educational applications of technology.

Despite the success of many open universities, open universities often lack the status of a campus-based institution. Their degree completion rates are often very low. The U.K. OU's degree completion rate is 22 percent, but nevertheless still higher for whole degree programs than for most single MOOC courses.

Lastly, some of the open universities have been established for more than 40 years and have not always quickly adapted to changes in technology, partly because of their large size and their substantial prior investment in older technologies such as print and broadcasting and partly because they do not wish to deny access to potential students without the latest technology.

Open Educational Practices

Open educational practices (OEP) is the use of Open educational Resources for teaching and learning in order to innovate the learning process. They are represented in teaching techniques that draw upon open technologies and adaptation to the contextual setting. OEP can also include the open sharing of teaching practices and aim to raise the quality of education and training and innovate educational practices on an institutional, professional and individual level. The OEP community includes policy makers, managers/ administrators of organisations, educational professionals and learners. OEP are also viewed as the next phase in OER development that continues to transform 21st century learning and learners. high-quality open educational resources (OER) in order to facilitate collaborative and flexible learning. They may involve students participating in online, peer production communities within activities intended to support learning or more broadly, any context where access to educational opportunity through freely available online content and services is the norm. Such activities may include (but are not limited to), the creation, use and repurposing of open educational resources and their adaptation to the contextual setting. OEP can also include the open sharing of teaching practices and aim "to raise the quality of education and training and innovate educational practices on an institutional, professional and individual level." The OEP community includes policy makers, managers/administrators of organisations, educational professionals and learners. OEP are also viewed as the next phase in OER development that continues to transform 21st century learning and learners.

The Scope of Open Educational Practices

A database or repository of open educational resources is not open educational practice. OER have a lifecycle of creation, use and management. Open educational practices aim to take the focus beyond building further access to OER and consider how in practice, such resources support education and promote quality and innovation in teaching and learning. They focus on reproduction/understanding, connecting information, application, competence and responsibility rather than the availability of good resources.

There is no canonical definition of open educational practice, however various groups and scholars have given their definition or view. One such scholar is Ehlers who defines OEP "as practices which support the (re)use and production of OER through institutional policies, promote innovative pedagogical models and respect and empower learners as co-producers on their lifelong learning path". A definition used by others either in its entirety or as basis for further development.

- The *Open Educational Quality (OPAL) Initiative* define Open Educational Practices as the use of Open Educational Resources to raise the quality of education and training and innovate educational practices on institutional, professional and individual level.

- The International Council for Open and Distance Education (ICDE): Open Educational Practices are defined as practices which support the production, use and reuse of high quality open educational resources (OER) through institutional policies, which promote innovative pedagogical models and respect and empower learners as co-producers on their lifelong learning path.

- The UK OER support and evaluation team suggest that (compared to ICDE) "a broader definition would encompass all activities that open up access to educational opportunity, in a context where freely available online content and services (whether 'open', 'educational' or not) are taken as the norm".

- The Institute for the Study of Knowledge Management in Education (ISKME) defines Open Educational Practices (OEP) as comprising a set of skills in collaboration, curation, curricular design and leadership around the use of Open Educational Resources. OEP build educator capacity for using OER to improve curriculum, instruction and pedagogy and to gain skills in digital resource curation and curriculum creation and to actively collaborate around and advocate for innovative approaches to open education and OER. ISKME developed the Open Educational Practice Rubric to articulate key learning objectives for integrating OER and open educational practice into teaching and learning improvement and leadership.

- The Center for Open Learning and Teaching (University of Mississippi) state that "Open Educational Practices (OEP) are teaching techniques that introduce students to online peer production communities. Such communities host dynamic communities and offer rich learning environments".

- The European Foundation for Quality in e-Learning (EFQUEL) write that Open Educational Practices are the next phase in OER development which will see a shift from a focus on resources to a focus on open educational practices being a combination of open resources use and open learning architectures to transform learning into 21st century learning environments in which universities', adult learners and citizens are provided with opportunities to shape their lifelong learning pathways in an autonomous and self-guided way.
- The Cape Town Open Education Declaration (with over 2,500 signatories) reads: open education is not limited to just open educational resources. It also draws upon open technologies that facilitate collaborative, flexible learning and the open sharing of teaching practices that empower educators to benefit from the best ideas of their colleagues. It may also grow to include new approaches to assessment, accreditation and collaborative learning.

OEP Areas

Best practice case studies identify a number of OEP areas.

- Business Model for OEP,
- Commitment,
- Creation of OER,
- Digital Literacy,
- Incentives and Motivation,
- IPR Framework for OEP,
- Mindsets and Attitudes,
- Open Educational Practices,
- Partnerships,
- Quality Concepts,
- Relevance: How to Convince Others of OEP?
- Repurposing OER,
- Sharing OER,
- Skills and Knowledge for OEP,
- Strategy and Policy for OEP,
- Support Mechanisms,
- Tools for Sharing,

- Using OER,
- Vision of OEP.

These areas surround the following topics, with other studies identifying categories and elements of Open Educational Practices.

Topics	Categories	Elements
• Using OER, • Innovation, • Learning, • Improving Quality, • Something Else.	• Open educational resources. • Open/public pedagogies. • Open learning. • Open scholarship. • Open sharing (of teaching practice). • Open technologies.	• Infrastructure (tools), • OER Use, • Open Design, • Adoption, • Policy.

Impact

Adopting OEP can lead to opportunities for collaborative learning through the affordances of Web 2.0 tools. In this context, open also refers to the learning environment where learner's set their own objectives rather than being restricted by those set externally (a closed environment).

Open educational practices can also provide the experience and tools to help bridge the gap between formal and informal learning and potentially an open source curriculum or emergent curriculum.

Levels of Openness

The trajectory to Open Education Practices lies between the use of open pedagogical models and, resource use and creation:

- Low - Teachers believe they know what learners have to learn. A focus on knowledge transfer.
- Medium - Predetermined Objectives (closed environment) but, using open pedagogical models and encourage dialogue and Problem-based learning.
- High - Learning Objectives and pathways highly governed by learners.

Initiatives

The OPAL Consortium

The define Open Educational Practices (OEP) as the use of Open Educational Resources (OER) to raise the quality of education and training and innovate educational practices on institutional, professional and individual level.

OPAL members		Country
International Council for Open and Distance Education	ICDE	Norway
United Nations Educational, Scientific and Cultural Organisation	UNESCO	France
Open University	OU	United Kingdom
European Foundation for Quality in e-Learning	EFQUEL	Belgium
Aalto University	AALTO	Finland
Universidade Católica Portugesa	UCP	Portugal
University Duisburg-Essen	UDE	Germany

For the mainstreaming of Open Educational Practices OPAL recommends:

- Enabling Legislation to Facilitate OEP:
  - Incentivising OEP through Legislation.
  - Reducing Legislative Burdens through Harmonisation.
  - Rethinking Intellectual Property Law for the 21st Century.
- Empowering Learners to take up OEP:
  - Addressing Fragmentation in Learning Resources.
  - Promoting the provision of Open Educational Assessment.
- Strengthening the Evidence-base of OEP:
  - Helping institutions nurture OEP.
  - Addressing Sustainability Concerns.
  - Making the Societal Benefit Explicit.
- Culturing Innovation through Networks:
  - Supporting Truly Open Collaboration.
  - Building a Coalition of Stakeholders around Principles of Openness.
- Improving Trust in OEP:
  - Integrate OEP into Institutional Quality Procedures.
  - Create Open Academic/Scientific Trust Infrastructures.

The International Council for Open and Distance Education sees OEP as those practices which support the production, use and reuse of high quality open educational resources and regards that OEP are often achieved through institutional policies, which promote innovative pedagogical models and respect. Learners are empowered as co-producers on their lifelong learning path. The scope of OEP covers all areas of OER governance: policy makers, managers and administrators of organizations, educational professionals and learners.

The OLCOS Consortium

Open e-Learning Content Observatory Services (OLCOS) project is a Transversal Action under the European eLearning Programme.

The OLCOS Roadmap focuses on Open Educational Practices, providing orientation and recommendations to educational decision makers on how to develop the use of OER. To further benefit from OERs one needs to better understand how their role could promote innovation and change in educational practices.

OLCOS members	Country
European Centre for Media Competence	Germany
European Distance and E-learning Network	Hungary
FernUniversität Hagen	Germany
Mediamaisteri Group	Finland
Open University of Catalonia	Spain
project co-ordinator Salzburg Research / EduMedia Group	Austria

The Roadmap states that; delivering OER to the dominant model of teacher-centred knowledge transfer will have little effect in equipping teachers, students and workers with the knowledge and skills required in the knowledge economy and, lifelong learning. Downloading Web-accessible, open teaching materials for classes and, continuing a one-way channel of content provision, will likely mirror the little impact achieved with regard to changing educational practices following the massive investments in the e-learning infrastructure by educational institutions. Open Educational Practices aim to deliver a competency-focused, constructivist paradigm of learning and promote a creative and collaborative engagement with digital content, tools and services to meet knowledge and skills required today.

Score

The Support Centre for Open Resources in Education (SCORE) at the Open University (UK), was the second major initiative to be funded by the Higher Education Funding Council for England (Hefce). (The first being the UKOER programme, jointly run by the Joint Information Systems Committee (JISC) and the Higher Education Academy (HEA)).

Discussions and actions were moving on from how open educational resources are published to how they are used. Placing OER as an enabler, within a wider set of open educational practices. Over a period of three years, SCORE, initiated a series of activities and events that involved several hundred educational practitioners from the majority of the higher education institutions in England.

There has been interest in how educational practitioners would accept and embed open resources into their practices. Sharing is at the heart of the philosophy OER and probably OEP and thus collective and cooperative activities between people and institutions are likely to be a key factor in the sustainability of such practices. SCORE reports it succeeded in raising the profile of OER and OEP within UK higher education institutions by assisting existing communities of practice and by creating new communities of practice to form a much larger network of practice that will be sustained by its participants.

Challenges

There are many challenges to the adoption of open educational practices. Certain aspects like technology have received greater attention than others but all of the factors below inhibit widespread use of open educational practices:

- Technology - Lack of or insufficient investment in broadband access as well as up-to-date software and hardware.
- Business Model - OER and OEP can incur a significant provider cost. Typically financial models focus on technology, but they also need to account for staff; i.e., those who create, reuse, mix and modify the content.
- Law and Policy - There is either ignorance on open access licenses, such as Creative Commons License and Gnu Public License, and restrictive intellectual property rights that limit the development of OEP.
- Pedagogy - Traditional models of learning are teacher-centric where teachers dispense knowledge to students and teachers/professors may not know how to integrate OEP into courses.
- Quality Assessment - There is not a quick and universal way to assess the quality of OER. MERLOT, based on the academic peer review process, has only reviewed 14% of submitted material.
- Cultural Imperialism - There is the concern that Western institutions use OEP to design educational courses for developing countries.

Strategies and Recommendations

In order for there to be widespread adoption of OEP, legal and educational policy must change and OEP needs to become sustainable.

- Funding - Develop a sustainable funding model for OEP that addresses technology and staffing. Various funding models being explored and examples:
    - Endowment Model, e.g. the Stanford Encyclopedia of Philosophy Project.
    - Membership Model, e.g. Sakai Educational Partners Program where member organizations pay a fee.
    - Donations Model, e.g. Wikipedia and Apache Foundation. Even though Apache has modified it so that there are fees for some services.

  - Conversion Model, e.g. Redhat, Ubuntu, SuSe. They convert free subscribers to paying customers for advanced features and support.
  - Contributor Pay Model, e.g. Public Library of Science (PLoS) where contributors pay for the cost of maintaining the contribution.
  - Sponsorship Model, e.g. MIT iCampus Outreach Initiative, which is sponsored by Microsoft and China Open Resources for Education and Stanford on iTunes, which is sponsored by Stanford and Apple. They are free for users with commercial messages by sponsors.
  - Institutional Model, e.g. MIT OpenCourseWare Project.
  - Government Model including UN programmes, e.g. Canada's SchoolNet Project.
  - Partnership and Exchange, e.g. Universities working together to create OER systems.
- Law and Policy - In terms of law, there should be an open access mandate for partially or fully publicly funded research. Also teachers and researchers should be better informed about their intellectual property rights. Researchers and teachers who use public funding should sign non-exclusive copyrights so their institutions make their work available under appropriate licenses.
- Open advocates should demand public-private partnerships.
- Build stakeholders.
- Quality Assessment.
- Pedagogy - Help teachers change to facilitate use of OEP to emphasize learners' developing competences, knowledge and skills. Therefore, teaching is no longer educator-centric, but instead it focuses on what learners can do for themselves.

Cooperative Education

Cooperative education (or co-operative education) is a structured method of combining classroom-based education with practical work experience. A cooperative education experience, commonly known as a "co-op", provides academic credit for structured job experience. Cooperative education is taking on new importance in helping young people to make the school-to-work transition. Cooperative learning falls under the umbrella of work-integrated learning (alongside internships, service learning and clinical placements) but is distinct as it alternates a school term with a work term in a structured manner, involves a partnership between the academic institution and the employer and generally is both paid and intended to advance the education of the student.

University of Waterloo operates the world's largest post-secondary co-op program in the world, with nearly 20,000 co-op students enrolled over three semesters in more than 120 programs.

Schneider's Foundations

While at Lehigh University at the beginning of the 20th century, Herman Schneider , engineer, architect and educator, concluded that the traditional learning space or classroom was insufficient for technical students. Schneider observed that several of the more successful Lehigh graduates had worked to earn money before graduation. Gathering data through interviews of employers and graduates, he devised the framework for cooperative education. About that time, Carnegie Technical Schools, now Carnegie Mellon University, opened and thereby minimized the need for Schneider's co-op plan in the region around Lehigh University. However, in 1903 the University of Cincinnati appointed Schneider to their faculty. In 1905 the UC Board of Trustees allowed Schneider to try this cooperative idea of education for one year only, for the failure of which they would not be held responsible. The cooperative education program was launched in 1906 and became an immediate success. The University of Cincinnati returned to the matter in its September 2005 board meeting, declaring the 100-year trial period of one hundred years of Cooperative Education officially ended, for the success of which the Board resumed full responsibility.

Schneider, beginning from the rank of assistant professor, would rise through the rank of dean of engineering to become interim president of the University of Cincinnati, based largely upon the strength of the co-op program. Throughout his career, he was an advocate for the co-op framework. His thirty years of service to the University of Cincinnati are partly credited for that institution's worldwide fame. In 2006 the University of Cincinnati unveiled a statue of dean Schneider outside the window of his office in Baldwin Hall.

In 1965, The Cooperative Education and Internship Association (CEIA) created "The Dean Herman Schneider Award" in honor of the contributions made by Dean Schneider in cooperative education. The award is given annually to an outstanding educator from faculty or administration. In 2006 The University of Cincinnati established the Cooperative Education Hall of Honor "to give a permanent place of honor to individuals and organizations that have made a significant qualitative difference in the advancement of Cooperative Education for the benefit of students".

Post-cincinnati Evolutions

In 1909, seeing the possibility of co-op education, Northeastern University began using co-op in their engineering program, becoming only the second institution in America to do so. By 1921, Antioch College had adapted the co-op practices to their liberal arts curricula, for which reason many called co-op the Antioch Plan. In 1919 the General

Motors Institute (GMI) was opened following this model to train new General Motors hires. This school was later renamed Kettering University.

The Drexel University four-year co-op program launched in the College of Engineering in 1919 with the participation of just three academic majors. This stemmed from the University's founder Anthony J. Drexel's belief that Drexel University should prepare its men and women for successful careers through an education that balanced class-room theory with real world practice. In 1925, the five-year co-op program took hold in the chemical engineering department, which would later become the foundation of Drexel's cooperative education program. Today, the cooperative education program supports students of more than 75 different disciplines, making it one of the largest programs in the nation.

In 1922, Northeastern University emphasized its commitment to co-op by extending it to the College of Business Administration. As new colleges opened at Northeastern, such as the College of Liberal Arts and College of Education, they became co-op schools as well. By the 1980s, Northeastern was the acknowledged leader in co-op education across the world.

In 1926, Dean Schneider invited those interested in forming an Association of Co-operative Colleges (ACC) to the University of Cincinnati for the first convention. The idea took hold and was followed by three more annual conventions. In 1929, the Society for the Promotion of Engineering Education, now called American Society for Engineering Education (ASEE), formed the Division of Cooperative Engineering Education, incorporating the membership of the ACC.

In 1957, the first Canadian co-operative education program began at the University of Waterloo with an inaugural class of 75. This program was seen as a joke and was not expected to succeed, however it quickly became a model for other co-op programs across Canada. These programs were based on both the sandwich education model popularized in Britain and the new American co-op programs. Canadian co-op programs generally follow a four-month school system interspersed with four month work terms. This common system allows employers to hire students from multiple institutions with common timelines and training programs.

In 1961, the Ford and Edison Foundations commissioned a study of co-operative education, published as *Work-study college programs; appraisal and report of the study of cooperative education.* That study resulted in the formation of the National Commission for Cooperative Education (NCCE). NCCE remains today to promote and lobby for co-operative education in the United States. Its membership comprises sponsoring corporations and organizations (not individuals) from academia and business.

Within Canada, the need for connections between co-op programs became clear by 1973. The Canadian Association for Co-operative Education (CAFCE) began with 29 educators from 15 institutions. In its first form, it did not include any employers or industry representatives. The institutions felt that they should decide on an integrative plan for co-op education prior to admitting employers as members. In 1977, employers, HR representatives and recruiters began to join CAFCE.

By 1962, about 150 academic institutions used co-op education, in one form or another. Many were outside of engineering. The need for professional support of non-engineering programs became obvious and the membership of ASEE, in 1963, began the Cooperative Education Association. To reflect its membership more accurately, it was eventually named the Cooperative Education and Internship Association, it remains today as the professional association for co-operative education outside of ASEE.

Much of those early efforts of NCCE focused on lobbying and promoting co-operative education. In 1965, the federal Higher Education Act provided support specifically for co-operative education. Funding continued from the federal government through 1992, when Congress ended its support of co-operative education. In all, a total of over $220 million was appropriated by the federal government toward co-operative education.

In Canada, regulation of co-operative education programs is overseen by CAFCE. Programs can apply for accreditation after the first class of co-op students has graduated. In order to be accredited, 30% of time spent in the program must be devoted to work experience and each experience must last at least 12 weeks.

In 1979, educators from Australia, Britain, Canada and the United States (Northeastern's President, Kenneth Ryder), met to discuss work-related programs in their respective countries. In 1981 and 1982, this group, headed by President Ryder, convened an international conference on cooperative education. In 1983, several college and university presidents, educational specialists and employers from around the world (including Australia, Canada, Hong Kong, the Netherlands, the Philippines, the United States and the United Kingdom) formed the World Council and Assembly on Cooperative Education to foster co-operative education around the world. In 1991, it renamed itself the World Association for Cooperative Education (WACE). By 2005, that Association boasted a membership of over 1,000 individuals from 43 different countries.

Co-op Models

From its beginnings in Cincinnati in 1906, cooperative education has evolved into a program offered at the secondary and post-secondary levels in two predominant models. In one model, students alternate a semester of academic coursework with an equal amount of time working, repeating this cycle several times until graduation. The parallel method splits the day between school and work, typically structured to accommodate the student's class schedule. Thus, like school-to-work (STW), the co-op model includes school-based and work-based learning and, in the best programs, connecting activities such as seminars and teacher-coordinator work site visits. These activities help students explicitly connect work and learning.

Other models, such as the sandwich model and the American-style semester model instead have students work a 40-hour work week for a set amount of time, typically between 12 weeks and six months. After this period is over, students return to the classroom for an academic semester after which they may have another work term. This cycle often repeats multiple times, adding a year or more to the students' university career. In this model, students' do not receive a summer break from school but instead are either working or in school for 12 months of the year. Before or during this work experience students may complete activities designed to maximize their learning on the job, such as online workplace conduct courses or reflective activities.

Co-op's proponents identify benefits for students (including motivation, career clarity, enhanced employability, vocational maturity) and employers (labor force flexibility, recruitment/retention of trained workers, input into curricula) as well as educational institutions and society (ibid.). Beyond informal and anecdotal evidence, however, a familiar refrain in the literature is the lack of well-done research that empirically demonstrates these benefits identifies some of the research problems for secondary co-op as follows: federal data collection on high school co-op enrollments and completions ceased in the 1980s; some studies use data in which co-op was not isolated from other work experience programs. Due to lack of a clear or consistent definition of cooperative education, researchers cannot accurately identify variables and findings cannot be compared; theory is not well developed; theory, research and practice are not integrated; and co-op research does not adhere to established standards.

Another set of problems involves perceptions of the field and its marginalization. Because of its "vocational" association, co-op is not regarded as academically legitimate; rather, it is viewed as taking time away from the classroom. Experiential activities are necessarily rewarded in post-secondary promotion and tenure systems (except in certain extenuating situations) and co-op faculty may be isolated from other faculty. Despite the current emphasis on contextual learning, work is not recognized as a vehicle for learning. Schaafsma and Van Gyn agree that the field places too much emphasis on placements rather than learning. Wilson, Stull and Vinsonhaler also decry the focus on administration, logistics, placements and procedures.

Some institutions are fully dedicated to the co-op ideal (such as Northeastern University, Drexel University, Georgia Institute of Technology, RIT, Kettering University, LaGuardia Community College and Purdue University). In others, the co-op program may be viewed as an add-on and therefore is vulnerable to cost cutting. Even where co-op programs are strong they can be threatened, as at Cincinnati Technical College when it became a comprehensive community college or LaGuardia during a budget crisis. For students, costs and time to degree completion may be deterrents to co-op participation. Other deterrents may include financial barriers, aversion to moving frequently due to family obligations or other pressures as well as difficulty managing the job search during a school semester.

New Approaches

Despite these problems, there is optimism about the future of co-op education; "Social, economic and historic forces are making cooperative education more relevant than ever", including emphasis on university-industry-government cooperation, a fluid and demanding workplace, new technology, the need for continuous on-the-job learning, globalization and demands for accountability. Federal investments in school-to-work and community service have resulted in a number of initiatives designed to provide "learning opportunities beyond the classroom walls". Because this has always been a principle of co-op, the field is in a position to capitalize on its strengths and the ways it complements other experiential methods in the effort to provide meaningful learning opportunities for students. To do this, however, cooperative education must be redesigned.

For Wilson, Stull and Vinsonhaler a new vision involves conceiving, defining and presenting co-op "as a curriculum model that links work and academics – a model that is based on sound learning theory". Ricks suggests affirming the work-based learning principles upon which co-op is based. These principles assert that cooperative education fosters self-directed learning, reflective practice and transformative learning; and integrates school and work learning experiences that are grounded in adult learning theories.

Fleming suggests that a new practical and research focus should be on the relationship between educational institutions and employers – institutions should take more initiative when it comes to training supervisors to be effective mentors. This would maximize the success of the work term and the amount the student learns, while also increasing the quality and quantity of the students' work. Drewery and Pretti echo this as they call for greater attention on the relationship between the student and the supervisor, explaining that this relationship can greatly impact the students' satisfaction with the co-op term and the benefits they gain from it.

Schaafsma also focuses on learning, seeing a need for a paradigm shift from content learning to greater understanding of learning processes, including reflection and critical thinking. Co-op is an experiential method, but learning from experience is not automatic. Therefore, Van Gyn recommends strengthening the reflective component that is already a part of some co-op models. If co-op is only a vehicle for experience to gain information about the workplace and to link technical knowledge with workplace application, then its effectiveness is not fully developed. A Higher Education Council of Ontario paper reviewing the University of Waterloo's PD programs states that the reflective element of the program is one of the main strengths, as it encourages students to review their own experiences and learn from their work terms. Maureen Drysdale suggests in a 2012 paper that the reflective elements of co-op allow students to increase their career and personal clarity relative to non-co-op students.

The Bergen County Academies, a public magnet high school in New Jersey, utilizes co-op education in a program called Senior Experience. This program allows all 12th grade students to participate in cooperative education or an internship opportunity for the full business day each Wednesday. Students explore a wide range of career possibilities. This new approach was recognized as an educational best practice and has been adopted as a state educational initiative for 12th grade students.

Negative Implications

Although there are many benefits to the co-operative education programme, there are some downsides. The negative implications do not fully compromise the number of students undertaking the study, but rather how the programme will affect the government's future funding for education. A huge burden that co-operative education brings to the education institution is financial struggles. The financial struggles come from the schools and universities who put pressure on the departments of education for funding to keep the programme going.

Implications directly to the students who participate in co-operative education is mainly based on direct learning at their institution, whether it is school or university. The co-operative education programme takes students away from school or university. As a student misses a consecutive number of school days, they can start to fall behind in school work and will eventually be unable to cope with their workload. For students who attend school and also participate in the co-operative education programme, commonly called Work Placement or VET courses, they are no longer eligible to be granted direct entry into university. This then gives the student an option of TAFE entry, a university certified bridging course or go on to full-time work after completion of graduation.

Integrating Experiential Methods

School-to-work and service learning have also been promoted as ways to link theory and practice through meaningful experiential learning experiences. Furco outlines the similarities between school-to-work and service learning. Although school-to-work, service learning and co-op have different goals, each of his points also applies to cooperative education:

- Based on the philosophy that learners learn best through active engagement in meaningful activities.
- View of students as active learners and producers of knowledge.
- Use of such instructional strategies as contextual learning and application of knowledge to real situations.
- Requirement for schools to establish formal partnerships with outside entities.
- Concern for integrating school experiences and external experiences.

The Community Service Scholarship Program at California State University-Fresno combines cooperative education with service learning. Students receive co-op/internship credit and scholarships for completing a placement at a community service site. As in traditional co-op work placements, students get real-world training, opportunities to explore career options and enhanced employability skills such as communication, problem solving and leadership as well as awareness of community and social problems. Combining co-op and service learning thus prepares students for roles as workers and citizens.

Research on highly successful co-op programs in Cincinnati and at LaGuardia Community College shows that they share the basic philosophy and fundamental characteristics of the educational strategy of school-to-work. The reconceptualization of co-op should recognize and build upon this connection. At the same time, lessons from successful co-op programs can benefit the broader STW movement.

There is a need for broader definition of acceptable models for integrating work and learning. Barton and Wilson, Stull and Vinsonhaler identify a variety of work-based learning activities taking different names: co-op, internships, externships, apprenticeship, career academies, etc. Work-based learning programs should look for connections and develop collaborative relationships. The alternating and parallel co-op models may not meet the needs of returning adult students and dislocated workers needing retraining. Alternatives such as extended-day programs emphasizing mentoring should be considered.

Connecting activities to integrate school- and work-based learning are an essential part of STW. At LaGuardia, the required co-op seminar helps students make connections by giving them a structure within which to reinforce employability skills, examine larger issues about work and society and undertake the crucial activities of critical reflection.

Grubb and Badway and Grubb and Villeneuve found that the value of cooperative education is embedded in the culture of the institution (LaGuardia) and the region (Cincinnati). In this supportive culture, employer support does not have to be repeatedly obtained and there are clearly understood long-term expectations on all sides (schools, employers, students). This informal culture of expectations around work-based learning may be more powerful in the long run than a complex set of regulations and bureaucratic requirements.

However, even LaGuardia has found it difficult to sustain co-op culture over time. “The only way in which STW programs can find a permanent place in schools and colleges is for the work-based component to become so central to the educational purposes of the institutions that it becomes as unthinkable to give it up as it would be to abandon math, English, or science”.

Finn believes that the answer lies in going beyond reconceiving co-op as an educational strategy, pedagogy, model, methodology, or curriculum”. She asserts that it is time for cooperative education to develop and define its body of knowledge, investigate its unique phenomena-e.g., the concept of learning from experience and clarify and strengthen the qualifications of co-op practitioners. For Ricks, cooperative education is inherently committed to improving the economy, people's working lives and lifelong learning abilities. It can thus position itself to serve the experiential learning needs of students into the 21st century.

Cates and Cedercreutz demonstrate that the assessment of student work performance as pursued by co-op employers, can be used for continuous improvement of curricula. The methodology, funded by the Fund for Postsecondary Education (FIPSE) has been developed to a level allowing institutionalization. The methodology could, when implemented over a larger front, provide a substantial competitive advantage for the entire field.

Examples:

- Work-study (federally subsidized campus employment) in the later twentieth century became a formal and major component of Student financial aid in the United States.
- The University of Waterloo has a co-operative education program with more than 19,000 students enrolled in co-op programs and more than 5,200 active co-op employers. Their five-year co-op program includes twenty four months of work experience. Enrolling in the co-op program at the University of Waterloo does not guarantee co-op employment. The school requires students to have a minimum of sixteen to twenty months of valid work experience (depending on the program of study) to successfully complete their academic program. Despite a high percentage of employment via the coop program, many students obtain employment by other methods, including a student's personal networks and unpaid full-time volunteering positions.
- Since its inception in 1975, the co-operative education program at Simon Fraser University (SFU) has grown to more than 8,400 students seeking paid work experiences across the globe. SFU's co-op programs span the faculties of Applied Sciences, Arts and Social Sciences, Business, Communication, Art and Technology, Education, Environment, Health Sciences and Science. The University has worked with over 6,000 employers worldwide. An SFU student has won the Canada-wide title Co-op Student of the Year four times.
- Wilfrid Laurier University and the Lazaridis School of Business and Economics provide a co-op business program with a competitive entry limited to about one-third of the students who start the BBA program in their first-year. It offers three four-month work terms. Additionally, the school offers a co-op MBA program for high calibre students with less than two years of work experience.

- The University of British Columbia's co-operative education program includes over three thousand students from the faculties of Arts, Commerce, Engineering, Forestry, Kinesiology and Science.
- The University of Victoria (UVic)'s co-operative education program offers hands-on learning opportunities for close to half of UVic students, with the number growing each year. Optional or mandatory co-op is available in almost every academic discipline. All UVic co-op students complete a professional practice course prior to their first work term, including intercultural training to help them contribute positively to diverse workplaces. Students also reflect on each work term experience using a competency-based framework. UVic's Co-op Program includes dedicated support for Indigenous and international students and has developed unique international co-op exchange partnerships with employers and post-secondaries around the globe. The program launched in 1976.
- All Antioch College students participate in the college's Co-op Program as part of their academic requirements for graduation. Under the program, students spend a total of four twelve-week terms, distributed throughout their undergraduate years, working as paid, full-time employees in local, national, or international settings. The program at Antioch, which is located in Yellow Springs, Ohio, began in 1921.
- The University of New South Wales (NSW) in Sydney provides an industry linked Co-op Scholarship. Students receive a scholarship of A$17,000 per annum for each year of their degree and current offerings span twenty four areas in business, engineering, science and the built environment. Along with industry experience, the Co-op Program incorporates leadership and professional development in addition to networking and mentoring opportunities.
- The Florida Institute of Technology has a condensed cooperative education program allowing students to graduate in four years with three-semester work terms. This program is only followed by engineering students and requires students to take online coursework while they are working full-time as a cooperative education student.
- Drexel University in Philadelphia, Pennsylvania has one of the nation's oldest, largest and best-known cooperative education programs. 91% of undergraduate students in over 75 majors participate in the co-op program. During their time at Drexel, students experience up to three different co-ops and gain up to 18 months of working experience. With over 1,700 employers in its network, Drexel's cooperative education program connects students with industry leaders across 35 states and 45 countries. Drexel's cooperative education program allows students to not only explore future careers, but also bring their cooperative education experiences back to the classroom. As a result of cooperative education, Drexel students graduate having already built

a professional network and they typically receive higher starting salaries than their counterparts from other schools. Students may also elect to participate in a Research Co-op to prepare them for a career in research or graduate school or an Entrepreneurship Co-op that will, in collaboration with the Close School of Entrepreneurship, assist them in establishing their own ongoing business. Specialized co-op experiences are also offered at the graduate level.

- Northeastern University in Boston, Massachusetts has a co-operative education program started in 1909. The program places about five thousand students annually with more than 2,500 co-op employers in Boston, across the United States and around the globe. A student graduating from Northeastern with a five-year bachelor's degree has a total of eighteen months of internship experience with up to three different companies.
- Rochester Institute of Technology (RIT) began cooperative education in 1912.
- Georgia Institute of Technology (Georgia Tech) started cooperative education in 1912.
- Kettering University in Flint, Michigan, enrolls students in co-operative education from their first year on campus, specializing in engineering, science and management degree programs.
- Baden-Wuerttemberg Cooperative State University (DHBW) (Germany) has a co-operative education program with more than 34,000 students enrolled and more than 9,000 co-op employers. The three-year co-op undergraduate programs include one and a half year of compulsory internships. DHBW offers job integrated learning (JIL) programs only. In JIL, every DHBW student has to be employed by a single company during the complete duration of the study program. Lectures and compulsory internships are geared to maximize applied learning. Founded on March 1, 2009, DHBW traces its roots back to the Berufsakademie Baden-Wuerttemberg.
- Steinbeis Center of Management and Technology of Steinbeis University Berlin offers an international masters program (Master of Business Engineering) for graduates and young professionals which integrates practical and theoretical learning, along with on the job training by managing projects for a sponsoring company.
- Wentworth Institute of Technology has a two-semester co-operative education program with an optional third semester in the sophomore summer. Every student in the Institute is required to do two co-ops. Co-operative education has been active since 1975 with over one thousand students in a co-op each year.
- EPUSP - Escola Politecnica da Universidade de São Paulo offers cooperative education in Sao Paulo, Brazil.

- TOBB University of Economics and Technology offers cooperative education in Ankara, Turkey.
- Purdue University has a top ten-ranked cooperative education program that was established in 1964. Originally exclusive to students in the College of Engineering, the co-op program is now available to students in 48 different disciplines in 8 of the academic colleges on campus. Purdue offers 5-session and 3-session co-op programs but differs from most universities in that students spend all 5 or 3 work sessions with the same employer, earning raises and gaining progressive responsibilities for each subsequent work rotation, for a total of 12–16 months of work experience. Both programs are 5-year academic programs, though students only pay tuition while studying on campus and pay a small administrative fee during each co-op work rotation. As of July 2014, there were over 600 students enrolled in co-op programs and over 500 qualified employers with locations around the nation and across the globe.
- To complete a bachelor of education at any Australian university, the individual must complete a minimum of 36 weeks of Practirum in a school faced environment doing work placement in their desired field, which includes helping the teacher to teaching a fully planned out class.
- For Australian high school students who are not completing ATAR courses, work placement is highly encouraged to gain necessary credits to complete graduation.

Industry-oriented Education

Industry Oriented Education is an approach to education from an industry perspective.

Industry oriented education is an approach to learning from an industry perspective where traditional subjects such as maths, physics and science are taught in the context of application of that knowledge to product design, development and operation.

With traditional technical teaching methodologies in educational environments, the conventional pathway is to build the foundation learning through subject based teaching of maths, physics and science independently. Subjects based on the knowledge required for the discipline usually follow on from this. The problem with this traditional methodology of learning is that there is no close relationship with industry requirements. Students may well graduate with no industrial oriented learning experience prior to their first job.

Practice

It has been applied to vocational education. It was only offered to sub-degree education and industry training until 2004. Since 2004 Industry Oriented Education has been introduced to higher education as part of study for undergraduate degrees and Master's degrees.

Examples:

As an example, the course of Electronics Technology in the Bachelor of Applied Technology is directly linked to industry and the focus is on an industrial product such as a Switch-mode power supply. The internal components form the topics for study: this includes the mechanical design for the enclosure, electronic design including the PCB (Printed Circuit Board) and embedded software design. The focus for learning is product design, application and operation of electronic components and circuitry. The industrial product will be activated under simulated industry conditions where students will gain invaluable insight of design technology, operational procedure and programming techniques. All foundation skills can be achieved within these studies and the students are well prepared to develop further knowledge and skills required for their industry project required in their final year through cooperative education with industry. Mathematics is not taught here as an independent course of study, but totally integrated into the compulsory technical courses. As an example, the course of Electronics Technology taught in the Bachelor of Applied Technology uses Fast Fourier Transform series to explore the method of Electromagnetic Interference (EMI) in Switch-mode power supplies. Initially students will receive a demonstration and the product which is a commercial product, will be opened for internal investigation of the enclosure. The internal components form the topics for study: this includes the mechanical design for the enclosure, electronic design including the PCB (Printed Circuit Board) and embedded software design. The focus for learning is product design, application and operation of electronic components and circuitry.

An example in post-graduate program is a "bridging" technology course designed for the first year students in Master of Design program before they start their projects. It is to enable a Bachelor of Design graduate to entry this technology oriented program.

Dual Education System

A dual education system combines apprenticeships in a company and vocational education at a vocational school in one course. This system is practiced in several countries, notably Germany, Austria, Switzerland and in the German-speaking Community of Belgium, but also for some years now in South Korea.

In the *Duales Ausbildungssystem,* students can learn one of 356 (as of 2005) apprenticeship occupations (*Ausbildungsberufe*), such as Doctor's Assistant, Dispensing Optician or Oven Builder. The precise skills and theory taught are strictly regulated and defined by national standards: An *Industriekaufmann* (Industrial Manager) has always acquired the same skills and taken the same courses in production planning, accounting and controlling, marketing, HR management, trade laws, etc. Especially in southern Germany this model is also used for a special college system called *Duale Hochschule.*

In France, dual education (*formation en alternance*) has gained a lot of popularity since the 1990s, with information technology being the greatest draw.

In South Korea, the German and Swiss dual apprenticeship system was studied and implemented by then President Park Geun-hye to address South Korea's more glaring employment needs including tackling the country's high youth employment rate and as well as reforming South Korea's entire education system. Since the rise of Meister schools and modern reforms through the implementation of vocational education in the South Korean education system, graduates from vocational high schools have been successful in navigating through South Korea's highly competitive and sluggish job market as they possess relevant skill sets that are in high demand in the South Korean economy.

In Germany, the dual education system formally emerged after the passage of the Vocational Training Act of 1969. A description of its functioning and value is given in Pritchard. It was significantly enhanced by reforms in 2005. Historically, vocational training was organized by the various guilds through apprenticeships, as their members sought to ensure that they had a talented labor pool to perpetuate their respective industries. The Vocational Training Act codified and standardized this system across Germany, serving as the foundation upon which the state, the private sector and trade unions could effectively coordinate to deliver the dual system for a modern Germany. This high level of coordination allowed for the development of public education programs and firm specific apprenticeships that are complementary and mutually reinforcing.

Present and Future Day Dual Education

Today's system of dual education in Germany functions by cooperation between small and medium companies. Cooperation is regulated by law and employers and trade unions are responsible for creating new training regulations. Since certificates and standardized across all industries, the dual education system ensures that apprentices receive the same training regardless of region or company. Employers trust the certificates since they provide evidence of an individual's knowledge. There is also a shared responsibility between the government, employers and trade unions which helps in responding to digital landscapes or changing job markets which impact how effective future employees may be in the future job market. Dual education was designed to make it easier for employers seeking new employees by allowing them to test potential candidates as apprentices and create a smoother flow for the hiring process. Good schools are a critical factor to this system as they better prepare candidates for changing job conditions. The dual education system is not perfect and flaws do exist. Although, creating specialization through early vocational training and apprenticeships programs can have its advantages, disadvantages also exist. As change accelerates in many industries, the skills of an individual apprentice become obsolete faster. Apprentices can excel early on in the job market but a lack of general skills and lifetime learning in new jobs cause them to do worse later on. Nonetheless, the dual education system is still very effective in stifling unemployment especially among the youth.

The modern era of rapid economic and technological change has expanded the role of the dual education system in the labor force. Increasingly, older workers are making use of the system to gain new skills in the ever evolving labor market. This is known as Continuous Vocational Educational Training, or CVET. Given the robustness of the systems in Germany, Austria and other similar countries, dual education may help these countries adapt more quickly to ongoing economic transformation.

Apprenticeship Section

As one part of the dual education course, students are trained in a company for three to five days a week. The company is responsible for ensuring that students get the standard quantity and quality of training set down in the training descriptions for each trade.

In Germany, this practical training may be complemented by more practical lessons at workshops run by the guilds and chamber of commerce, in order to compensate for the bias caused by training at only one company. These extra courses usually take three or four weeks a year. The time spent at vocational school is approximately 60 days a year, in blocks of one or two weeks at a time spread out over the year.

In France, the same amount of time is spent in practical training and theory, with the following possible systems:

- 2.5 days in a company, 2.5 days at school,
- one week in a company, one week at school,
- six months in a company, six months at school.

French companies must provide a tutor or other person responsible for the students, or a human resources officer to deal with them. Their duties may involve daily tutoring and targeted training. French apprentices on the dual education course are paid a certain percentage of the minimum wage for the job they are learning.

School Section

The other part of the dual education course involves lessons at a vocational school (German: *Berufsschule*). The responsibility for this part of the course lies with the school authorities in every German state or Swiss canton. Both general lessons (for example German, politics, economics, religion or even sport) and trade-specific theory are taught.

Lessons may be taught part-time (one or two days a week) or in blocks of several weeks. The latter is preferred for trades learned by only a small number of students, where students may have to travel long distances to get to the nearest vocational school which teaches their subject.

Testing

In Germany, for most trades, the first examination takes place about half-way through the vocational training and is only to test how well the student is doing so far: the marks do not go towards the final exam. Both exams are organised by the small business trade group and chamber of commerce and industry. Examinations for trained artisans are traditionally known as journeyman's tests (*Gesellenprüfung*).

Examinations for trades which have been recognised more recently are organised slightly differently. Here, the first examination counts as 40% of the total result, with the final examination making up the other 60%.

Those who fail the exam can apply to have their training extended until the following year when they can retake it. Only one extension is allowed.

Advantages

The student is an employee of the company from the beginning and receives tasks that are according to his growing abilities. If a company is willing to make an employment-contract with the student after his dual education time, the company gets an employee who knows the company's workflow. The student can also benefit from the knowledge about born hard and soft skills of more experienced co-workers. The student develops under real conditions. Therefore, he can see if he is not able or willing to do this job quite early and not only after exams. Furthermore, the student earns money from the beginning.

Given that students in dual education systems receive high quality vocational training and education, they are well prepared to enter the job market at a young age and the firms that participate in their training are more willing to hire them when they graduate. As a consequence, Germany has the lowest rate of youth unemployment in the European Union and Austria has similarly low rates. Furthermore, the system effectively provides huge savings for firms on recruitment costs, as they are aware of and invested in the skills of potential hires. It is also seen as a contributor to the economic success of Germany's world renowned firms, as the highly skilled workforce can contribute directly to improvements in production and service delivery.

Disadvantages

Although the dual education system is generally considered to be exemplary, more young people are taking vocational education and training courses at training sites and schools rather than in real companies, as they are becoming less willing to take on apprentices for various reasons. The Cabinet of Germany considered making it compulsory for firms to take on apprentices. The idea was dropped when the trade associations agreed to a voluntary training pact.

Companies that take on apprentices have to follow many regulations and the training itself is very expensive.

Requirements for several positions have become more complex and many high school graduates do not provide the right level of education. The less complex positions have only graduates with very little education are willing to do it and even they are not able to keep up with the course.

Also, companies are often highly specialised and unable to train apprentices in all the required areas.

Two solutions put forward so far are "contractual education" (*Auftragsausbildung*) and state-run courses. The former would involve companies training apprentices that they do not plan to employ; the contract would also not be an employment contract. The latter would involve training outside companies: in schools and colleges.

Switzerland also has more and more young people finding it hard to get a place in a company of their choice. In 2004, a conference took place and was attended by all the parties in the Swiss Federal Council; as no agreement could be reached on which measures to take, the only result was a call for all companies to take on apprentices.

The lack of places has changed the conditions in which apprentices are taken on. In 2004, one new company even advertised apprenticeships in information technology in which apprentices had to pay for the training themselves. The uproar was so great, however, that the company was not able to start up.

Today, most apprentices have to take aptitude tests before they are accepted and the company can usually chose from several candidates.

Difficulties in Exporting Dual Education

Although the dual education system seems promising at partnering future employees with potential jobs in their industry, it does not mean every country can simply create a dual education system within their borders. The system is successful in Germany because VET (the model for dual education) is regulated and strongly funded by both the federal government and German states and works closely with the German industry for maximum success. The model is unlikely to easily be adapted in other countries for a variety of reasons. Firstly, the high degree of success can be attributed to Germany's long-historical culture of apprenticeships. This system was grown in Germany over a period of time under very specific conditions and cannot easily be adapted in other modernized countries. One important degree of the dual education system is the high standard of education provided by the German government in Germany. This allows apprentices to not only specialize early on but maintain the basic education needed to react flexibly in the future. Another important aspect is that in other developed or developing countries, large social problems exist which prevent the creation or minimize the effectiveness of a potential dual education system. High-college costs and economic inequality mean that the local government must provide even more for certain individuals to succeed for the system to work. Finally, the long culture of apprenticeship makes sense in Germany but produces social stigmas in other foreign nations as it seen as inferior as opposed to the traditional educational pathway.

Problem-based Learning

A PBL group at Sydney Dental Hospital.

Problem-based learning (PBL) is a student-centered pedagogy in which students learn about a subject through the experience of solving an open-ended problem found in trigger material. The PBL process does not focus on problem solving with a defined solution, but it allows for the development of other desirable skills and attributes. This includes knowledge acquisition, enhanced group collaboration and communication. The PBL process was developed for medical education and has since been broadened in applications for other programs of learning. The process allows for learners to develop skills used for their future practice. It enhances critical appraisal, literature retrieval and encourages ongoing learning within a team environment.

The PBL tutorial process involves working in small groups of learners. Each student takes on a role within the group that may be formal or informal and the role often alternates. It is focused on the student's reflection and reasoning to construct their own learning. The Maastricht seven-jump process involves clarifying terms, defining problems, brainstorming, structuring and hypothesis, learning objectives, independent study and synthesis. In short, it is identifying what they already know, what they need to know and how and where to access new information that may lead to the resolution of the problem. The role of the tutor is to facilitate learning by supporting, guiding and monitoring the learning process. The tutor aims to build students' confidence when addressing problems, while also expanding their understanding. This process is based on constructivism. PBL represents a paradigm shift from traditional teaching and learning philosophy, which is more often lecture-based. The constructs for teaching PBL are very different from traditional classroom or lecture teaching and often require more preparation time and resources to support small group learning.

Wood defines problem-based learning as a process that uses identified issues within a scenario to increase knowledge and understanding. The principles of this process are listed below:

- Learner-driven self-identified goals and outcomes.
- Students do independent, self-directed study before returning to larger group.
- Learning is done in small groups of 8–10 people, with a tutor to facilitate discussion.
- Trigger materials such as paper-based clinical scenarios, lab data, photographs, articles or videos or patients (real or simulated) can be used.
- The Maastricht 7-jump process helps to guide the PBL tutorial process.
- Based on principles of adult learning theory.
- All members of the group have a role to play.
- Allows for knowledge acquisition through combined work and intellect.
- Enhances teamwork and communication, problem-solving and encourages independent responsibility for shared learning - all essential skills for future practice.
- Anyone can do it as long it is right depending on the given causes and scenario.
- We can be champions and holders of a vocational degree.
- It depends upon the cases and the scenario the building of curriculum lesson.

The PBL process was pioneered by Barrows and Tamblyn at the medical school program at McMaster University in Hamilton in the 1960s. Traditional medical education disenchanted students, who perceived the vast amount of material presented in the first three years of medical school as having little relevance to the practice of medicine and clinically based medicine. The PBL curriculum was developed in order to stimulate learning by allowing students to see the relevance and application to future roles. It maintains a higher level of motivation towards learning and shows the importance of responsible, professional attitudes with teamwork values. The motivation for learning drives interest because it allows for selection of problems that have real-world application.

Problem-based learning has subsequently been adopted by other medical school programs adapted for undergraduate instruction, as well as K-12. The use of PBL has expanded from its initial introduction into medical school programs to include education in the areas of other health sciences, math, law, education, economics, business, social studies and engineering. PBL includes problems that can be solved in many different ways depending on the initial identification of the problem and may have more than one solution.

Advantages

There are advantages of PBL. It is student-focused, which allows for active learning and better understanding and retention of knowledge. It also helps to develop life skills that are applicable to many domains. It can be used to enhance content knowledge while simultaneously fostering the development of communication, problem-solving, critical thinking, collaboration and self-directed learning skills. PBL may position students to optimally function using real-world experiences. By harnessing collective group intellect, differing perspectives may offer different perceptions and solutions to a problem. Following are the advantages and limitations of problem-based learning.

Fosters Student-centered Learning

In problem-based learning the students are actively involved and they like this method. It fosters active learning and also retention and development of lifelong learning skills. It encourages self-directed learning by confronting students with problems and stimulates the development of deep learning.

Upholds Lifelong Learning

Problem-based learning gives emphasis to lifelong learning by developing in students the potential to determine their own goals, locate appropriate resources for learning and assume responsibility for what they need to know. It also greatly helps them better long term knowledge retention.

Prominence on Comprehension not Facts

Problem-based learning focuses on engaging students in finding solutions to real life situations and pertinent contextualized problems. In this method discussion forums collaborative research take the place of lecturing.

In-depth Learning and Constructivist Approach

PBL fosters learning by involving students with the interaction of learning materials. They relate the concept they study with everyday activities and enhance their knowledge and understanding. Students also activate their prior knowledge and build on existing conceptual knowledge frameworks.

Augments Self-learning

Students themselves resolve the problems that are given to them, they take more interest and responsibility for their learning. They themselves will look for resources like research articles, journals, web materials, text books etc. for their purpose. Thus it equips them with more proficiency in seeking resources in comparison to the students of traditional learning methods.

Better Understanding and Adeptness

By giving more significance to the meaning, applicability and relevance to the learning materials it leads to better understanding of the subjects learnt. When students are given more challenging and significant problems are given it makes them more proficient. The real life contexts and problems makes their learning more profound, lasting and also enhance the transferability of skills and knowledge from the classroom to work. Since there is more scope for application of knowledge and skills the transferability is increased. It will be also very helpful to them not only to visualise what it will be like applying that knowledge and expertise on their field of work or profession.

Reinforces Interpersonal Skills and Teamwork

Project based learning is more of teamwork and collaborative learning. The teams or groups resolve relevant problems in collaboration and hence it fosters student interaction, teamwork and reinforces interpersonal skills. like peer evaluation, working with group dynamic etc. It also fosters in them the leadership qualities, learn to make decision by consensus and give constructive feed back to the team members etc.

Self-motivated Attitude

Researchers say that students like problem-based learning classes rather than the traditional classes. The increase in the percentage of attendance of students and their attitude towards this approach itself makes it very clear that they are self-motivated. In fact it is more fascinating, stimulating and one of the good learning methods because it is more flexible and interesting to students. They enjoy this environment of learning for it is less threatening and they can learn independently. All these aspects make students more self-motivated and they pursue learning even after they leave the school or college.

Enriches the Teacher-student Relationship

Since the students are self-motivated, good teamwork, self-directed learning etc. the teachers who have worked in both traditional and project based learning formats prefer project based learning. They also feel that problem-based learning is more nurturing, significant curriculum and beneficial to the cognitive growth of the student.

Higher Level of Learning

The PBL students score higher than the students in traditional courses because of their learning competencies, problem solving, self-assessment techniques, data gathering, behavioral science etc. It is because they are better at activating prior knowledge and they learn in a context resembling their future context and elaborate more on the information presented which helps in better understanding and retention of knowledge. In medical education, PBL cases can incorporate dialogue between patients and physicians, demonstrate the narrative character of the medical encounter and examine the political economic contributors to disease production. PBL can serve as a platform for a discursive practices approach to culture that emphasizes the emergent, participant-constructed qualities of social phenomena while also acknowledging large-scale social forces.

Disadvantages

According to Wood, the major disadvantage to this process involves the utilization of resources and tutor facilitation. It requires more staff to take an active role in facilitation and group-led discussion and some educators find PBL facilitation difficult and frustrating. It is resource-intensive because it requires more physical space and more accessible computer resources to accommodate simultaneous smaller group-learning. Students also report uncertainty with information overload and are unable to determine how much study is required and the relevance of information available. Students may not have access to teachers who serve as the inspirational role models that traditional curriculum offers.

Time-consuming

Although students generally like and gain greater ability to solve real-life problems in problem-based learning courses, instructors of the methodology must often invest more time to assess student learning and prepare course materials, as compared to LBL instructors. Part of this frustration also stems from the amount of time dedicated to presenting new research and individual student findings regarding each specific topic, as well as the disorganised nature of brain-storming

Traditional Assumptions of the Students

The problem of the problem-based learning is the traditional assumptions of the students. Most of the students might have spent their previous years of education assuming their teacher as the main disseminator of knowledge. Because of this understanding towards the subject matter students may lack the ability to simply wonder about something in the initial years of problem-based learning.

Role of the Instructor

The instructors have to change their traditional teaching methodologies in order to incorporate problem-based learning. Their task is to question students' knowledge, beliefs, give only hints to correct their mistakes and guide the students in their research. All these features of problem-based learning may be foreign to some instructors; hence they find it difficult to alter their past habits.

Pupil's Evaluation

The instructors have to adapt new assessment methods to evaluate the pupils' achievement. They have to incorporate written examinations with modified essay questions, practical examinations, peer and self-assessments etc. Problem-based has also been considered slightly more favourable to female participants, whilst having equivocal impacts on their male counterparts when compared to lecture based learning.

Cognitive Load

Sweller and others published a series of studies over the past twenty years that is relevant to problem-based learning, concerning cognitive load and what they describe as the guidance-fading effect. Sweller et al. conducted several classroom-based studies with students studying algebra problems. These studies have shown that active problem solving early in the learning process is a less effective instructional strategy than studying worked examples. Certainly active problem solving is useful as learners become more competent and better able to deal with their working memory limitations. But early in the learning process, learners may find it difficult to process a large amount of information in a short time. Thus the rigors of active problem solving may become an issue for novices. Once learners gain expertise the scaffolding inherent in problem-based learning helps learners avoid these issues. These studies were conducted largely based on individual problem solving of well-defined problems.

Sweller proposed cognitive load theory to explain how novices react to problem solving during the early stages of learning. Sweller, et al. suggests a worked example early and then a gradual introduction of problems to be solved. They propose other forms of learning early in the learning process (worked example, goal free problems, etc.); to later be replaced by completions problems, with the eventual goal of solving problems on their own. This problem-based learning becomes very useful later in the learning process.

Many forms of scaffolding have been implemented in problem-based learning to reduce the cognitive load of learners. These are most useful to enable decreasing ("fading") the amount of guidance during problem solving. A gradual fading of guidance helps learners to slowly transit from studying examples to solving problems. In this case backwards fading was found to be quite effective and assisting in decreasing the cognitive load on learners.

Evaluation of the effects of PBL learning in comparison to traditional instructional learning have proved to be a challenge. Various factors can influence the implementation of PBL: extent of PBL incorporation into curriculum, group dynamics, nature of problems used, facilitator influence on group and the motivation of the learners. There are also various outcomes of PBL that can be measured including knowledge acquisition and clinical competence. Additional studies are needed to investigate all the variables and technological scaffolds, that may impact the efficacy of PBL.

Demands of Implementing

Implementing PBL in schools and Universities is a demanding process that requires resources, a lot of planning and organization. Azer discusses the 12 steps for implementing the pure PBL:

- Prepare faculty for change.
- Establish a new curriculum committee and working group.
- Designing the new PBL curriculum and defining educational outcomes.
- Seeking advice from experts in PBL.
- Planning, organizing and managing.
- Training PBL facilitators and defining the objectives of a facilitator.
- Introducing students to the PBL program.
- Using 3-learning to support the delivery of the PBL program.
- Changing the assessment to suit the PBL curriculum.
- Encouraging feedback from students and teaching staff.
- Managing learning resources and facilities that support self-directed learning.
- Continuing evaluation and making changes.

Constructivism

Problem-based learning addresses the need to promote lifelong learning through the process of inquiry and constructivist learning. PBL is considered a constructivist approach to instruction because it emphasizes collaborative and self-directed learning while being supported by tutor facilitation. Yew and Schmidt, Schmidt and Hung elaborate on the cognitive constructivist process of PBL:

- Learners are presented with a problem and through discussion within their group, activate their prior knowledge.
- Within their group, they develop possible theories or hypotheses to explain the problem. Together they identify learning issues to be researched. They construct

a shared primary model to explain the problem at hand. Facilitators provide scaffolding, which is a framework on which students can construct knowledge relating to the problem.

- After the initial teamwork, students work independently in self-directed study to research the identified issues.
- The students re-group to discuss their findings and refine their initial explanations based on what they learned.

A PBL group.

PBL follows a constructivist perspective in learning as the role of the instructor is to guide and challenge the learning process rather than strictly providing knowledge. From this perspective, feedback and reflection on the learning process and group dynamics are essential components of PBL. Students are considered to be active agents who engage in social knowledge construction. PBL assists in processes of creating meaning and building personal interpretations of the world based on experiences and interactions. PBL assists to guide the student from theory to practice during their journey through solving the problem.

Supporting Evidence

Several studies support the success of the constructivist problem-based and inquiry learning methods. One example is a study on a project called GenScope, an inquiry-based science software application, which found that students using the GenScope software showed significant gains over the control groups, with the largest gains shown in students from basic courses.

One large study tracked middle school students' performance on high-stakes standardized tests to evaluate the effectiveness of inquiry-based science. The study found a 14 percent improvement for the first cohort of students and a 13 percent improvement for the second cohort. The study also found that inquiry-based teaching methods greatly reduced the achievement gap for African-American students.

A systematic review of the effects of problem-based learning in medical school on the performance of doctors after graduation showed clear positive effects on physician competence. This effect was especially strong for social and cognitive competencies such as coping with uncertainty and communication skills.

Another study from Slovenia looked at whether students who learn with PBL are better at solving problems and if their attitudes towards mathematics were improved compared to their peers in a more traditional curriculum. The study found that students who were exposed to PBL were better at solving more difficult problems; however, there was no significant difference in student attitude towards mathematics.

Examples in Curricula

Medical Schools

Several medical schools have incorporated problem-based learning into their curricula following the lead of McMaster University Medical School, using real patient cases to teach students how to think like a clinician. More than eighty percent of medical schools in the United States now have some form of problem-based learning in their programs. Research of 10 years of data from the University of Missouri School of Medicine indicates that PBL has a positive effect on the students' competency as physicians after graduation.

In 1998, Western University of Health Sciences opened its College of Veterinary Medicine, with curriculum based completely on PBL.

In 2002, UC Berkeley – UCSF Joint Medical Program (JMP), an accredited five year Master of Science/Medical Doctorate Program housed at University of California, Berkeley School of Public Health, began offering a 100% case based curriculum to their students in their pre-clerkship years. The curriculum integrates the basic and preclinical sciences while fostering an understanding of the biological, social and moral contexts of human health and disease. The students spend their last two clerkship years at University of California, San Francisco.

In 2002, Gadjah Mada University of Yogyakarta, Indonesia began offering an International Medicine program based on problem-based learning.

Ecological Economics

The transdisciplinary field of ecological economics has embraced problem-based learning as a core pedagogy. A workbook developed by Joshua Farley, Jon Erickson and Herman Daly organizes the problem-solving process into (1) building the problem base, (2) analyzing the problem, (3) synthesizing the findings and (4) communicating the results. Building the problem base includes choosing, defining and structuring an ecological economic problem. Analysis is breaking down of a problem into understandable components. Synthesis is the re-integration of the parts in a way that helps better understand the whole. Communication is the translation of results into a form relevant to stakeholders, broadly defined as the extended peer community.

Other Outcomes

One of the aims of PBL is the development of self-directed learning (SDL) skills. In Loyens, Magda and Rikers' discussion, SDL is defined as "a process in which individuals take the initiative in diagnosing their learning needs, formulating goals, identifying human and material resources, choosing and implementing appropriate learning strategies and evaluating learning outcomes". By being invited into the learning process, students are also invited to take responsibility for their learning, which leads to an increase in self-directed learning skills. In Severiens and Schmidt's study of 305 first year college students, they found that PBL and its focus on SDL led to motivation for students to maintain study pace, led to social and academic integration, encouraged development of cognitive skills and fostered more study progress than students in a conventional learning setting. PBL encourages learners to take a place in the academic world through inquiring and discovery that is central to problem-based learning.

PBL is also argued as a learning method that can promote the development of critical thinking skills. In PBL learning, students learn how to analyze a problem, identify relevant facts and generate hypotheses, identify necessary information/knowledge for solving the problem and make reasonable judgments about solving the problem.

Employers have appreciated the positive attributes of communication, teamwork, respect and collaboration that PBL experienced students have developed. These skills provide for better future skills preparation in the ever-changing information explosion. PBL curriculum includes building these attributes through knowledge building, written and interpersonal interactions and through the experience of the problem solving process.

Computer-supported Collaborative Learning

Computer-supported PBL can be an electronic version (ePBL) of the traditional face-to-face paper-based PBL or an online group activity with participants located distant apart. ePBL provides the opportunity to embed audios and videos, related to the skills (e.g. clinical findings) within the case scenarios improving learning environment and thus enhance students' engagement in the learning process. Comparing face-to-face setting with strict online PBL, the group activities play the key role in the success of the social interaction in PBL. Online PBL is also seen as more cost-effective. Collaborative PBL has been shown to improve critical thinking scores as compared with individual PBL and increased students' achievement levels and retention scores.

For the instructors, instructional design principles for the instructors regarding the design and development of online PBL must include collaborative characteristics. For example, the scheduling must be conducive to collaborative activities. Additionally, instructors should ensure that the problems should be relevant to real-life experiences and the nature of solutions and problem contexts. Furthermore, a sound technological infrastructure is paramount.

The establishment and application of PBL in teaching and training started as early as in the 1960s. As instructional technology developed over time coupled with the emergence of the internet in the mid-1990s, online education became popular gaining huge attention from organizations and institutions. However, the use of PBL in complete online education does not seem as established based on the relatively scarce references available in the literature. In 2001, the University of Southern Queensland (USQ) was one of the first few faculties that utilized a learning management system (LMS) to facilitate collaboration and group problem-solving. The result showed the significant impact of online PBL on the learning outcomes of students in many aspects including enhancing their communication skills, problem-solving skills and ability to work as a team. The most successful feature of the LMS in terms of user rate was the discussion boards where asynchronous communications took place. Technology has advanced for another decade since then and it should help us take online PBL to a greater height as many more activities such as synchronous online meetings have been made readily available today on numerous platforms. The key focus here is to examine how technology can further facilitate the effective use of PBL online by zooming into the learner needs in each phase of PBL.

Tools

Collaborative Tools

The first and possibly most crucial phase in PBL, is to identify the problem. Before learners can begin to solve a problem, all members must understand and agree on the details of the problem. This consensus forms through collaboration and discussion. With online learning on the rise, it is important that learners can engage in collaborative brainstorming and research through the use of technology. Technology allows for groups to collaborate synchronously or asynchronously from anywhere in the world; schedules and geography no longer prevent collaboration in PBL. Today, there is a plethora of tools available to promote group collaboration online, each with unique strengths and limitations. Learning management systems and cloud-based solutions are the two most popular and accessible technological solution for online collaboration. Learning management systems, such as Canvas, Edmodo, Moodle, Schoology and itslearning, provide schools and classrooms collaborative tools to support synchronous and asynchronous communication and learning.

The learning management systems (LMS) allow for supervision and support by the course administrator or professor. One limitation of these systems is their availability; most LMS are restricted by course enrollment. Students must be enrolled in a particular course or subscribe to a specific class to gain access to the tools and content stored in the system. Cloud-based solutions on the other hand, such as Google Apps, OneNote and the Office 365 suit offer collaborative tools outside the traditional education setting. Educators of all kinds (K-12 schools, colleges and universities, vocational training, HR training teams, etc.) can access these cloud-based solutions and collaborate with anyone around the world by simply sharing a link. These tools range in availability from free with an email account to subscription costs based on the suit purchased. In addition to potential financial limitations, these cloud-based systems are always as secure or private as an LMS that requires course enrollment. Both LMS and cloud-based solutions present learners with opportunities to collaborate in a variety of ways while brainstorming the meaning of the problem and developing a plan for research and future collaboration.

Research Tools

Once the problem has been identified, learners move into the second step of PBL: the information gathering phase. In this phase, learners research the problem by gathering background information and researching potential solutions. This information is shared with the learning team and used to generate potential solutions, each with supporting evidence. The most popular online tool for gathering information today is Google, but there are many other search-engines available online. Free search engines, such as Google, Yahoo, or Bing, offer access to seemingly countless links to information. While these research tools provide ample sources of potential information, the quantity can be overwhelming. It also becomes difficult to identify quality sources without adding filters and higher-level search strategies when using these broad search-engines. Libraries are a more selective option and often offer online-databases, but typically require an account or subscription for online access to articles and books. Wolframalpha.com is a smart search-engine with both free and subscription level access options. Wolfram claims to be more than a platform for searching the web, rather, getting knowledge and answers by doing dynamic computations based on a vast collection of built-in data, algorithms and methods.

Presentation Tools

The third most important phase of PBL is resolving the problem, the critical task is presenting and defending your solution to the given problem. Students need to be able to state the problem clearly, describe the process of problem-solving considering different options to overcome difficulties, support the solution using relevant information and data analysis. Being able to communicate and present the solution clearly is the key to the success of this phase as it directly affects the learning outcomes. With the help of technology, presentation has been made much easier and more effective as it can incorporate visual aids of charts, pictures, videos, animations, simulations etc. Ideas and connections between ideas can be clearly demonstrated using different tools. Microsoft PowerPoint 2016, Apple Keynote, Prezi and Google Slides are among the top-rated presentation applications of 2017.

These popular presentation tools have their distinctive features and advantages over one another and can be summarized into three broad types. The first type has almost everything a presenter needs, ranging from tables, charts, picture tools, animations, video tools, add in functions and so forth. Such tools can replace many authoring tools as more complicated functions such as creating simulations, drag and drop etc. are all made possible. Hence, the presentation can be made highly interactive, engaging and compatible with most devices. The best examples are Microsoft PowerPoint and Apple Keynote. However, one drawback is that such tools often come at a subscription charge and need to be installed locally on devices. Both PowerPoint and Keynote point more towards the standard form of slide by slide presentations. Prezi represents the second major type of tools with a storytelling style and less traditional or structured form of presentation that allows one to zoom in and out of any part of the screen. These tools are generally web-based and have collaborative functions of value-add for the PBL process. Nevertheless, this type of tools also charge subscription fees based on privilege levels. The third broad type of tools would be the web-based ones free of charge with less fanciful effects, allowing access to presentations collaboratively online anytime. Google Slides is such an option which is easy to use. Though it has fewer functions, it offers the convenience of being available anytime anywhere on any online device. This type can be effective when students have limited time to prepare for their presentations as it removes many technical difficulties such as arranging for face-to-face meetings, installing the presentation tool or the time needed to learn to create the presentation. Students can spend more time on meaningful discussions about their problem and solution instead of the presentation itself.

P^{5}BL Approach

P^{5}BL stands for People, Problem, Process, Product and Project Based Learning.

The P^{5}BL approach was a learning strategy introduced in Stanford School of Engineering in their P^{5}BL laboratory in 1993 as an initiative to offer their graduate students from the engineering, architecture and construction disciplines to implement their skills in a "cross-disciplinary, collaborative and geographically distributed teamwork experience". In this approach, which was pioneered by Stanford Professor Fruchter, an environment across six universities from Europe, the United States and Japan along with a toolkit to capture and share project knowledge was developed. The students (people) from the three disciplines were assigned a team project that works on solving a problem and delivering an end-product to a client.

The main stress of this approach is to have an inter-disciplinary integrated development of deliverables, in order to improve the overall competency and skills of the students. P^5BL mentoring is a structured activity that involves situated learning and constructivist learning strategies to foster the culture of practice that would extend beyond the university campus to real life. P^5BL is all about encouraging teaching and learning teamwork in the information age, by facilitating team interaction with professors, industry mentors and owners who provide necessary guidance and support for the learning activity.

Key advantages of this method are that it familiarizes students with real world problems and improves their confidence in solving these. It also improves their networking skills, thereby establishing rapport with key persons of the industry. They also learn the value of teamwork. The method also creates in them an appreciation of interdisciplinary approach.

The approach however needs due consideration of the mentoring provided to the students. Appropriate scaffolding should be done by the mentors to ensure that students are successful in attaining their project goals to solve the problem. Communication between the team should also be open and constructive in nature for achieving the necessary milestones.

Distance Education

Distance education or long-distance learning is the education of students who may not always be physically present at a school. Traditionally, this usually involved correspondence courses wherein the student corresponded with the school via post. Today it involves online education. A distance learning program can be completely distance learning, or a combination of distance learning and traditional classroom instruction (called hybrid or blended). Massive open online courses (MOOCs), offering large-scale interactive participation and open access through the World Wide Web or other network technologies, are recent developments in distance education. A number of other terms (distributed learning, e-learning, online learning, virtual classroom etc.) are used roughly synonymously with distance education.

One of the earliest attempts was advertised in 1728. This was in the *Boston Gazette* for Caleb Philipps, Teacher of the new method of Short Hand, who sought students who wanted to learn through weekly mailed lessons.

The first distance education course in the modern sense was provided by Sir Isaac Pitman in the 1840s, who taught a system of shorthand by mailing texts transcribed into shorthand on postcards and receiving transcriptions from his students in return for correction. The element of student feedback was a crucial innovation of Pitman's system. This scheme was made possible by the introduction of uniform postage rates across England in 1840.

This early beginning proved extremely successful and the Phonographic Correspondence Society was founded three years later to establish these courses on a more formal basis. The Society paved the way for the later formation of Sir Isaac Pitman Colleges across the country.

The first correspondence school in the United States was the Society to Encourage Studies at Home, which was founded in 1873.

University Correspondence Courses

The University of London was the first university to offer distance learning degrees, establishing its External Programme in 1858. The background to this innovation lay in the fact that the institution (later known as University College London) was non-denominational and, given the intense religious rivalries at the time, there was an outcry against the godless university. The issue soon boiled down to which institutions had degree-granting powers and which institutions did not.

The London University.

The compromise solution that emerged in 1836 was that the sole authority to conduct the examinations leading to degrees would be given to a new officially recognized entity called the "University of London", which would act as examining body for the University of London colleges, originally University College London and King's College London and award their students University of London degrees. As Sheldon Rothblatt states: Thus arose in nearly archetypal form the famous English distinction between teaching and examining, here embodied in separate institutions."

With the state giving examining powers to a separate entity, the groundwork was laid for the creation of a programme within the new university which would both administer examinations and award qualifications to students taking instruction at another institution or pursuing a course of self-directed study.

Referred to as "People's University" by Charles Dickens because it provided access to higher education to students from less affluent backgrounds, the External Programme was chartered by Queen Victoria in 1858, making the University of London the first university to offer distance learning degrees to students. Enrollment increased steadily during the late 19th century and its example was widely copied elsewhere. This program is now known as the University of London International Programme and includes Postgraduate, Undergraduate and Diploma degrees created by colleges such as the London School of Economics, Royal Holloway and Goldsmiths.

William Rainey Harper, encouraged the development of external university courses at the new University of Chicago in the 1890s.

In the United States, William Rainey Harper, first president of the University of Chicago, celebrated the concept of extended education, whereby the research university had satellite colleges in the wider community.

In 1892, Harper encouraged correspondence courses to further promote education, an idea that was put into practice by Chicago, Wisconsin, Columbia and several dozen other universities by the 1920s Columbia University. Enrollment in the largest private for-profit school based in Scranton, Pennsylvania, the International Correspondence Schools grew explosively in the 1890s. Founded in 1888 to provide training for immigrant coal miners aiming to become state mine inspectors or foremen, it enrolled 2500 new students in 1894 and matriculated 72,000 new students in 1895. By 1906 total enrollments reached 900,000. The growth was due to sending out complete textbooks instead of single lessons and the use of 1200 aggressive in-person salesmen. There was a stark contrast in pedagogy:

> "The regular technical school or college aims to educate a man broadly; our aim, on the contrary, is to educate him only along some particular

> line. The college demands that a student shall have certain educational qualifications to enter it and that all students study for approximately the same length of time; when they have finished their courses they are supposed to be qualified to enter any one of a number of branches in some particular profession. We, on the contrary, are aiming to make our courses fit the particular needs of the student who takes them."

Education was a high priority in the Progressive Era, as American high schools and colleges expanded greatly. For men who were older or were too busy with family responsibilities, night schools were opened, such as the YMCA school in Boston that became Northeastern University. Outside the big cities, private correspondence schools offered a flexible, narrowly focused solution. Large corporations systematized their training programs for new employees. The National Association of Corporation Schools grew from 37 in 1913 to 146 in 1920. Starting in the 1880s, private schools opened across the country which offered specialized technical training to anyone who enrolled, not just the employees of one company. Starting in Milwaukee in 1907, public schools began opening free vocational programs.

Only a third of the American population lived in cities of 100,000 or more population In 1920; to reach the rest, correspondence techniques had to be adopted. Australia, with its vast distances, was especially active; the University of Queensland established its Department of Correspondence Studies in 1911. In South Africa, the University of South Africa, formerly an examining and certification body, started to present distance education tuition in 1946. The International Conference for Correspondence Education held its first meeting in 1938. The goal was to provide individualized education for students, at low cost, by using a pedagogy of testing, recording, classification and differentiation. The organization has since been renamed as the International Council for Open and Distance Education (ICDE), with headquarters in Oslo, Norway.

Open Universities

The Open University in the United Kingdom was founded by the-then Labour government led by Prime Minister, Harold Wilson, based on the vision of Michael Young. Planning commenced in 1965 under the Minister of State for Education, Jennie Lee, who established a model for the Open University (OU) as one of widening access to the highest standards of scholarship in higher education and set up a planning committee consisting of university vice-chancellors, educationalists and television broadcasters, chaired by Sir Peter Venables. The British Broadcasting Corporation (BBC) Assistant Director of Engineering at the time, James Redmond, had obtained most of his qualifications at night school and his natural enthusiasm for the project did much to overcome the technical difficulties of using television to broadcast teaching programmes.

Walton Hall, renovated in 1970 to act as the headquarters of the newly established Open University.

The Open University revolutionised the scope of the correspondence program and helped to create a respectable learning alternative to the traditional form of education. It has been at the forefront of developing new technologies to improve the distance learning service as well as undertaking research in other disciplines. Walter Perry was appointed the OU's first vice-chancellor in January 1969 and its foundation secretary was Anastasios Christodoulou. The election of the new Conservative government under the leadership of Edward Heath, in 1970; led to budget cuts under Chancellor of the Exchequer Iain Macleod (who had earlier called the idea of an Open University blithering nonsense). However, the OU accepted its first 25,000 students in 1971, adopting a radical open admissions policy. At the time, the total student population of conventional universities in the United Kingdom was around 130,000.

Athabasca University, Canada's Open University, was created in 1970 and followed a similar, though independently developed, pattern. The Open University inspired the creation of Spain's National University of Distance Education and Germany's FernUniversität in Hagen. There are now many similar institutions around the world, often with the name Open University (in English or in the local language).

Most open universities use distance education technologies as delivery methods, though some require attendance at local study centres or at regional summer schools. Some open universities have grown to become *mega-universities*, a term coined to denote institutions with more than 100,000 students.

Technologies

Internet technology has enabled many forms of distance learning through open educational resources and facilities such as e-learning and MOOCs. Although the expansion of the Internet blurs the boundaries, distance education technologies are divided into two modes of delivery: synchronous learning and asynchronous learning.

In synchronous learning, all participants are "present" at the same time. In this regard, it resembles traditional classroom teaching methods despite the participants being located remotely. It requires a timetable to be organized. Web conferencing, videoconferencing, educational television, instructional television are examples of synchronous technology, as are direct-broadcast satellite (DBS), internet radio, live streaming, telephone and web-based VoIP. Web conferencing software helps to facilitate meetings in distance learning courses and usually contain additional interaction tools such as text chat, polls, hand raising, emoticons etc. These tools also support asynchronous participation by students being able to listen to recordings of synchronous sessions. Immersive environments (notably SecondLife) have also been used to enhance participant presence in distance education courses. Another form of synchronous learning that has been entering the classroom over the last couple of years is the use of robot proxies including those that allow sick students to attend classes.

Some universities have been starting to use robot proxies to enable more engaging synchronous hybrid classes where both remote and in person students can be present and interact using telerobotics devices such as the Kubi Telepresence robot stand that looks around and the Double Robot that roams around. With these telepresence robots, the remote students have a seat at the table or desk instead of being on a screen on the wall.

In asynchronous learning, participants access course materials flexibly on their own schedules. Students are not required to be together at the same time. Mail correspondence, which is the oldest form of distance education, is an asynchronous delivery technology, as are message board forums, e-mail, video and audio recordings, print materials, voicemail and fax.

The two methods can be combined. Many courses offered by both open universities and an increasing number of campus based institutions use periodic sessions of residential or day teaching to supplement the sessions delivered at a distance. This type of mixed distance and campus based education has recently come to be called blended learning" or less often "hybrid learning". Many open universities uses a blend of technologies and a blend of learning modalities (face-to-face, distance and hybrid) all under the rubric of "distance learning".

Distance learning can also use interactive radio instruction (IRI), interactive audio instruction (IAI), online virtual worlds, digital games, webinars and webcasts, all of which are referred to as e-Learning.

Radio and Television

The rapid spread of film in the 1920s and radio in the 1930s led to proposals to use it for distance education. By 1938, at least 200 city school systems, 25 state boards of education and many colleges and universities broadcast educational programs for the public schools. One line of thought was to use radio as a master teacher.

> Experts in given fields broadcast lessons for pupils within the many schoolrooms of the public school system, asking questions, suggesting readings, making assignments and conducting tests. This mechanizes education and leaves the local teacher only the tasks of preparing for the broadcast and keeping order in the classroom.

A typical setup came in Kentucky in 1948 when John Wilkinson Taylor, president of the University of Louisville, teamed up with NBC to use radio as a medium for distance education, The chairman of the Federal Communications Commission endorsed the project and predicted that the college-by-radio would put American education 25 years ahead. The University was owned by the city and local residents would pay the low tuition rates, receive their study materials in the mail and listen by radio to live classroom discussions that were held on campus. Physicist Daniel Q. Posin also was a pioneer in the field of distance education when he hosted a televised course through DePaul University.

Charles Wedemeyer of the University of Wisconsin–Madison also promoted new methods. From 1964 to 1968, the Carnegie Foundation funded Wedemeyer's *Project* (AIM) which brought in a variety of communications technologies aimed at providing learning to an off-campus population. The radio courses faded away in the 1950s. Many efforts to use television along the same lines proved unsuccessful, despite heavy funding by the Ford Foundation.

From 1970 to 1972 the Coordinating Commission for Higher Education in California funded Project Outreach to study the potential of telecourses. The study included the University of California, California State University and the community colleges. This study led to coordinated instructional systems legislation allowing the use of public funds for non-classroom instruction and paved the way for the emergence of telecourses as the precursor to the online courses and programs of today. The Coastline Community Colleges, The Dallas County Community College District and Miami Dade Community College led the way. The *Adult Learning Service* of the US Public Broadcasting Service came into being and the "wrapped" series and individually produced telecourse for credit became a significant part of the history of distance education and online learning.

Internet

The widespread use of computers and the internet have made distance learning easier and faster and today virtual schools and virtual universities deliver full curricula online. The capacity of Internet to support voice, video, text and immersion teaching methods made earlier distinct forms of telephone, videoconferencing, radio, television and text based education somewhat redundant. However, many of the techniques developed and lessons learned with earlier media are used in Internet delivery.

The first completely online course for credit was offered by the University of Toronto in 1984 through the Graduate School of Education (then called OISE: the Ontario Institute for Studies in Education). The topic was "Women and Computers in Education", dealing with gender issues and educational computing. The first new and fully online university was founded in 1994 as the Open University of Catalonia, headquartered in Barcelona, Spain. In 1999 Jones International University was launched as the first fully online university accredited by a regional accrediting association in the US.

Between 2000 and 2008, enrollment in distance education courses increased rapidly in almost every country in both developed and developing countries. Many private, public, non-profit and for-profit institutions worldwide now offer distance education courses from the most basic instruction through to the highest levels of degree and doctoral programs. New York University, International University Canada, for example, offers online degrees in engineering and management-related fields through NYU Tandon Online. Levels of accreditation vary: widely respected universities such as Stanford University and Harvard now deliver online courses—but other online schools receive little outside oversight and some are actually fraudulent, i.e., diploma mills. In the US, the Distance Education Accrediting Commission (DEAC) specializes in the accreditation of distance education institutions.

In the United States in 2011, it was found that a third of all the students enrolled in postsecondary education had taken an accredited online course in a postsecondary institution. Even though growth rates are slowing, enrollment for online courses has been seen to increase with the advance in technology. The majority of public and private colleges now offer full academic programs online. These include, but are not limited to, training programs in the mental health, occupational therapy, family therapy, art therapy, physical therapy and rehabilitation counseling fields.

Distance education has a long history, but its popularity and use has grown exponentially as more advanced technology has become available. By 2008, online learning programs were available in the United States in 44 states at the K-12 level.

Internet forums, online discussion group and online learning community can contribute to an efficacious distance education experience. Research shows that socialization plays an important role in some forms of distance education.

E-courses are also a viable option for distance learning. There are many available that cover a broad range of topics.

Paced and Self-paced Models

Distance education can be delivered in a paced format similar to traditional campus based models in which learners commence and complete a course at the same time. Paced delivery is currently the most common mode of distance education delivery. Alternatively, some institutions offer self-paced programs that allow for continuous enrollment and the length of time to complete the course is set by the learner's time, skill and commitment levels. Paced courses may be offered in either synchronous mode, but self-paced courses are almost always offered asynchronously. Each delivery model offers both advantages and disadvantages for students, teachers and institutions.

Kaplan and Haenlein classify distance education into four groups along the dimensions Time dependency and Number of participants: 1) MOOCs (Massive Open Online Courses): Open-access online course (i.e., without specific participation restrictions) that allows for unlimited (massive) participation; 2) SPOCs (Small Private Online Courses): Online course that only offers a limited number of places and therefore requires some form of formal enrollment; 3) SMOCs (Synchronous Massive Online Courses): Open-access online course that allows for unlimited participation but requires students to be present at the same time (synchronously); 4) SSOCs (Synchronous Private Online Courses): Online course that only offers a limited number of places and requires students to be present at the same time (synchronously).

Paced models are a familiar mode as they are used almost exclusively in campus based schools. Institutes that offer both distance and campus programs usually use paced models as teacher workload, student semester planning, tuition deadlines, exam schedules and other administrative details can be synchronized with campus delivery. Student familiarity and the pressure of deadlines encourages students to readily adapt to and usually succeed in paced models. However, student freedom is sacrificed as a common pace is often too fast for some students and too slow for others. In addition life events, professional or family responsibilities can interfere with a student's capability to complete tasks to an external schedule. Finally, paced models allows students to readily form communities of inquiry and to engage in collaborative work.

Self-paced courses maximize student freedom, as not only can students commence studies on any date, but they can complete a course in as little time as a few weeks or up to a year or longer. Students often enroll in self-paced study when they are under pressure to complete programs, have not been able to complete a scheduled course, need additional courses or have pressure which precludes regular study for any length of time. The self-paced nature of the programming, though is an unfamiliar model for many students and can lead to excessive procrastination resulting in course incompletion. Assessment of learning can also be challenging as exams can be written on any day, making it possible for students to share examination questions with resulting loss of academic integrity. Finally, it is extremely challenging to organize collaborative work activities, though some schools are developing cooperative models based upon networked and connectivist pedagogies, for use in self-paced programs.

Benefits

Distance learning can expand access to education and training for both general populace and businesses since its flexible scheduling structure lessens the effects of the many time-constraints imposed by personal responsibilities and commitments. Devolving some activities off-site alleviates institutional capacity constraints arising from the traditional demand on institutional buildings and infrastructure. Furthermore, there is the potential for increased access to more experts in the field and to other students from diverse geographical, social, cultural, economic and experiential backgrounds. As the population at large becomes more involved in lifelong learning beyond the normal schooling age, institutions can benefit financially and adult learning business courses may be particularly lucrative. Distance education programs can act as a catalyst for institutional innovation and are at least as effective as face-to-face learning programs, especially if the instructor is knowledgeable and skilled.

Distance education can also provide a broader method of communication within the realm of education. With the many tools and programs that technological advancements have to offer, communication appears to increase in distance education amongst students and their professors, as well as students and their classmates. The distance educational increase in communication, particularly communication amongst students and their classmates, is an improvement that has been made to provide distance education students with as many of the opportunities as possible as they would receive in in-person education. The improvement being made in distance education is growing in tandem with the constant technological advancements. Present-day online communication allows students to associate with accredited schools and programs throughout the world that are out of reach for in-person learning. By having the opportunity to be involved in global institutions via distance education, a diverse array of thought is presented to students through communication with their classmates. This is beneficial because students have the opportunity to combine new opinions with their own and develop a solid foundation for learning. It has been shown through research that as learners become aware of the variations in interpretation and construction of meaning among a range of people [they] construct an individual meaning, which can help students become knowledgeable of a wide array of viewpoints in education. To increase the likelihood that students will build effective ties with one another during the course, instructors should use similar assignments for students across different locations to overcome the influence of co-location on relationship building.

The high cost of education affects students in higher education, to which distance education may be an alternative in order to provide some relief. Distance education has been a more cost-effective form of learning and can sometimes save students a significant amount of money as opposed to traditional education. Distance education may be able to help to save students a considerable amount financially by removing the cost of transportation. In addition, distance education may be able to save students from the economic burden of high-priced course textbooks. Many textbooks are now available as electronic textbooks, known as e-textbooks, which can offer digital textbooks for a reduced price in comparison to traditional textbooks. Also, the increasing improvements in technology have resulted in many school libraries having a partnership with digital publishers that offer course materials for free, which can help students significantly with educational costs.

Within the class, students are able to learn in ways that traditional classrooms would not be able to provide. It is able to promote good learning experiences and therefore, allow students to obtain higher satisfaction with their online learning. For example, students can review their lessons more than once according to their need. Students can then manipulate the coursework to fit their learning by focusing more on their weaker topics while breezing through concepts that they already have or can easily grasp. When course design and the learning environment are at their optimal conditions, distance education can lead students to higher satisfaction with their learning experiences. Studies have shown that high satisfaction correlates to increased learning. For those in a healthcare or mental health distance learning program, online-based interactions have the potential to foster deeper reflections and discussions of client issues as well as a quicker response to client issues, since supervision happens on a regular basis and is not limited to a weekly supervision meeting. This also may contribute to the students feeling a greater sense of support, since they have ongoing and regular access to their instructors and other students.

Distance learning may enable students who are unable to attend a traditional school setting, due to disability or illness such as decreased mobility and immune system suppression, to get a good education. Children who are sick or are unable to attend classes are able to attend them in person through the use of robot proxies. This helps the students have experiences of the classroom and social interaction that they are unable to receive at home or the hospital, while still keeping them in a safe learning environment. Over the last few years[ ] more students are entering safely back into the classroom thanks to the help of robots. An article from the *New York Times*, “A Swiveling Proxy Will Even Wear a Tutu”, explains the positive impact of virtual learning in the classroom and another that explains how even a simple, stationary telepresence robot can help. Distance education may provide equal access regardless of socioeconomic status or income, area of residence, gender, race, age, or cost per student. Applying universal design strategies to distance learning courses as they are being developed (rather than instituting accommodations for specific students on an as-needed basis) can increase the accessibility of such courses to students with a range of abilities, disabilities, learning styles and native languages. Distance education graduates, who would never have been associated with the school under a traditional system, may donate money to the school.

Distance learning may also offer a final opportunity for adolescents that are no longer permitted in the general education population due to behavior disorders. Instead of these students having no other academic opportunities, they may continue their education from their homes and earn their diplomas, offering them another chance to be an integral part of society.

Distance learning offers individuals a unique opportunity to benefit from the expertise and resources of the best universities currently available. Students have the ability to collaborate, share, question, infer and suggest new methods and techniques for continuous improvement of the content. The ability to complete a course at a pace that is appropriate for each individual is the most effective manner to learn given the personal demands on time and schedule. Self-paced distance learning on a mobile device, such is a smartphone, provides maximum flexibility and capability.

Criticism

Barriers to effective distance education include obstacles such as domestic distractions and unreliable technology, as well as students' program costs, adequate contact with teachers and support services and a need for more experience.

Some students attempt to participate in distance education without proper training with the tools needed to be successful in the program. Students must be provided with training opportunities (if needed) on each tool that is used throughout the program. The lack of advanced technology skills can lead to an unsuccessful experience. Schools have a responsibility to adopt a proactive policy for managing technology barriers. Time management skills and self-discipline in distance education is just as important as complete knowledge of the software and tools being used for learning.

The results of a study of Washington state community college students showed that distance learning students tended to drop out more often than their traditional counterparts due to difficulties in language, time management and study skills.

According to Dr. Pankaj Singhm, director of Nims University, "distance learning benefits may outweigh the disadvantages for students in such a technology-driven society; however before indulging into use of educational technology a few more disadvantages should be considered. He describes that over multiple years, all of the obstacles have been overcome and the world environment for distance education continues to improve. Dr. Pankaj Singhm also claims there is a debate to distance education stating, due to a lack of direct face-to-face social interaction. However, as more people become used to personal and social interaction online (for example dating, chat rooms, shopping, or blogging), it is becoming easier for learners to both project themselves and socialize with others. This is an obstacle that has dissipated.

Not all courses required to complete a degree may be offered online. Health care profession programs in particular, require some sort of patient interaction through field work before a student may graduate. Studies have also shown that students pursuing a medical professional graduate degree who are participating in distance education courses, favor face to face communication over professor-mediated chat rooms and independent studies. However, this is little correlation between student performance when comparing the previous different distance learning strategies.

There is a theoretical problem about the application of traditional teaching methods to online courses because online courses may have no upper size limit. Daniel Barwick noted that there is no evidence that large class size is always worse or that small class size is always better, although a negative link has been established between certain types of instruction in large classes and learning outcomes; he argued that higher education has not made a sufficient effort to experiment with a variety of instructional methods to determine whether large class size is always negatively correlated with a reduction in learning outcomes. Early proponents of Massive Open Online Courses (MOOC)s saw them as just the type of experiment that Barwick had pointed out was lacking in higher education, although Barwick himself has never advocated for MOOCs.

There may also be institutional challenges. Distance learning is new enough that it may be a challenge to gain support for these programs in a traditional brick-and-mortar academic learning environment. Furthermore, it may be more difficult for the instructor to organize and plan a distance learning program, especially since many are new programs and their organizational needs are different from a traditional learning program.

Additionally, though distance education offers industrial countries the opportunity to become globally informed, there are still negative sides to it. Hellman states that "These include its cost and capital intensiveness, time constraints and other pressures on instructors, the isolation of students from instructors and their peers, instructors' enormous difficulty in adequately evaluating students they never meet face-to-face and drop-out rates far higher than in classroom-based courses."

A more complex challenge of distance education relates to cultural differences between student and teachers and among students. Distance programmes tend to be more diverse as they could go beyond the geographical borders of regions, countries and continents and cross the cultural borders that may exist with respect to race, gender and religion. That requires a proper understanding and awareness of the norms, differences, preconceptions and potential conflicting issues.

Educational Technology

The modern use of electronic educational technology (also called e-learning) facilitates distance learning and independent learning by the extensive use of information and communications technology (ICT), replacing traditional content delivery by postal correspondence. Instruction can be synchronous and asynchronous online communication in an interactive learning environment or virtual communities, in lieu of a physical classroom. The focus is shifted to the education transaction in the form of virtual community of learners sustainable across time.

One of the most significant issues encountered in the mainstream correspondence model of distance education is transactional distance, which results from the lack of appropriate communication between learner and teacher. This gap has been observed to become wider if there is no communication between the learner and teacher and has direct implications over the learning process and future endeavors in distance education. Distance education providers began to introduce various strategies, techniques and procedures to increase the amount of interaction between learner and teacher. These measures e.g. more frequent face-to-face tutorials, increased use of information and communication technologies including teleconferencing and the Internet, were designed to close the gap in transactional distance.

Credentials

Online credentials for learning are digital credentials that are offered in place of traditional paper credentials for a skill or educational achievement. Directly linked to the accelerated development of internet communication technologies, the development of digital badges, electronic passports and massive open online courses (MOOCs) have a very direct bearing on our understanding of learning, recognition and levels as they pose a direct challenge to the status quo. It is useful to distinguish between three forms of online credentials: Test-based credentials, online badges and online certificates.

Vocational Qualification Transfer System

The Vocational Qualification Transfer System (VQTS) model is a proposal for a structured description of work-related competences. The core elements are the Competence Matrix and the Competence Profiles. A Competence Matrix displays competences structurally in a table according to core work tasks in a specific occupational field ("competence area") and the progress of competence development ("step of competence development"). Competence Profiles are formed from individual parts of this Competence Matrix. In the context of ECVET the VQTS project sought to support the transnational mobility of learners. A Competence Matrix can be used for the development of qualifications, training programmes and job profiles, as well as for human resource planning, the allocation of qualifications to the Qualifications Framework and for developing higher permeability between vocational education and higher education.

Goals

The main goal of the VQTS model is the development of a systematic process for the comparison of competences and qualifications and for the transnational transfer of competences acquired abroad (for example between education and working environment, or between vocational and higher education).

Structure

Competence Matrix

Competence Matrix "Mechatronics"

Competence area	Steps of competence development					
1. Maintaining and assuring the reliability of mechatronic systems	He/She can perform the basic scheduled maintenance on mechatronic machines and systems and adhere to the equipment maintenance plans.	He/She can master the maintenance procedures for mechatronic systems such as the use of service documents and maintenance plans and, if faced with new challenges, can make the necessary adaptations.	He/She can use preventive maintenance to assure the trouble-free operation of mechatronic systems. In addition, he/she can modify operational sequences to implement quality-assurance measures	He/She can develop the necessary procedures for maintenance of mechatronic devices and systems, and can schedule the maintenance and quality-assurance procedures.		
2. Installing and dismantling mechatronic systems and facilities	He/She can use written instructions to install and dismantle individual components (e.g., sensors, actuators, drives, motors, transport systems, racks) that form a functional group of mechatronic systems.	He/She can master the installation and dismantling of mechatronic systems that use several technologies (e.g., mechanics, hydraulics, pneumatics, electrical-mechanics, electronics), set up the connexion technology, and check the efficiency of the overall system.	He/She can provide independent mechatronic solutions for the construction of production lines, assure their overall ability to function, and, in addition, can use both existing and modified standard components.			
3. Installing and adjusting mechatronic components in systems and production lines	He/She is able to install and adjust standardized mechatronic components (e.g., individual electro-pneumatic valves, sensor and actuator units).	He/She can install and adjust components of mechatronic subsystems (e.g., linear drives, measuring systems, transport systems).	He/She can install and adjust complex mechatronic facilities that include diverse technologies and instrumentation and control (I&C) equipment, adjust the associated parameters, test the facilities overall functions, and assure their reliability			
4. Designing, adapting, and building mechatronic systems and facilities on the basis of client needs and site plans	He/She can use machine tools controlled either manually or via computer-program to fabricate (according to production designs and customer requirements) the individual components for mechatronic systems. He/she can provide simple designs and descriptions of mechatronic subsystems and can use basic CAD applications.	He/She can build simple mechatronic subsystems by using engineering drawing and can install the devices according to specific production needs. He/She can act on extensive knowledge of standards and regulations (e.g., on surface treatments) and is able to use CAD's more advanced functions (e.g., interference check).	He/She can build mechatronic systems by using both original construction techniques and previously designed parts. He/She fully understands CAD functions and can document system developments (e.g., parts lists, descriptions of function, operating instructions).	He/She can design and build autonomous mechatronic subsystems and, with suitable measuring and testing facilities, can assess the necessary production accuracy. He/She can document the results with quality-control systems.	He/She can make independent adaptations to the various devices (including selection of drives, sensors, PLC) and can use CNC programs for building the system. He/She can, through a digital mock up, assemble and simulate the functioning system and use computer-aided computations (e.g., FEM). He/She can perform cost-benefit analyses (e.g., as a basis for deciding whether components should be bought or individually constructed.)	He/She can independently develop complex mechatronic systems and can calculate the economic usefulness of the system. He/She can optimise CNC programs for the manufacturing of complex mechatronic devices and systems and monitor the automated quantity of an open loop control system.
5. Putting mechatronic systems into operation and providing clients with technical and economic support	He/She can, according to specifications and blueprints, put mechatronic devices into operation and provide support to the client in the hand-over phase.	He/She, after considering the enterprise's needs and basic conditions, can put the mechatronic systems into operation, create the necessary documentation, advise the customer on safe operations of the devices, and advise on future technology selection.	He/She, after considering all basic conditions, can master the start-up of interconnected mechatronic systems and machines, and can provide the necessary documentation including a manual. He/She can review client needs and configure machines that provide solutions. He/She can train the customer where necessary and provide support for safe operating procedures.	He/She can evaluate customer requirements for mechatronic facilities, develop solutions, and can plan the system's implementation and operation.	He/She can direct, including scheduling and time management, the start-up of the project from the creation of a proposal to the client's acceptance.	
6. Supervising and evaluating both the process sequences of mechatronic systems and facilities and the operational sequence (including quality assurance)	He/She can supervise process sequences according to specifications as well as implement any requested quality-control measures.	He/She can independently supervise the process sequences, evaluate the results, operate an accompanying statistic process control (SPC) for the quality control plan, and prepare simple work schedules, including production schedule and time management.	He/She can operate and supervise mechatronic facilities, choose testing and monitoring plans, set up the accompanying SPC, seek the optimal results of the production line according to material-flow, and provide work schedules including standard production times.	He/She can master the monitoring of complex mechatronic systems using virtual instruments and PPS systems as well as open loop control for the optimisation of machinery arrangement, material flow analysis, and scheduling.	He/She can optimise the process cycles of mechatronic production lines, provide instructions on modifying the PPS systems (e.g., adjustment to SAP systems) and introduce quality systems for continuous improvement processes (CIP/KVP).	
7. Installing, configuring, programming and testing hardware and software components for control and regulation of mechatronic systems and facilities	He/She is able to install and configure programs for hardware and software components as well as set up simple programmable logic control programs (PLC).	He/She can master the selection of hardware and software for mechatronic systems (e.g., sensors, actuators, interfaces, communication procedures) and can provide and test simple programmable logic control programs (PLC) according to production process requirements.	He/She can integrate and configure program-, control-, and regulation-mechanisms in mechatronic systems, program simple devices (in co-operation with developers), and simulate the program sequence before start-up.	He/She can develop, test, and configure hardware and software solutions for networked mechatronic systems; and can monitor system conditions with suitable measuring and visualisation tools.		
8. Preparing and distributing the technical information for adjustment of each enterprise's mechatronic systems	He/She can provide descriptions and designs of mechatronic subsystems and is familiar with the basic CAD applications.	He/She can fully understand the management of technical information documents for mechatronic systems and can prepare and adapt these documents according to an enterprise's specific operating requirements.	He/She is able to analyse complex operational sequences separately in order to understand the connections and draw up maintenance and production procedures. He/She can understand that the system parameters are important for the equipments' functions and can independently assess and document the wear and general conditions of the mechatronic equipment.			
9. Diagnosing and repairing malfunctions with mechatronic systems and facilities, advising clients on avoiding malfunctions, and modifying and expanding mechatronic systems	He/She can diagnose and repair errors and malfunctions on the simple components and devices in the mechatronic systems. He/She can use the necessary checking, measuring, and diagnostic tools.	He/She can independently correct problems in mechatronic production equipment with the help of (computer-aided) diagnostic systems and the use of expert systems, databases, and error documentations.	He/She can diagnose and repair errors and disturbances in complex mechatronic equipment and is able to advise clients on how to avoid sources of malfunctions through changes or upgrades in the equipment and system.	He/She can develop, through analyses of malfunctions in the mechatronic equipment, a monitoring and diagnostic system		

Chart 1: Competence Matrix Mechatronics.

A Competence Matrix displays competences in a table according to core work tasks and the progress of competence development. Competence areas and steps of competence development are described in the table.

- The left hand column of the table contains competence areas, based on the various core work tasks.
- The acquisitions of competences, from beginner level to "skilled worker" level, are described for each competence area. Each competence described is a "step of competence development".

Competence Matrix "Electronics/Electrical Engineering"

Competence areas (core work tasks)	Steps of competence development			
1. Preparing, planning, mounting and installing electrical and/or electronic systems for buildings and industrial applications	He/She can prepare and carry out simple electrical and/or electronic installations (e.g., cables, electrical outlets, connection and distribution systems, modular electronic components, computer components) as well as carry out and check the necessary wirings and mountings.	He/She can plan, prepare and connect electrical and modular electronic installations (e.g., energy supply in private and business premises, incl. lighting; alternating and three-phase current; electronic systems as units, wireless LAN, multimedia systems). He/She can advice the costumer and select the best implementation according to customer specifications.	He/She can plan complex electrical and/or electronically networked installations (e.g., systems of energy distribution, building management systems / KNX, regulation and monitoring systems, building access systems, RFID-systems) and fully wire them. He/She can configure, service and diagnose the functionality of the installation according to customer requirements and for this purpose can use computer-assisted tools.	
2. Inspecting, maintaining and servicing electrical and/or electronic systems and machinery	He/She can carry out basic and scheduled maintenance tasks, inspections and checks at electrical and/or electronic equipment according to maintenance schedules and predefined instructions (e.g., checking voltage tolerances, changing wearing parts in industrial plants, switching and control systems, electrical machinery, computer systems). He/She can use the measuring and testing tools necessary for it.	He/She can carry out and document preventative maintenance and alignment tasks at electrical and/or electronic industrial appliances and systems according to established quality assurance methods (e.g., continuous monitoring of a CNC machine tool)	He/She can analyse and determine availability and condition of electrical and/or electronic systems. He/She can analyse influencing factors on reliability and performance of electrical and/ or electronic systems and find causes of malfunctions (e.g., leakage current analysis, power factor correction, EMC analysis).	He/She can develop and document maintenance and inspection methods for electrical/electronic systems based on production and service process analysis as well as on quality management and customer requirements. He/She is able to develop related maintenance, inspection and quality assurance plans (e.g., optimizing MTBF of a production line, planning reserve power supply).
3. Setting up, putting into operation and adjusting electrical and/or electronic systems	He/She can set up, adjust and put into operation electrical and/or electronic systems (e.g., allocating frequency channels for a TV set, basic settings of a frequency converter or a thermo relay for a motor) following customer requirements and instructions from the technical documentation.	He/She can obtain and set system test parameters for setting up and operating electrical and/or electronic systems and select and carry out test procedures for installation and adjustment (e.g., adjusting interfaces in multimedia system, sensitivity setting of alarm equipment, elevator control unit).	He/She can select, set up and adjust electrical and/ or electronic systems and their control including accompanying sensors and actuators according to requirement analysis (e.g., energy supply systems, drive systems, electrical machinery, radio relay systems).	
4. Designing, modifying and adapting wirings and circuit boards for electrical and/ or electronic systems including their interfaces	He/She can modify, plan and build up simple electrical and/ or electronic circuits according to standards and guidelines (e.g., wiring for rooms, connection diagram of basic motor circuits, simple operational amplifier applications, small programmable control units).	He/She can modify, plan and build up standard electrical and/or electronic appliances according to customer requirements and official regulations (e.g., fire-warning devices, layouts for electrical/ electronic wirings with the help of CAD programmes, energy supply in private and business premises).	He/She can design, build up and improve electrical and/or electronic applications and its interfaces together with experts working in interdisciplinary teams according to EMC standards and confirming tests (e.g., electronic control circuits and equipment, micro-controller applications, PLC and related software).	He/She can design, build up and configure devices, facilities and units for process control systems including related programming and considering complex system requirements (e.g., controlled drive systems, process monitoring, automated production line, real time microcontroller applications for car control, GSM data transmission for monitoring and remote control).
5. Developing custom designed electrical and/ or electronic projects	He/She can develop and propose solutions for simple electrical and/or electronic system based on customer requirements (e.g., lighting installations, power supply unit, basic automation and control systems).	He/She can design electrical and/or electronic systems (e.g., PLC program for industrial applications, microcontroller application, ensuring expansion capability) and provide the necessary documentation (operational, maintenance, safety instructions, function, integration and acceptance tests).	He/She can develop technical solutions for electrical and/or electronic systems and applications (e.g., microcontroller board for heating and air condition, RFID access system, new production line) and provide appropriate documentation and customer training.	
6. Supervising and supporting work and business processes including quality management	He/She can check process steps in the production with suitable process tools (e.g., PPS, ERP, MRP) and carry out quality controls.	He/She can evaluate results of the process monitoring with software tools and determine quality assurance actions (work, production and time schedules).	He/She can develop controlling methods in the production (e.g. PPS, MRP, ERP) and process planning/control and supervision (e.g. CAP) and implement these with the help of software supported systems.	
7. Installing, configuring modifying and testing of application software for setting up and operating electrical and/ or electronic systems	He/She can install programmes for hardware and software environments and carry out simple configuration tasks as well as updates (e.g., starter software, graphical programming for measurement and automation).	He/She can select hardware and software for production systems following the business requirements and test programmes.	He/She can integrate hardware and software into existing system environments and use simulation and diagnostic programs (e.g. implement and adapt a driver for a CAD/CAM interface).	He/She can combine hardware and software to networked system environments and carry out network specific checks of all signals and adapt by means of software (e.g., OPC-Server, process control system).
8. Diagnosing and repairing of electrical/electronic systems and equipment	He/She can carry out standardized test procedures and diagnostic methods using wiring diagrams and test tools and carry out simple repairs at electrical and/or electronic systems (e.g., power measurement, level measurement).	He/She can use testing and diagnostic tools as well as expert systems for the fault diagnosis at electrical and/or electronic systems up to the component level and carry out the necessary repairs (e.g., software control test, spectrum analyzer).	He/She can select and use diagnostic methods for complex electrical and/ or electronic systems and carry out preventative measures for the avoidance of disturbances and malfunctions in arrangement with customers (e.g., detection of bit error rate, over-voltage protection analyse).	He/She can carry out system analyses (e.g., FMEA, FTA) of electrical and/or /electronic systems, determine error types and develop suitable diagnosis and repair methods including preventative measures.

Acronyms

CAD: Computer Aided Design
CAP: Computer Aided Planning
CAM: Computer Aided Manufacturing
CNC: Computer Numeric Control
EMC: Electro Magnetic Compatibility
ERP: Enterprise Resource Planning
FMEA: Failure Mode and Effect Analysis
FTA: Failure Tree Analysis
GSM: Global System for Mobile Communications
MRP: Machine Resource Planning
MTBF: Mean Time Between Failures
OPC: Object Linking Embedding for Process Control
KNX: Konnex is the most established standard for home and building electronic systems. The Konnex technology is based on the well-tried EIB-System (European Installation bus - EIB)
LAN: Local Area Network
PLC: Programmable Logic Control
PPS: Production Planning System
RFID: Radio Frequency Identification

Chart 2: Competence Matrix Electronics.

The structure and different ranges of Competence Matrices can be shown by these examples:

- Competence Matrix "mechatronics (chart 1)": Developed in VQTS I, this Matrix focuses on the development of competences required from workers at beginner level to skilled worker level.
- Competence Matrix for "electronics/electrical engineering" (chart 2): The VQTS II project intended to develop a Competence Matrix to be used to identify areas of overlap between VET and HE programmes. Therefore, the scope of the Competence Matrix 'electronics/electrical engineering' had to be broadened to include at least some steps of competence development relevant to HE.

A Competence Matrix can be developed via a moderated workshop using experts from the respective areas. Within the VQTS model it is assumed that 5-25 competence areas will be defined per occupational field and 2-6 steps of the competence development process described for each competence area. It is not easy to describe competences, because they depend on a variety of characteristics and may be localised in different manners. There are no specific determinants for differentiating the steps in the model. Several dimensions could be:

- Ability to:
    - Perform independent work tasks.
    - Deal with a certain complexity.
    - Deal with quality standard demands.
    - Deal with dynamic situations.
    - Deal with non-transparency.

Competences in this model refer to cognitive competences (knowledge), functional competences (skills) as well as social competences (behaviour).

Competence Profiles

Competence Profiles are formed from particular parts of a Competence Matrix by identifying competences that are relevant to a certain training programme or qualification (organisational profile) or are reflective the competences acquired so far by a person in training (individual profile). Organisational profiles, developed by the authorities responsible for the respective training programmes or qualification, indicate the relevant competences of the specific training programme or qualification on the Competence Matrix and the corresponding number of Credit Points. Individual profiles, developed by the responsible training provider, assess which stage of competence development and Credit Points the student or apprentice has reached so far. Based on the competence profile of the person in training a Competence Profile Certificate can be issued.

Applications

A Competence Matrix can be used for those purposes where the transparency of competence profiles is very important, such as:

- Transferring vocational competences acquired abroad (mobility in VET).
- Transferring and recognising competences acquired within the official VET system as well as competences achieved through non-formal or informal learning.
- Developing qualifications (for use in the development of the EQF).

- Composing job profiles as well as personnel (human resources) planning.
- Referencing qualifications to qualifications frameworks.
- Enhancing permeability between VET and HE.

Context of Educational Policy

The VQTS project was closely aligned with the aims of the 'Copenhagen Process' wherein the EU countries declared their willingness to foster employability and lifelong learning in Europe by strengthening cooperation and increasing mobility in vocational education and training (VET). According to the 'Copenhagen Process', it should be possible to utilise competences acquired through formal, non-formal and informal learning throughout Europe. The VQTS model is one of the best instruments to implement ECVET and increase the (international) transparency and comparability of qualifications and training offers.

Technical and Vocational Education and Training

TVET (Technical and Vocational Education and Training) is education and training which provides knowledge and skills for employment. TVET uses formal, non-formal and informal learning. TVET is recognised to be a crucial vehicle for social equity, inclusion and sustainable development.

Development of the Term TVET

The term 'Technical and Vocational Education and Training or TVET was officiated at the World Congress on TVET in 1999 in Seoul, Republic of Korea. The congress recognised the term TVET to be broad enough to incorporate other terms that had been used to describe similar educational and training activities including Workforce Education (WE) and Technical-Vocational Education (TVE). The term TVET parallels other types of education and training e.g. Vocational Education but is also used as an umbrella term to encompass education and training activities.

The decision in 1999 to officiate the term TVET led to the development of the UNESCO-UNEVOC International Centre for Technical and Vocational Education and Training in Bonn, Germany.

Aims and Purposes of TVET

Technical and Vocational Education and Training serves multiple purposes. A key purpose is preparation of youth for work. This takes the form of learning and developing work related skills and mastery of underlying knowledge and scientific principles. Work is broadly defined and therefore refers to both formal employment and self-employment. To support self-employment, TVET curricula often include entrepreneurship training. Related to this is the social reproduction and transformation of occupational and vocational practices.

A related role is continuing professional development. The rapid technological changes demand that workers continuously update their knowledge and skills. Unlike the past where a job could be held for life, it is common place to change vocations several times. TVET enables that flexibility in two ways. One is providing broad based technical knowledge and transversal skills on which different occupations can be based on. The second is providing continuing vocational training to workers. In contrast with the industrial paradigm of the old economy, today's global economy lays the onus on the worker to continually reinvent himself or herself. In the past, workers were assured of a job for life, with full-time employment, clear occupational roles and well established career paths. This is no longer the case. The knowledge dependent global economy is characterized by rapid changes in technology and related modes of work. Often, workers find themselves declared redundant and out of work. TVET today has the responsibility of re-skilling such workers to enable them find and get back to work Apart from providing work related education, TVET is also a site for personal development and emancipation. These concerns the development of those personal capacities that relate to realizing one's full potential with regard to paid or self-employment, occupational interests and life goals outside of work. At the same time TVET seeks to enable individual overcome disadvantages due to circumstances of birth or prior educational experiences.

From a development point of view, TVET facilitates economic growth by increasing the productivity of workers. The returns from increased output far exceed the costs of training, direct and indirect, leading to economic growth. TVET like any other form of education also facilitates socio-economic development by enhancing the capacity of individuals to adopt practices that are socially worthwhile. As a form of education similar to all others, TVET aims to developing the broad range of personal capabilities that characterize an educated person. Thus, the provision of broad based knowledge seeks to ensure critic-creative thinking. TVET also aims at developing capacities for effective communication and effective interpersonal relations.

Hybridisation

Because of TVET's isolation with other education streams it was not widely adopted, in particularly in secondary education. Steps were taken to reduce segmentation of education and training and to address institutional barriers that restricted TVET learners' options including choices to move vertically to higher levels of learning, or horizontally to other streams.

Policy-makers have introduced forms of hybridization with other education systems, additionally some of the distinctions between TVET and 'academic' education streams have been blurred. This hybridisation has been termed the 'vocationalization of secondary education', a similar process has happened to a lesser extent in tertiary education.

The baccalauréat professionnel in France and the middelbaar beroepsonderwijs (MBO) count work experience in the area they are specializing in.

Apprenticeships enhanced content within occupational training courses and considerable emphasis has been placed on personal skills.

Work education has been included in the primary standards (grades 1–8) to make the students aware of work. At the lower secondary level (grades 9–10) pre-vocational education has been included with the aim to increase students' familiarity with the world of work.

Around 40% of secondary students are currently enrolled in TVET education, in some schools, academic and vocational students share almost 75% of the curriculum.

A new approach to vocationalization of secondary schooling has been introduced within the framework of general educational reform. This has been guided by the Ministry of Education's strategy of modernization. Vocationalization in the Russian Federation refers to the introduction of profile education at the upper-secondary level (the last two years of schooling, grades 10 and 11) and the process of preparation for profile selection. Profile education provided students with the opportunity to study a chosen area in depth, usually one that would be related to their further study (TVET or academic). Schools could design their own profiles, e.g. science, socio-economics, humanities and technology, or keep a general orientation curriculum. In preparation for the upper-secondary specialization, a 'pre-profiling' programme in grade 9 has been introduced to help students make their choices in grade 10.

Tech-prep programmes in the United States of America are examples of how the 'blending' approach was used to help students make the connections between school and work. In year nine, programmes in broad occupational fields such as the health professions, automotive technology, computer systems networking are offered within general technology studies. The programmes continue for at least two years after the end of secondary school, through a tertiary education or an apprenticeship programme, with students achieving an associate degree or certificate by the end of the programme.

It is a new experiment in Iraq about TVET, there are three ministries related to TVET in Iraq, Ministry of higher Education and scientific research which represented by the technical universities, Ministry of Education which represented by the vocational education foundation and Ministry of Labor and Social Guaranty which represented by vocational training centers. Theses associations are trained by UNESCO for the last three years on the main topics and fields of TVET, so they now waiting the Iraqi Perelman to put the suitable law for the TVET Council in Iraq to start it system and control these associations with the required outputs of TVET.

Private Sector

Private TVET providers include for-profit and non-profit institutions. Several factors triggered actions to support the expansion of private TVET including the limited capacities of public TVET providers and their low responsiveness to enterprises and trainees. Private TVET providers were expected to be more responsive because they were subject to fewer bureaucratic restrictions than public institutions (particularly in centralized systems). Their presence was expected to help raise quality system-wide, in many developing countries, government budgets constituted a vulnerable and unreliable source of financing for TVET, an important objective was to finance TVET systems by increasing the contribution of beneficiaries, including employers and trainees.

Private TVET provision over since 2005 has become a significant and growing part of TVET in sub-Saharan Africa, the Middle East and North Africa. In some countries, e.g. Lebanon, enrolments in private TVET institutions have exceeded enrolments in public institutions. In Jordan, private provision at the community college level has been promoted by the government. However, not all experiences has been positive with private proprietary institutions or NGOs, their courses have often been concentrated in professional areas that typically do not require large capital investment, permitting easy entry and exit by private providers from the sector. Quality issues have also emerged, where market information about quality has been unavailable.

Technological Advancement and its Impact

TVET has an important role to play in technology diffusion through transfer of knowledge and skills. Rapid technological progress has had and continues to have significant implications for TVET. Understanding and anticipating changes has become crucial for designing responsive TVET systems and, more broadly, effective skills policies. The flexibility to adapt the supply of skills to the rapidly and in some cases radically, changing needs in sectors such as information technology and the green economy has become a central feature of TVET systems. Globally, the skills requirements and qualifications demanded for job entry are rising. This reflects a need for not just a more knowledgeable and skilled workforce, but one that can adapt quickly to new emerging technologies in a cycle of continuous learning.

TVET courses have been created to respond to the diverse ICT needs of learners, whether these are related to work, education or citizenship. New courses have been introduced to address occupational changes in the ICT job market, while many TVET providers have shifted provision towards a blended approach, with significantly more self-directed and distance learning. In developed countries, new ICT approaches have been introduced to modernize TVET organizations and to manage administration and finance, including learner records.

Education for All

The Education for All (EFA) movement has had its own implications for TVET at both international and national levels. The third EFA goal lacked precision and measurable targets for TVET, however it called for ensuring 'that the learning needs of all young people and adults are met through equitable access to appropriate learning and life-skills programmes'. This goal had a symbolic value, helping to raise the visibility of TVET and skills development and create a more prominent place for them on the global education policy agenda. The current bulge of young people requiring TVET learning opportunities is partly fuelled by the success of the EFA movement in opening access to basic education, particularly at the primary level. In 2009, 702 million children were enrolled worldwide in primary education, compared with 646 million in 1999.

Continuing TVET

Continuing TVET involves ongoing training to upgrade existing skills and to develop new ones and has a much higher profile in ageing societies and knowledge-based economies. Increased recognition of the importance of human capital for economic growth and social development made it necessary to increase learning opportunities for adults in workplaces within the wider context of policies and strategies for lifelong learning.

In many countries policy-makers have considered ways to expand workplace learning opportunities for workers and to assess and give credit for knowledge and skills acquired in workplaces. Efforts were geared towards training for workers in companies, encouraged by legislation, financial incentives and contractual agreements.

Challenges

Labour Market Demands and Trends

Following the global financial crisis in 2008, labour markets across the world experienced structural changes that influenced the demand for skills and TVET. Unemployment worsened and the quality of jobs decreased, especially for youth. Gender differentials in labour force participation placed men ahead of women and skill mismatches deepened. The crisis impacted labour markets adversely and led to deepening uncertainty, vulnerability of employment and inequality. Furthermore, measures to improve efficiency and profitability in the economic recovery have often led to jobless growth, as happened in Algeria, India and post-apartheid South Africa.

In seeking to address the level of vulnerable employment, TVET systems have focused on increasing the employability of graduates and enhancing their capacity to function effectively within existing vulnerable labour markets and to adjust to other labour market constraints. This has meant enhanced coordination among government departments responsible for TVET and employment policies. It has also created the need for TVET systems to develop mechanisms that identify skills needs early on and make better use of labour market information for matching skills demands and supply. TVET systems have focused more on developing immediate job skills and wider competencies. This has been accomplished by adopting competency-based approaches to instruction and workplace learning that enable learners to handle vulnerable employment, adjust to changing jobs and career contexts and build their capacity to learn and agility to adapt.

Migration Flow

Increasing migration are significant challenges to the national character of TVET systems and qualifications. TVET qualifications are progressively expected not only to serve as proxies for an individual's competencies but to also act as a form of a currency that signals national and international value. TVET systems have been developing mechanisms to enable credible and fair cross-border recognition of skills. In 2007, the ILO identified three types of recognition that TVET system may use: unilateral (independent assessment by the receiving country), mutual (agreements between sending and receiving countries) and multilateral (mostly between a regional grouping of countries). The most prevalent of these is unilateral recognition, which is mostly under the control of national credential evaluation agencies. Countries have been slow to move from input-based skill evaluations to outcome-based methodologies that focus on competencies attained.

TVET systems are responding to migration by providing qualifications that can stand the rigour of these recognition systems and by creating frameworks for mutual recognition of qualifications. Regional Qualifications Frameworks such as those in Southern Africa, Europe, Asia and the Caribbean aim to significantly support the recognition of qualifications across borders. These efforts are further supported through the introduction of outcome-based learning methodologies within the broader context of multilateral recognition agreements.

Providing Broader Competencies Alongside Specialist Skills

Skills for economic development include a mix of technical and soft skills. Empirical evidence and TVET policy reviews conducted by UNESCO suggest that TVET systems may not as yet sufficiently support the development of the so-called soft competencies. Many countries have, however, adopted competency-based approaches as measures for reforming TVET curricula.

The HEART Trust National Training Agency of Jamaica adopted this approach, with a particular emphasis on competency standards and balanced job-specific and generic skills. Competency standards aimed to ensure that the training was linked to industry and was up to date and that competences were integrated into training programmes, along with the needed knowledge, skills and attitudes. The balancing of skill types was to ensure adequate attention was given to job-specific skills as well as the conceptual and experiential knowledge necessary to enable individuals to grow and develop in the workplace and more generally in society.

Globalization

Globalization of the economy and the consequent reorganization of the workplace require a more adaptable labour force, requiring countries to rethink the nature and role of TVET. Globalization intensifies pressure on the TVET sector to supply the necessary skills to workers involved in globalized activity and to adapt existing skills to rapidly changing needs. As a consequence, there is an increasing requirement for more demand-driven TVET systems with a greater focus on modular and competency-based programmes, as well as on cognitive and transferable skills, which are expected to help people adapt to unpredictable conditions.

Promoting Social Equity and Inclusive Workplaces

Preparing marginalized groups of youths and adults with the right skills and helping them make the transition from school to work is part of the problem faced by TVET in promoting social equity. Ensuring that the workplace is inclusive poses numerous policy challenges, depending on the contextual dynamics of inclusion and exclusion and the capabilities of individuals. For example, the experiences of exclusion by people with disabilities and disadvantaged women may be similar in some ways and different in others. Many individuals experience multiple forms of disadvantage in the workplace, to different degrees of severity, depending on social attitudes and traditions in a specific context or organization. Approaches to inclusiveness in the workplace will therefore vary according to population needs, social diversity and context. To give one example, the Netherlands set about the task of making workplaces more inclusive for low-skilled adults by offering programmes that combine language instruction with work and in certain cases on-the-job training.

A review of employer surveys in Australia, the Netherlands, the United Kingdom and the United States of America, reported that employers valued people with disabilities for their high levels of motivation and their diverse perspectives and found their attendance records to be the same or better than those of other employees. Many employers mentioned that being seen as pro-inclusion was positive for the company or organization's image, an advantage that goes well beyond providing employment opportunities to disadvantaged groups. In many cases, however, social and cultural perceptions are an obstacle to making workplaces more inclusive and this will require sensitive and concerted attention. Some low- and middle-income countries have sought to address this through legislation.

The 2012 Education for All Global Monitoring Report concluded that ‹all countries, regardless of income level, need to pay greater attention to the needs of young people who face disadvantage in education and skills development by virtue of their poverty, gender or other characteristics'. The report found that several barriers and constraints reduced the success of TVET in meeting social equity demands. First, national TVET policies in most cases failed to address the skills needs of young people living in urban poverty and in deprived rural areas. Second, additional funds were needed to support TVET learning opportunities on a much larger scale. Third, the training needs of disadvantaged young women were particularly neglected. The 2012 EFA Global Monitoring Report also noted that skills training alone was not sufficient for the most disadvantaged of the rural and urban poor. Coherent policies that link social protection, micro-finance and TVET are considered critical for ensuring better outcomes for marginalized groups.

Gender Disparities

Recent years have seen rising numbers of young women enrolling in TVET programmes, especially in service sector subjects. At times the challenge is to bring more males into female-dominated streams. However, beyond number games, the real gender parity test that TVET systems are yet to pass is balancing the gender participation in programmes that lead to employability, as well as to decent and high-paying jobs. Gender disparities in learning opportunities and earnings, are a cause for concern. The persistent gender-typing of TVET requires concerted attention if TVET is to really serve a key facilitative role in shared growth, social equity and inclusive development.

The absence of work, poor quality of work, lack of voice at work, continued gender discrimination and unacceptably high youth unemployment are all major drivers of TVET system reforms from the perspective of social equity. This is an area where TVET systems continue to be challenged to contribute proactively to the shaping of more equitable societies.

Gender equality has received significant international attention in recent years and this has been reflected in a reduction in gender participation gaps in both primary and secondary schooling. Efforts to analyse and address gender equality in TVET are relevant to other aspects of equity and dimensions of inclusion/exclusion. In almost all parts of the world, the proportion of girls to total enrolment in secondary education defined as TVET is less than for 'general' secondary education.

Responses

Bangladesh

Integrating women or men into areas of specialization in which they were previously under-represented is important to diversifying opportunities for TVET. The National Strategy for Promotion of Gender Equality in TVET in Bangladesh set clear priorities and targets for breaking gender stereotypes. The Strategy developed by a Gender Working Group comprising fifteen representatives from government ministries and departments, employers, workers and civil society organizations. It provided an overview of the current status and nature of gender inequalities in TVET, highlighted the priority areas for action, explored a number of steps to promote equal participation of women in TVET and outlined the way forward.

Cambodia

In Cambodia, TVET programmes set out to empower young women in traditional trades by upgrading their skills and technology in silk weaving. This led to the revitalization and reappraisal of a traditional craft by learners and society.

The Shanghai Consensus of the Third International Congress on TVET

The Shanghai Consensus of the Third International Congress on TVET made the following recommendations on expanding access and improving quality and equity, including to:

> "Improve gender equality by promoting equal access of females and males to TVET programmes, particularly in fields where there is strong labour market demand and by ensuring that TVET curricula and materials avoid stereotyping by gender.

School-to-work Transition

School-to-work transition is a phrase referring to on-the-job training, apprenticeships, cooperative education agreements or other programs designed to prepare students to enter the job market. This education system is primarily employed in the United States, partially as a response to work training as it is done in Asia.

School to Work is a system to introduce the philosophy of school-based, work-based and connecting activities as early as kindergarten to expose students to potential future careers. School to Work emphasizes lifelong learning.

School to Work is funded and sponsored at the federal level by the U.S. Department of Labor and U.S. Department of Education. At the state level in states like Arizona, the grant is administered by the Arizona Department of Commerce, School to Work Division. This grant was funded for a maximum of five years with decreasing funds years three through five;

An example of county level involvement is the Cochise County School to Work Consortia in Arizona. It is composed of more than fifty Cochise County public and private schools, kindergarten through four-year university level, local and community-based organizations and more than one hundred supporting business partners.

STW is part of a comprehensive education reform movement which includes formulating new standards which emphasize higher order thinking skills, new standards based assessments and graduation exams, such as the Certificate of Initial Mastery which insure that students are ready for job training or college prep by age 16. Reformers believe that it is important and egalitarian that all students graduate ready for jobs and ready for college, rather than tracking students one way or the other.

Critics

"Back to basics" traditionalists observe that in Europe, apprenticeships typically mean that the worker essentially ends their formal education after age 16 and works full-time at reduced pay in exchange for learning "job skills" such as assembling automobiles. Some believe that it was better to have students who were not bound for college concentrate on career schools, while academic students should spend class time learning core academic subjects such as history or science rather than job-shadowing at a hospital or auto dealer. A student in North Dakota would have little opportunity to learn to be an auto designer, while one in Alabama would have little opportunity to do job shadowing at a major software company if job training were allocated according to local human resource needs, as many programs are structured. Local businesses also need to structure their operations to accommodate student workers and transportation since typically schools are situated close to homes and not businesses which are typically a car or transit commute away from homes.

The Michigan STW Initiative states "students work without pay for two to three hours each day" and "students are able to perform what might otherwise be hazardous order work." which would contradict child labor laws. Data would be shared with state STW partnership network and local labor market areas which might be an invasion of privacy. The state would utilize the national industry-recognized skill certificates when developed, which would be the Certificate of Initial Mastery. Critics call this a government-controlled passport to work. Michigan Rep. Harold J. Voorhees expressed concern that, with full implementation, a child would not be employed without this Certificate.

Virtual Learning Environment

A virtual learning environment is an online-based platform that offers students and professors digital solutions that enhance the learning experience. Unlike a virtual classroom, which is meant to replicate and replace the physical classroom environment for distance learners, a virtual learning environment (or VLE) harnesses technology to supplement an in-class experience, with, for example, digital communication, interaction and quizzes or polls run through the VLE.

A virtual learning environment refers to a system that offers educators digitally-based solutions aimed at creating interactive, active learning environments. VLEs can help professors create, store and disseminate content, plan courses and lessons and foster communication between student and professor (in the form of e-mails and discussions), even in real-time. Virtual learning environments are often part of a higher education institution's wider learning management system (LMS).

References

- What-open-education, resources: opensource.com, Retrieved 09 June, 2019
- Duch, Barbara J.; Groh, Susan; Allen, Deborah E. (2001). The power of problem-based learning : a practical "how to" for teaching undergraduate courses in any discipline (1st ed.). Sterling, VA: Stylus Pub. ISBN 978-1579220372
- Vaughan, Dr Norman D. (2010). "Blended Learning". In Cleveland-Innes, MF; Garrison, DR (eds.). An Introduction to Distance Education: Understanding Teaching and Learning in a New Era. Taylor & Francis. p. 165. ISBN 978-0-415-99598-6. Retrieved 23 January 2011
- Marope, P.T.M.; Chakroun, B.; Holmes, K.P. (2015). Unleashing the Potential: Transforming Technical and Vocational Education and Training (PDF). UNESCO. pp. 9–10, 41, 43, 47–48, 56–58, 63, 80, 95, 98–103. ISBN 978-92-3-100091-1
- Ng, Thomas W.H.; Feldman, Daniel C. (2007-08-01). "The school-to-work transition: A role identity perspective". Journal of Vocational Behavior. 71 (1): 114–134. doi:10.1016/j.jvb.2007.04.004. ISSN 0001-8791
- Virtual-learning-environment: tophat.com, Retrieved 27 July, 2019

3
Learning Styles

There are different learning styles that are used in vocational education such as visual learning, auditory learning, competency-based learning, work-based learning, experiential learning, etc. This chapter closely examines these learning styles of vocational education for a thorough understanding of the subject.

Visual Learning

Visual Learning is one of the three different learning styles popularized by Neil D. Fleming in his VAK model of learning. The visual learning style means that people need to see information to learn it and this "seeing" takes many forms from spatial awareness, photographic memory, color/tone, brightness/contrast and other visual information. Naturally, a classroom is a very good place for a visual learner to learn. Teachers use overheads, the chalkboard, pictures, graphs, maps and many other visual items to entice a visual learner into knowledge.

Strengths of Visual Learners

Visual learners typically do well in a modern classroom setting. After all, there are just so many visuals in classrooms — whiteboards, handouts, photos and so on. These students have much strength that can boost their performances in school. Here are just a few of the strengths of this learning type:

- Instinctively follows directions.
- Easily visualizes objects.
- Has a great sense of balance and alignment.
- Is an excellent organizer.
- Has a strong sense of color and is very color-oriented.
- Can see the passage from a page in a book in his or her mind.

- Notices minute similarities and differences between objects and people easily.
- Can envision imagery easily.

Visual Learning Strategies for Students

If you are a visual learner, you may find these things helpful when sitting in class or studying for a test. Visual learners need things in front of them to help solidify them in their brains, so don't try to go it alone when listening to lectures or studying for your next midterm. Be sure to integrate these tips into your study routine:

- Color-code your notes, vocabulary words and textbook.
- Be sure to read the diagrams, maps and other visuals that go along with text to help you remember it.
- Make to-do lists in an agenda.
- Study in solitude. You need to see things to remember them and often, any noise will distract you.
- Take notes during lectures to capitalize on your learning style.
- Sit near the front so you're better able to see everything.
- Use outlines and concept maps to organize your notes.

Visual Learning Strategies for Teachers

Students with the visual learning style make up about 65 percent of your class. These students are the ones traditional classrooms are designed to teach. They will pay attention to your overhead slides, whiteboard, Smartboard, PowerPoint presentations, handouts, graphs and charts. They will usually take good notes and will appear to be paying attention during class. If you use a lot of verbal directions without visual cues, visual learners may get confused, as they prefer to have something in writing to refer to.

Try these strategies for reaching those students with the visual learning type:

- Supplement verbal lectures with a handout, diagram, or other visuals.
- Incorporate color into your presentations, the classroom and handouts.
- Give written instructions and expectations.
- Vary your reading in class with solitary reading time so visual learners will take in the information better.
- Vary your instructional methods (lectures, group work, solitary work, pairs, circles) and assignments so every learner is challenged.

- Show your students how to complete a task instead of just telling your students how to complete a task.
- Show students how to make great vocabulary flashcards.
- Use video and still images to enhance your presentations.
- Provide written feedback on assignments.

Auditory Learning

Auditory learning is a learning style in which a person learns through listening. An auditory learner depends on listening and speaking as a main way of learning. Auditory learners must be able to hear what is being said in order to understand and may have difficulty with instructions that are drawn but if the writing is in a logical order it can be easier to understand. They also use their listening and repeating skills to sort through the information that is sent to them. They are good listeners when people speak.

The Fleming VAK/VARK model, one of the most common and widely used categorizations of the various types of learning styles, categorized the various types of learning styles as follows: visual learners, auditory learners, reading/writing-preference learners and kinesthetic learners (also known as "tactile learners").

Characteristics

Auditory learners may have a knack for ascertaining the true meaning of someone's words by listening to audible signals like changes in tone. When memorizing a phone number, an auditory learner will say it out loud and then remember how it sounded to recall it.

Auditory learners are good at writing responses to lectures they've heard. They're also good at oral exams, effectively by listening to information delivered orally, in lectures, speeches and oral sessions.

Proponents claim that when an auditory/verbal learner reads, it is almost impossible for the learner to comprehend anything without sound in the background. In these situations, listening to music or having different sounds in the background (TV, people talking, music, etc.) will help learners work better.

Auditory learners are good at storytelling. They solve problems by talking them through. Speech patterns include phrases "I hear you; That clicks; It's ringing a bell" and other sound or voice-oriented information. These learners will move their lips or talk to themselves to help accomplish tasks.

Recommended Techniques

Proponents say that teachers should use these techniques to instruct auditory learners: verbal direction, group discussions, verbal reinforcement, group activities, reading aloud and putting information into a rhythmic pattern such as a rap, poem, or song.

Prevalence

Auditory learners make up about 30% of the population.

Lack of Evidence

Although learning styles have "enormous popularity" and both children and adults express personal preferences, there is no evidence that identifying a student's learning style produces better outcomes and there is significant evidence that the widely touted "meshing hypothesis" (that a student will learn best if taught in a method deemed appropriate for the student's learning style) is invalid. Well-designed studies "flatly contradict the popular meshing hypothesis". Rather than targeting instruction to the "right" learning style, students appear to benefit most from mixed modality presentations, for instance using both auditory and visual techniques for all students.

Competency-based Learning

Competency-based learning or competency-based education and training is an approach to teaching and learning more often used in learning concrete skills than abstract learning. It differs from other non-related approaches in that the unit of learning is extremely fine-grained. Rather than a course or a module, every individual skill or learning outcome (known as a competency) is one single unit. Learners work on one competency at a time, which is likely a small component of a larger learning goal. The student is evaluated on the individual competency and can only move on to other competencies after they have mastered the current skill being learned. After that, higher or more complex competencies are learned to a degree of mastery and are isolated from other topics. Another common component of competency-based learning is the ability to skip learning modules entirely if the learner can demonstrate mastery. This can be determined through prior learning assessment or formative testing.

People learning to drive manual transmission might first have to demonstrate their mastery on the "rules of the road," safety, defensive driving, parallel parking etc. In this manner, they can focus on two independent competencies – "using the clutch, brake with right foot" and "shifting up and down through the gears." Once the learners have demonstrated that they are comfortable with those two skills, the next overarching skill that needs to be learned might be "finding first: from full stop to a slow roll" followed by "sudden stops," "shifting up" and "down shifting." Because this is kinetic learning, the instructor likely would demonstrate the skill to the learner a few times after which the student can perform guided practice followed by independent practice until mastery is demonstrated.

As a Learning Method

Competency-based learning is learnerfocused and works naturally with independent study and with the instructor in the role of facilitator. Learners often find different individual skills more difficult than others. This learning method allows a student to learn those individual skills they find challenging at their own pace, practising and refining as much as they like. Then move rapidly to other skills to which they are more adept.

While most other learning methods use summative testing, competency-based learning requires mastery of every individual learning outcome, making it very well suited to learning credentials in which safety is an issue. With summative testing, a student who got 80% in the evaluation may have an 80% mastery of all learning outcomes or may have no mastery what-so-ever of 20% of the learning outcomes. Further, this student may be permitted to move on to higher learning and still be missing some abilities that are crucial to that higher learning. For example, a student who knows most traffic laws and has mostly mastered controlling a vehicle could be treated equally with a student who has mastered vehicle control but no understanding of traffic laws, but only one of these students will be permitted to drive.

What it means to have mastered a competency depends on the learning domain (subject matter). In a subject matter that could affect safety, it would be usual to expect complete learning that can be repeated every time. In abstract learning, such as algebra, the learner may only have to demonstrate that they can identify an appropriate formula, for example, 4 of 5 times since when using that skill in the next competency, resolving a formula, will usually allow an opportunity for the learner to discover and correct his/her mistakes.

It is important to understand that this learning methodology is common in many kinetic and skills-based learning and is also sometimes applied to abstract and academic learning for students who find themselves out-of-step with their grade, course or program of study. Increasingly, educational institutions are evaluating ways to include competency-based learning methodologies in many different types of programs in order to make learning success a constant while students' pace can vary.

Best Practices

Competency profiles assist in effective learning and development by identifying the behaviors, knowledge, skills and abilities that are necessary for successful performance in a job. Employees can assess their competencies against those required for their own job, or for another job in which they are interested and then take steps to acquire or improve any necessary competencies.

Competencies support learning by:

- Focusing learning on the critical competencies needed for success in the job and organization.
- Providing standards for measuring employee performance and capabilities.
- Providing the framework for identifying learning options/curriculum/programs to meet employee and organizational needs.
- Supporting effective forecasting of organizational, as well as project-related learning requirements.
- Providing standards for determining how well learning has occurred, both at the individual and organizational level.

Some of the common benchmark competency-based practices in learning and development are:

- Once the competencies have been defined for particular job / roles, it becomes possible for employees and others to assess the employee's competencies against those required for current or future roles within the organization. This assessment can occur in the following ways:
    - Self-assessment – Typically, the behavioral indicators for the competencies and proficiency levels needed within the target role / job are used as the standard for assessing the performance of the employee using a common rating scale (e.g., five-point Likert scale) for assessing each indicator. These behavioral examples ensure people self-assess consistently and accurately. They create self-awareness, which drives intrinsic motivation to improve. The results show employee strengths as well as skill gaps. This information can then be used to support the development of an individual learning plan.
    - Multi-source/360 – Multi-source or 360-degree feedback is similar to the self-assessment process except there is more than one assessor. The process includes at a minimum the employee and their supervisor and can include others with whom the employee interacts within the workplace (e.g., peers, team members, clients both within and outside the organization, reporting employees; etc).

Implementation Stages

The following implementation stages are suggested for organizations implementing competencies in Learning and Development on a corporate-wide basis.

Stage 1

- Determine policy for integrating competencies in Learning and Development.

- Design or acquire tools to support assessment and personalized, competency-based learning.
- Build/buy/curate learning activities to that correspond to each task and behavior in the competency model. Ensure these also include informal learning resources, such as skill practices or activities, job aids, checklists, templates, performance support tutorials, as well as the opportunity to work with others for collaborative learning. This facilitates learning in the flow of work.
- Create a plan for introduction, embedding and sustaining the program.
- Have people assess, be recommended personalized competency-based learning and create their development plans. Engage managers or multi-raters to participate if relevant.

Stage 2

- Use aggregated assessment results and development plan selections to identify organizational skill gaps and needs assessment.
- Engage leaders in results regularly so they understand how skill gaps impact their ability to achieve corporate strategy and how strong organizational capability can be leveraged for competitive advantage.
- Continue emphasis through communication and change management on creating a habit of learning, so development activity continues.
- Identify new learning opportunities, including those that need to be created to support gaps, or activities to replace those with lower than desired user feedback.
- Ensure periodic reassessments occur; measure the impact of competency-based skill development over time.
- Make regular improvements in communication.
- At least annually, revisit the competency model and competency-based learning recommendations to ensure currency.

Schools with this System

Adams county school district 50 and the Chugach School District are a part of the Competency-based learning project but have their own name called Re-Inventing schools coalition (RISC). They have replaced grade levels with 10 learning levels that students work through at their own pace. Western Governors University (WGU), has used this model of learning since it was chartered in 1996 by 19 governors in the Western United States.

Other institutions are also offering competency-based approaches to postsecondary degrees. Capella University's FlexPath bachelor's and master's programs were the second direct assessment degree to be given the go-ahead by the Department of Education. Southern New Hampshire University developed a competency-based pathway to an associate or bachelor's degree through College for America, launched in 2013. Additionally, the University of Wisconsin-Extension's Flex Option provides a competency-based approach to earning a bachelor's degree. Since 1971, the Upper Valley Educator's Institute in Lebanon, NH has offered a teacher certification program that is competency based and now offers a competency based Master in Arts in Teaching (MAT).

Work-based Learning

"Work-based learning (WBL) is an educational strategy that provides students with real-life work experiences where they can apply academic and technical skills and develop their employability." It is a series of educational courses which integrate the school or university curriculum with the workplace to create a different learning paradigm. "Work-based learning deliberately merges theory with practice and acknowledges the intersection of explicit and tacit forms of knowing."

Most WBL programs are generally university accredited courses, aiming at a win-win situation where the learner's needs and the industry requirement for skilled and talented employees both are met. WBL programs are targeted to bridge the gap between the learning and the doing. "Work-based learning strategies provide career awareness, career exploration opportunities, career planning activities and help students attain competencies such as positive work attitudes and other employable skills."

Work-based learning encompasses a diversity of formal, nonformal and informal arrangements including apprenticeships, work placement and informal learning on the job. The key driver is the need for active policies to secure learning that meets the need of the workplace.

Classification

Work-based learning is classified in three ways based on the:

- Duration of assignment: The work-based learning experience maybe of a duration of a few hours to 2/4 years.
- Relation to course work: Work-based learning is generally related to a specific subject taught at school or university.
- Stipend: WBL assignments may be paid or unpaid.

WBL Learning Strategies

Work-based learning strategies include the following:

- Apprenticeship or internship or mentorship: An apprenticeship involves the student working for an employer where he or she is taught and supervised by an experienced employee of the chosen organization. The student is periodically evaluated for progress as per the skills and knowledge acquired and maybe granted wages accordingly. At the end of the course, the student receives a certificate of service. The student learns in a realistic environment and gets the opportunity to apply his or her knowledge in real-world scenarios.
- Job shadowing: Job Shadowing is a short term opportunity that introduces the student to a particular job or career by pairing the student with an employee of the workplace. By following or ‹shadowing' the employee, the student gets familiar with the duties and responsibilities associates with that job.
- Business/industry field trip: Field trips offer the students an insight in the latest technical advancements and business strategies of an enterprise. Students also gain awareness of the various career opportunities available and understand the driving forces of the community's economy.
- Entrepreneurial experience: This includes setting up of specific business, right from the planning, organizing and managing stage to the risk control and management aspects of a business.
- Cooperative education: In cooperative education, the work experience is planned in conjunction with the technical classroom instruction. This method is used by universities that do not have access to state-of-art equipment required to transact the technical course practically.
- School-based enterprise: A school-based enterprise is a simulated or actual business run by the school. It offers students a learning experience by letting them manage the various aspects of a business
- Service learning: This strategy combines community service with career, where students provide volunteer service to public and non-profit agencies, civic and government offices etc.

Key Persons

- Student: The student is central to the WBL process. The student engages in a WBL program and completes all requirements of the program, maintains high degree of professionalism and acquires necessary competencies for which the WBL program was designed.

- Business Mentor: A business mentor sets realistic goals for the student to acquire, engages and supervises them to complete their tasks and is a role model for the student to emulate.
- Teacher Coordinator: A teacher coordinator is a certified educator who manages the WBL program and checks on the student progress and supports whenever required to ensure successful completion of the WBL program.
- School Administrator: The school administrator is key in introducing WBL programs within the curriculum after identifying the appropriate courses that can be learnt through the program.
- Parents: Parental support enables successful completion of the WBL program as offer suitable guidance, support and motivation to their wards and approve the WBL program that would be most suitable for meeting their ward's learning needs and career aspirations.

Merits

- Application of classroom learning in real-world setting.
- Establishment of connection between school and work.
- Improvement in critical thinking, analytical reasoning and logical abilities.
- Expansion of curriculum and learning facilities.
- Meeting the diverse needs of the learner.
- Creating a talented and skilled pool of future employees.
- Reduces pre-service training time and cost.
- Improvement of student awareness of career opportunities.
- Making education relevant and valuable to the social context.
- Community building exercise for productive economy.

Demerits

- Time-consuming activity to identify key courses that can be taught via WBL programs.
- Needs careful consideration and planning when introducing WBL strategies within the existing curriculum.
- Certain WBL programs may not be in sync with the formal education timelines and pattern.

- It is unclear what key elements of this learning may be and that readily available indicators which equate with academic learning outcomes are not necessarily evoking it accuracy.
- Needs effective coordination between all key persons involved in the WBL program.
- Effective evaluation strategy needs to be developed for assessing student performance. This should encompass both formative and summative feedback.

Experiential Learning

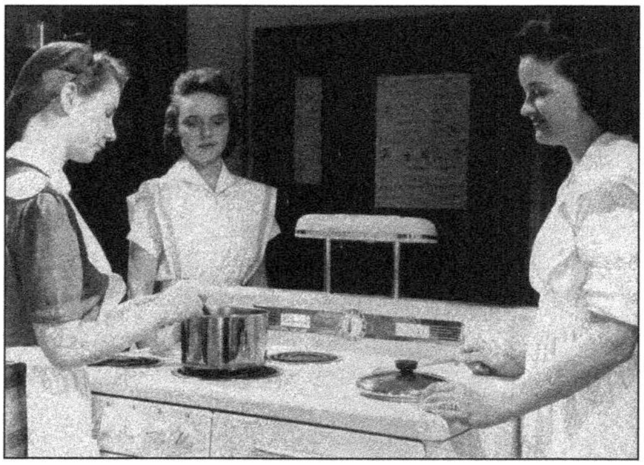

Shimer College students learning to cook by cooking.

Experiential learning also known as (EXL) is the process of learning through experience and is more specifically defined as "learning through reflection on doing". Hands-on learning can be a form of experiential learning, but does not necessarily involve students reflecting on their product. Experiential learning is distinct from rote or didactic learning, in which the learner plays a comparatively passive role. It is related to, but not synonymous with, other forms of active learning such as action learning, adventure learning, free-choice learning, cooperative learning, service-learning and situated learning.

Experiential learning is often used synonymously with the term "experiential education", but while experiential education is a broader philosophy of education, experiential learning considers the individual learning process. As such, compared to experiential education, experiential learning is concerned with more concrete issues related to the learner and the learning context.

The general concept of learning through experience is ancient. Around 350 BCE, Aristotle wrote in the *Nicomachean Ethics* "for the things we have to learn before we can do them, we learn by doing them". But as an articulated educational approach, experiential learning is of much more recent vintage. Beginning in the 1970s, David A. Kolb helped to develop the modern theory of experiential learning, drawing heavily on the work of John Dewey, Kurt Lewin and Jean Piaget.

Experiential learning has significant teaching advantages. Peter Senge, author of *The Fifth Discipline,* states that teaching is of utmost importance to motivate people. Learning only has good effects when learners have the desire to absorb the knowledge. Therefore, experiential learning requires the showing of directions for learners.

Experiential learning entails a hands-on approach to learning that moves away from just the teacher at the front of the room imparting and transferring their knowledge to students. It makes learning an experience that moves beyond the classroom and strives to bring a more involved way of learning.

Kolb's Experiential Learning Model

Experiential learning focuses on the learning process for the individual. One example of experiential learning is going to the zoo and learning through observation and interaction with the zoo environment, as opposed to reading about animals from a book. Thus, one makes discoveries and experiments with knowledge firsthand, instead of hearing or reading about others' experiences. Likewise, in business school, internship and job-shadowing, opportunities in a student's field of interest can provide valuable experiential learning which contributes significantly to the student's overall understanding of the real-world environment.

A third example of experiential learning involves learning how to ride a bike, a process which can illustrate the four-step experiential learning model (ELM) as set forth by Kolb and outlined in figure below. Following this example, in the "concrete experience" stage, the learner physically experiences the bike in the "here-and-now". This experience forms "the basis for observation and reflection" and the learner has the opportunity to consider what is working or failing (reflective observation) and to think about ways to improve on the next attempt made at riding (abstract conceptualization). Every new attempt to ride is informed by a cyclical pattern of previous experience, thought and reflection (active experimentation).

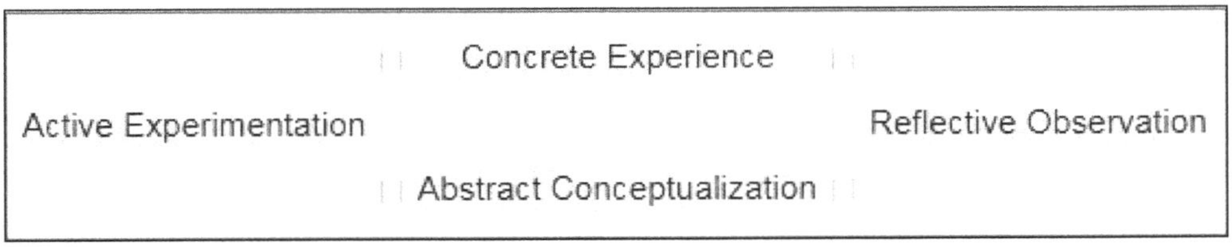

David Kolb's Experiential Learning Model (ELM).

Elements

Experiential learning can exist without a teacher and relates solely to the meaning-making process of the individual's direct experience. However, though the gaining of knowledge is an inherent process that occurs naturally, a genuine learning experience requires certain elements. According to Kolb, knowledge is continuously gained through both personal and environmental experiences. Kolb states that in order to gain genuine knowledge from an experience, the learner must have four abilities:

- The learner must be willing to be actively involved in the experience.
- The learner must be able to reflect on the experience.
- The learner must possess and use analytical skills to conceptualize the experience.
- The learner must possess decision making and problem solving skills in order to use the new ideas gained from the experience.

Implementation

Experiential learning requires self-initiative, an "intention to learn" and an "active phase of learning". Kolb's cycle of experiential learning can be used as a framework for considering the different stages involved. Jennifer A. Moon has elaborated on this cycle to argue that experiential learning is most effective when it involves: 1) a "reflective learning phase" 2) a phase of learning resulting from the actions inherent to experiential learning and 3) "a further phase of learning from feedback". This process of learning can result in "changes in judgment, feeling or skills" for the individual and can provide direction for the "making of judgments as a guide to choice and action".

Most educators understand the important role experience plays in the learning process. The role of emotion and feelings in learning from experience has been recognised as an important part of experiential learning. While those factors may improve the likelihood of experiential learning occurring, it can occur without them. Rather, what is vital in experiential learning is that the individual is encouraged to directly involve themselves in the experience and then to reflect on their experiences using analytic skills, in order that they gain a better understanding of the new knowledge and retain the information for a longer time.

Reflection is a crucial part of the experiential learning process and like experiential learning itself, it can be facilitated or independent. Dewey wrote that "successive portions of reflective thought grow out of one another and support one another", creating a scaffold for further learning and allowing for further experiences and reflection. This reinforces the fact that experiential learning and reflective learning are iterative processes and the learning builds and develops with further reflection and experience. Facilitation of experiential learning and reflection is challenging, but "a skilled facilitator, asking the right questions and guiding reflective conversation before, during and after an experience, can help open a gateway to powerful new thinking and learning". Jacobson and Ruddy, building on Kolb's four-stage Experiential Learning Model and Pfeiffer and Jones's five stage Experiential Learning Cycle, took these theoretical frameworks and created a simple, practical questioning model for facilitators to use in promoting critical reflection in experiential learning. Their "5 Questions" model is as follows:

- Did you notice?
- Why did that happen?
- Does that happen in life?
- Why does that happen?
- How can you use that?

These questions are posed by the facilitator after an experience and gradually lead the group towards a critical reflection on their experience and an understanding of how they can apply the learning to their own life. Although the questions are simple, they allow a relatively inexperienced facilitator to apply the theories of Kolb, Pfeiffer and Jones and deepen the learning of the group.

While it is the learner's experience that is most important to the learning process, it is also important not to forget the wealth of experience a good facilitator also brings to the situation. However, while a facilitator, or "teacher", may improve the likelihood of experiential learning occurring, a facilitator is not essential to experiential learning. Rather, the mechanism of experiential learning is the learner's reflection on experiences using analytic skills. This can occur without the presence of a facilitator, meaning that experiential learning is not defined by the presence of a facilitator. Yet, by considering experiential learning in developing course or program content, it provides an opportunity to develop a framework for adapting varying teaching/learning techniques into the classroom.

In Schools

Experiential learning is supported in different school organizational models and learning environments.

- Think Global School is a four-year traveling high school that holds classes in a new country each term. Students engage in experiential learning through activities such as workshops, cultural exchanges, museum tours and nature expeditions.
- The Dawson School in Boulder, Colorado, devotes two weeks of each school year to experiential learning, with students visiting surrounding states to engage in

community service, visit museums and scientific institutions and engage in activities such as mountain biking, backpacking and canoeing.

- In the ELENA-Project, the follow-up project of "animals live", experiential learning with living animals will be developed. Together with project partners from Romania, Hungary and Georgia, the Bavarian Academy of Nature Conservation and Landscape Management in Germany brings living animals in the lessons of European schools. The aim is to brief children for the context of the biological diversity and to support them to develop ecologically oriented values.
- Loving High School in Loving, New Mexico, publishes career and technical education opportunities for students. These include internship for students who are interested in science, STEM majors, or architecture. The school is making good connections with local businesses, which helps students get used to working in such environments.
- Chicago Public Schools operates eight early college STEM high schools through its Early College STEM School Initiative. The eight high schools offer four-years of computer science classes to every student. Additionally, students are able to earn college credits from local community colleges. Each school partners with a technology company which offers students internships and mentors from the company to expose students to jobs in STEM fields.
- Robert H. Smith School of Business offers select undergraduate students a year-round advanced course whereby students conduct financial analyses and security trades on Bloomberg Terminals to manage real investment dollars in the Lemma Senbet Fund.
- Nonprofits such as Out Teach, Life Lab, Nature Explore and the National Wildlife Federation, provide training for teachers on how to use outdoor spaces for experiential learning.

Experiential business learning is the process of learning and developing business skills through the medium of shared experience. The main point of difference between this and academic learning is more "real-life" experience for the recipient.

This may include for example, learning gained from a network of business leaders sharing best practice, or individuals being mentored or coached by a person who has faced similar challenges and issues, or simply listening to an expert or thought leader in current business thinking.

Providers of this type of experiential business learning often include membership organisations who offer product offerings such as peer group learning, professional business networking, expert/speaker sessions, mentoring and coaching.

Comparisons

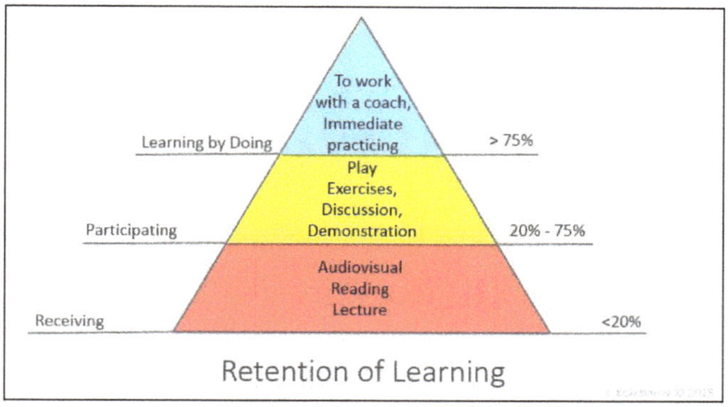

Experiential Learning is more efficient than passive learning such as reading or listening.

Experiential learning is most easily compared with academic learning, the process of acquiring information through the study of a subject without the necessity for direct experience. While the dimensions of experiential learning are analysis, initiative and immersion, the dimensions of academic learning are constructive learning and reproductive learning. Though both methods aim to instill new knowledge in the learner, academic learning does so through more abstract, classroom-based techniques, whereas experiential learning actively involves the learner in a concrete experience.

Benefits

- Experience real world: For example, students who major in Chemistry may have chances to interact with the chemical environment. Learners who have a desire to become businesspeople will have the opportunity to experience the manager position.
- Opportunities for creativity: There is always more than one solution for a problem in the real world. Students will have a better chance to learn that lesson when they get to interact with real life experiences.

References

- Visual-learning-style-3212062: thoughtco.com, Retrieved 01 March, 2019
- Harold Pashler; Mark McDaniel; Doug Rohrer; Robert Bjork (2009). "Learning Styles: Concepts and Evidence". Psychological Science in the Public Interest. 9 (3): 105–119. doi:10.1111/j.1539-6053.2009.01038.x. ISSN 1539-6053. PMID 26162104
- Gervais, J. (2016). "The operational definition of competency-based education". The Journal of Competency-Based Education. 1 (2): 98–106. doi:10.1002/cbe2.1011
- Keevy, James; Chakroun, Borhene (2015). Level-setting and recognition of learning outcomes: The use of level descriptors in the twenty-first century (PDF). Paris, UNESCO. p. 115. ISBN 978-92-3-100138-3
- Beard, Colin (2010). The Experiential Learning Toolkit: Blending Practice with Concepts. p. 20. ISBN 9780749459345

4
Apprenticeship

Apprenticeship is the system of vocational training for preparing a new generation of tradesmen, artisans, technicians, etc. Cognitive apprenticeship, engineering apprenticeship, seaman apprenticeship, degree apprenticeship, higher apprenticeship, etc. fall under its domain. All the concepts related to apprenticeship have been carefully analyzed in this chapter.

Apprenticeship is a process of teaching a trade to young practitioners. It comprises mostly of on-the-job training accompanied by some amount of the conventional reading and classroom study. Ideal duration of the training is 3-6 years. The origin of apprenticeship can be traced back to the middle ages when master craftsmen employed young people as what can be termed as assistants who worked as labors and in exchange provide them with food, lodging and formal training of the craft. At a later period of time, the governments stepped in to regulate and license vocational training institutes and made the process formal and legal.

Importance of Apprenticeship for Trainees

Apprenticeship programs are valued among employees not only as an educational or training process but also as gateways to the professional world as it prepares them with the industry knowledge and other essentials. Some benefits of the program for the trainees can be listed as:

- Specialized learning,
- On-the-job experience,
- First hand industry experience,
- Greater exposure,
- Earning during training,
- Better relationship building with employer.

Importance of Apprenticeship for Employers

In the current market employers are not only looking for a highly qualified workforce but a workforce with quality and experience in relevant domains. Apprenticeships helps them to fill up this gap. Some benefits of the program for the employers can be listed as below:

- Ability to understand the worker better before the formal hiring process.
- Provide specializes training as per the organizations requirement.
- Create a loyal workforce.
- Better understanding and tackling skill gaps.
- Newer ideas for problem solving.
- Relevant domain knowledge.

Types of Apprenticeships

Vocational training is part of tertiary training that puts full emphasis on the skills and knowledge required for a particular job function or trade. It covers a wide range of careers and industries like technology, office work, retail and hospitality.

Therefore, here are the types of vocational training commonly offered today.

Types of Vocational Training

Trade Schools

- This is a school that provides education in skilled trades such as plumbing, car repair and construction.
- It provides approximately 3 years of classroom work accompanied by workshop instructions before you seek any job from a potential employer.
- After completing this training, you will obtain a license to freely practice the trade.

Administration Schools

- This is a program that is intended to equip and prepare students for such careers as; administrative assistants, medical assistants, office clerks or legal assistants.
- This program takes one to two years for you to complete.

Nursing Schools

- Nurses are in high demand in the U.S. and in most parts of the world.
- As the population grows bigger and the average lifespan is increasing medical careers are on the rise.
- Being a nurse is very demanding yet it's also very rewarding.
- If money is what you're after, know that nursing is not an easy profession but salaries are on the rise in recent years.

Aesthetic Schools

- This is a program that offers creative vocations.
- It offers programs such as interior decorations, cosmetology and hairstyling.

- It is a training that takes two to three years of study and does not usually require an apprenticeship after you complete your degree.

Adult Education

- Adult Education, also known as continuing education.
- It's a form of vocational training for those adults that are already employed.
- Many employed people choose to undergo this training due to such reasons as to be considered for promotion or for career development.
- Often, employers choose to pay for their employees to undergo such training so as to keep them motivated and remain competitive in the market.

Internships

- This is a form of training for people with the need to get hands-on training from the ultimate source.
- It is a vocational training that is intended to give you the desired experience in your field of study hence helps you acquire a position in an industry of your desire.

Educational Theory of Apprenticeship

The apprentice perspective is an educational theory of apprenticeship concerning the process of learning through physical integration into the practices associated with the subject, such as workplace training. By developing similar performance to other practitioners, an apprentice will come to understand the tacit (informally taught) duties of the position. In the process of creating this awareness, the learner also affect their environment; as they are accepted by master practitioners, their specific talents and contributions within the field are taken into account and integrated into the overall practice.

The Apprenticeship Perspective can be used to teach procedures to students. For example, tying a shoe, building a fire and taking blood can all use the Apprenticeship Perspective to teach students these skills. However, it can be used to develop master practitioners in fields that involve increased complexity, numerous webs of interaction, or shifting environments demanding constant attention. Driver education, flight training and sports training all use the Apprenticeship Perspective for learners to learn a specific skill.

Apprenticeship learning has several formal definitions. Here are the most popular definitions:

- The Apprenticeship Perspective involves the learner within an actual, physical context of practice.
- Apprentices work side by side with an expert in order to learn a specific task.
- Apprenticeships include:
    - The development of learning contexts that model proficiency.
    - Providing coaching and scaffolding as students become immersed in authentic activities.
    - Independent practice so that students gain an appreciation of the use of domain-related principles across multiple contexts.
- Apprenticeship is a teaching method utilized by educators to teach students how to solve problems, understand tasks, perform specific tasks and deal with difficult situations.
- Furthermore, apprenticeship learning can be a useful supplement for adult educators with other types of instruction.

In summary, apprenticeship learning is a method used by teachers to teach students about a specific task. It is utilized in a problematic situation so students know how to react when faced with a similar situation. Students work very closely with an expert at learning a specific skill. Apprenticeship learning is very beneficial to the learner. Information the student acquires is then applied through practical applications in the field of study.

Unlike most other perspectives of education, the apprenticeship perspective is rarely formally taught. This is because the concepts communicated through apprenticeship are often practical, tacit strategies for achieving goals that do not always conform to standard procedure. For example, in an office environment lunch breaks may be limited to thirty minutes, but through apprenticeship one learns that up to forty-five minutes is acceptable. It would be inconvenient for the company to formally allow that allotment, but through informal training the message may still be communicated.

Educational theories of apprenticeship often involve the combination of formal and information training for the development of schema, mental structures that represent individual understanding of experiences that frame a person's conceptualization of reality. For example, a bicycle mechanic accustomed to road cycling may study texts covering mountain biking, but he will probably find it difficult to apply that formal training on a rough course. Educational theory's response to this is apprenticeship; by riding with a friend on the mountain side, the cyclist can watch and learn, constantly reiterating his performance to meet the demands of the sport. In this way he is developing his schema through formal and informal training.

The Apprentice Perspective is a holistic field of learning because it involves the education of both the student and the teacher. As the learner develops a schema that begins to incorporate the intricacies of the environment, they will be more capable of performing similarly to their peers. Once this is recognized by the trainer, the student will become accepted as a peer; at this point, as the new worker tackles problems through their new and previously existing schema, their individual talents may start to be applied within the group practices. In this way, apprenticeship retains fresh information and ideas within a common body of knowledge.

Factors of Success in Apprenticeship

Successful development through apprenticeship involves three key factors. To become a master of the field, the learning process must be active, social and authentic. These points will lead to the learner's greater understanding of the field and improved future contributions:

- Activity concerns the level to which the learner is physically and mentally stimulated within the environment. Successful trainers allow the student to be highly involved in the processes of decision making and action because they know that it is the doing that will have the most effect on the student's schema. In training to drive an automobile, students will never be able to pass without a physical examination of driving ability. To prepare for this, learners are given the opportunity to drive in safe areas. This active use of the tool prepares the student for its later, tested use.
- Second is the concept of sociality. Students must interact constantly with the tools for success, the teachers and the beneficiaries of the work. This holistic approach will further integrate the student into the interrelated web of action and consequence within the field. For example, a server training at a restaurant will not only follow a more experienced server, but interact with the customers, fellow employees and management in the same time frame. The server will thus establish connections between all these groups and the personnel that embody them, preparing the server for day-to-day activities.
- Finally, authenticity is essential to apprenticeship. This is the establishment of a mental connection between the work of the student in a particular field and

the comprehension of the greater public. An electrical engineer may understand the intricacies and challenges of computer panels, but this is only half of the required knowledge. They must also learn how most people perceive these panels and their interaction with them. From this understanding of the other end of spectrum, the engineer will better understand the achievement and thus authenticity of the community of electrical engineering.

Apprenticeship Phases

The apprenticeship perspective includes a series of phases that help articulate the roles of the learner and teacher during the process of observing and enacting concepts.

- Phase I: Modeling – The complete act is observed and contemplated. This means that the smaller parts that make up the whole are not yet examined in depth. The observer first frames the larger experience and will be able to specify from there. "Modeling occurs in two parts: behavioral modeling allows learners to observe performance of an activity by experienced members to share "tricks of the trade" with new members". The learner is using articulation and domain-specific heuristics in this phase.
- Phase II: Approximating – In private or in non-critical scenarios, the observer begins to mimic the actions of the teacher. Through close guidance, the learner begins to articulate more clearly the teacher's actions. This phase allows the learner to try the activity and lets them think about what they plan to do and why they plan to do it. Then after the activity the learner reflects about the activity. They examine what they did in comparison to what the expert did.
- Phase III: Fading – The learner, still within the safety net, starts operating in a more detailed manner, playing within the structure that has been taught. The learner's capabilities are increased as the experts assistance decreases.
- Phase IV: Self-directed Learning – The learner attempts the actions within real society, limiting him/herself to the scope of actions in the field that are well understood. The learner is performing the actual task and only seeking assistance when needed from the expert.
- Phase V: Generalizing – The learner generalizes what has been learned, trying to apply those skills to multiple scenarios and continuing to grow in ability in the field. The learner uses discussion in this phase to relate what they have learned to other relevant situations.

Goals of Apprenticeship

There are three main goals of apprenticeship learning according to Brandt et al;

- The first goal is for the adult learner to discover what works. This does not mean for the learner to use problem solving learning and figure out the situation on their own. There is guidance provided. The learner uses skills learned from the expert in order to successfully solve a problem.

- Secondly, the learner recognizes tasks, problems or situations and knows how to handle them. The learner learns the appropriate practical and theoretical knowledge. Learners are not learning this knowledge in isolation from other students. Students are working in a social setting with lifelike scenarios in order to learn a specific task.
- Finally, the learner is able to perform at an acceptable level. The learner is not learning basic skills at a novice level but working with an expert in order to perform at an acceptable level. Students are not learning skills at a basic level but rather at a level that is accepted in the specific industry.

These three goals have been accomplished based on published literature, learners feel that the apprenticeship "learning experience" expands their awareness of the factors that should be considered helps them organize and pay attention to their thought processes while handling difficult tasks, problems and problematic situations; and emphasizes the importance of particular aspects of such tasks, problems and problematic situations previously ignored or regarded as unimportant". Clearly the three goals of apprenticeship learning have been accomplished. Learners have been able to discover what works in situations and knows how to handles problems and finally the learner can perform at a satisfactory level.

Cognitive Apprenticeship

Cognitive apprenticeship is a theory that emphasizes the importance of the process in which a master of a skill teaches that skill to an apprentice.

Constructivist approaches to human learning have led to the development of the theory of cognitive apprenticeship. This theory accounts for the problem that masters of a skill often fail to take into account the implicit processes involved in carrying out complex skills when they are teaching novices. To combat these tendencies, cognitive apprenticeships "are designed, among other things, to bring these tacit processes into the open, where students can observe, enact and practice them with help from the teacher". This model is supported by Albert Bandura's theory of modeling, which posits that in order for modeling to be successful, the learner must be attentive, access and retain the information presented, be motivated to learn and be able to accurately reproduce the desired skill.

Part of the effectiveness of the cognitive apprenticeship model comes from learning in context and is based on theories of situated cognition. Cognitive scientists maintain that the context in which learning takes place is critical. Based on findings such as these, Collins, Duguid and Brown argue that cognitive apprenticeships are less effective when skills and concepts are taught independently of their real-world context and situation. As they state, "Situations might be said to co-produce knowledge through activity. Learning and cognition, it is now possible to argue, are fundamentally situated". In cognitive apprenticeships, teachers model their skills in real-world situations.

By modelling and coaching, masters in cognitive apprenticeships also support the three stages of skill acquisition described in the expertise literature: the cognitive stage, the associative stage and the autonomous stage. In the cognitive stage, learners develop a declarative understanding of the skill. In the associative stage, mistakes and misinterpretations learned in the cognitive stage are detected and eliminated, while associations between the critical elements involved in the skill are strengthened. Finally, in the autonomous stage, the learner's skill becomes honed and perfected until it is executed at an expert level.

Like traditional apprenticeships, in which the apprentice learns a trade such as tailoring or woodworking by working under a master teacher, cognitive apprenticeships allow masters to model behaviors in a real-world context with cognitive modeling. After listening to the master explain exactly what they are doing and thinking as they model the skill, the apprentice identifies relevant behaviors and develops a conceptual model of the processes involved. The apprentice then attempts to imitate those behaviors as the master observes and coaches. Coaching provides assistance at the most critical level– the skill level just beyond what the learner/apprentice could accomplish by themself. Vygotsky referred to this as the Zone of Proximal Development and believed that fostering development within this zone would lead to the most rapid development. The coaching process includes providing additional modeling as necessary, giving corrective feedback and giving reminders, which all intend to bring the apprentice's performance closer to that of the master's. As the apprentice becomes more skilled through the repetition of this process, the feedback and instruction provided by the master "fades" until the apprentice is, ideally, performing the skill at a close approximation of the master level.

Teaching Methods

Collins, Brown and Newman developed six teaching methods rooted in cognitive apprenticeship theory and claim these methods help students attain cognitive and metacognitive strategies for "using, managing and discovering knowledge". The first three, modeling, coaching, scaffolding, are at the core of cognitive apprenticeship and help with cognitive and metacognitive development. The next two, articulation and reflection, are designed to help novices with awareness of problem-solving strategies and execution similar to that of an expert. The final step, exploration, intends to guide the novice towards independence and the ability to solve and identify problems within the domain on their own. The authors note, however, that this is not an exhaustive list of methods and that the successful execution of these methods is highly dependent on the domain.

Modeling

Modeling is when an expert, usually a teacher, within the cognitive domain or subject area demonstrates a task explicitly so that novices, usually a student, can experience and build a conceptual model of the task at hand. For example, a math teacher might write out explicit steps and work through a problem aloud, demonstrating their heuristics and procedural knowledge. Modeling includes demonstrating expert performances or processes in the world.

Coaching

Coaching involves observing a novice's task performance and offering feedback and hints to sculpt the novice's performance to that of an expert's. The expert oversees the novice's tasks and may structure the task accordingly to assist the novice's development.

Scaffolding

Instructional scaffolding is the act of applying strategies and methods to support the student's learning. These supports could be teaching manipulatives, activities, or group work. The teacher may have to execute parts of the task that the student is not yet able to do. This requires the teacher to have the skill to analyze and assess students' abilities in the moment.

Articulation

Articulation includes "any method of getting students to articulate their knowledge, reasoning, or problem-solving process in a domain". Three types of articulation are inquiry teaching, thinking aloud and critical student role. Through inquiry teaching, teachers ask students a series of questions that allow them to refine and restate their learned knowledge and form explicit conceptual models. Thinking aloud requires students to articulate their thoughts while solving problems. Students assuming a critical role monitor others in cooperative activities and draw conclusions based on the problem-solving activities. Articulation is described by McLellan as consisting of two aspects: separating component knowledge from skills to learn more effectively and more commonly verbalizing or demonstrating knowledge and thinking processes in order to expose and clarify ideas.

Reflection

Reflection allows students to "compare their own problem-solving processes with those of an expert, another student and ultimately, an internal cognitive model of expertise". A technique for reflection would be examining the past performances of both an expert and a novice and highlighting similarities and differences. The goal of reflection is for students to look back and analyze their performances with desire to understand and improve the behavior of an expert.

Exploration

Exploration involves giving students room to problem solve on their own and teaching students exploration strategies. The former requires the teacher to slowly withdraw the use of supports and scaffolds not only in problem solving methods, but problem setting methods as well. The latter requires the teacher to show students how to explore, research and develop hypotheses. Exploration allows the student to frame interesting problems within the domain for themselves and then take the initiative to solve these problems.

Success

- In a technologically rich learning environment.
- Online.
- For clinical skills.

Apprentices Mobility

Apprentices mobility is the movement of students and teachers in vocational education or training (VET) to another institution inside or outside their own country to study or teach for a limited time. The term is usually used in the context of European Union (EU) policy.

Under the EU Lisbon agenda attempts have been made to lower cultural, socio-economical and academic barriers to mobility. Mobile learners are usually divided into two groups: *free-movers* are learners who travel entirely on their own initiative, while *programme students* use exchange programmes at department, faculty, institution or national level (such as Leonardo da Vinci II).

The practice of going abroad to learn has been denoted by different terms in different contexts over the years, such as "exchange" or "transnational mobility". For the specific practice of sending people abroad on placements in public and private enterprise, the more neutral term of "placements abroad" has been preferred.

Many different practices use the term "placement" as a denominator for their activities and some form of definition is necessary to distinguish between these and to mark it off from ordinary employment abroad as well as other forms of transnational mobility. Placements may be set up by an organiser who has made the necessary arrangements for a placement, defined the intended learning outcome and thought out the pedagogic implications. Placements may also be self-organised by the participant. When a student organises a work stay in another country during holidays or a study break, this may or may not qualify as a placement according to the criterion of intent. If the purpose is to acquire vocational skills and improve language and intercultural skills in general, it should be seen as a placement and count it as such, rather than a holiday job. It may be inscribed in an educational context through accreditation of prior experiential learning (APEL), if the organisation can be convinced that the person in question has sought out learning situations during the stay rather than just focused on having a good time or earning as much money as possible. Other activities in this borderline category are au pair placements and voluntary work in charitable institutions and organisations, e.g. as financed under the European Voluntary Service. The practice of some companies to send employees abroad in foreign subsidiaries for a period of time in order to acquire specific competences may also be considered under this label. It should be distinguished from employment abroad in general, which is another matter. The line is blurred and different definitions may collide here. Any labour market activity where the participant draws some kind of wages or salary is juridically considered as employment. But payment is not necessarily a way of distinguishing between placements and proper jobs; placements may be paid or unpaid, even though the learning role of participants is often signified by the fact that they receive no – or a considerably reduced – payment.

Mobility of VET learners can be traced to the tradition of the travelling journeyman of the medieval guilds. Dedicated transnational placement programmes appeared after the Second World War when the organisations AIESEC and IAESTE were set up under the auspices of Unesco in 1948 to facilitate placements for students of commerce and technology in higher education.

Another placement programme was set up in 1964 by the Commission of the European Communities in the shape of the Young workers' exchange programme (YWEP). In 1981 a binational Franco- German programme for placements (exchanges) in VET was established within the framework of the Franco-German Treaty of 1963.

The Comett programme from 1987 – also set up by the European Commission – grant aided placements of students in higher education in order to promote cooperation between universities and industry and to facilitate transfer of technology. Action 4 of the Lingua programme from 1990 contained funding provisions for young people in VET to undertake placement periods abroad in order to improve foreign language proficiency.

Up to the early 1990s, however, mobility in VET – and in particular in initial VET and for young workers – was very limited and certainly not a realistic proposition except for a very small minority of the total population engaged in VET. Mobility took a quantum leap upwards on the agenda of European and national VET-policies more or less precisely a decade ago, notably with the introduction of the enlarged Petra programme (Petra II) in 1992. That year, 8500 placements were grant-aided through the programme and by the end of the programme period in 1995, the total number approached 35 000 for the then 12 EU Member States. A significant development at national level was the establishment by the Danish government in 1992 of the PIU programme, which gave people in initial vocational training not just the opportunity but the right to undertake all or part of their mandatory work placements in another EU or EFTA country. Funding was provided by Danish employers through the Employers' reimbursement scheme for apprentices and trainees (AER). This was the first of several national programmes for placements abroad that have since been set up in various countries.

Criteria for Defining Placements Abroad in VET

Criteria have been established to define what a work placement is, in order to differentiate it from other activities. A placement:

- Is carried out in an authentic work environment. The placement period is not an artificially created situation, where the central feature is the learning of the participant. The most important thing here is continuing production and learning is placed second or third or even lower down on the scale of priorities;
- Implies involvement in concrete work processes. The participants are not merely onlookers to the activities, but are given an active role;
- Is for a limited time. Placements are planned and carried out as a period abroad that is set in a (national) learning context – i.e. surrounded by this on both sides. They are not open-ended. Duration, however, may vary considerably, from two weeks to two years. To this we may add another features, which we should term characteristics rather than criteria, since they need not always be applicable.

A placement thus as a rule:

- Demands professional experience as the "entry ticket". Workplaces where it is possible to become integrated in work processes immediately without any prior training or experience are few and far between. Therefore, participation in most placement projects is contingent upon either a wholly or partly completed training course or solid practical experience;
- Is not under the supervision of trained pedagogical staff. Contrary to a school environment or youth exchanges, there are usually no pedagogically trained staff (teachers) or experienced youth leaders around to offer guidance and practical support during the placement period. Mentors may be appointed, but the supervision of the participants is only a secondary task for them;
- Does not take place among peer groups. In school stays or youth exchanges, the participants will often be surrounded by people in the same age bracket and societal position who are in a similar life situation. At the workplace, however, there is a broad spectrum of colleagues, who are largely in a different position from the participant and have different dreams, expectations and interests.

Some activities are excluded from the definition, For example, "work camps" organised to improve intercultural understanding bring together young people from many countries to accomplish a practical task such as building a playground, or restoring a building to be used by the local community. However, the work situation is an artificially created one, there are trained supervisors present and the group is composed of young people in the same age bracket. Study visits are also excluded: even though they may be in authentic work environments, the participants are merely engaged as onlookers.

A definition of the term "placement abroad" is "a shorter or longer period spent abroad in a public or private enterprise, which has been consciously organised for learning purposes, which implies active involvement in concrete work processes and which can be paid or unpaid". The phenomenon is often associated with past and present programmes of the European Commission. These have grant-aided placements abroad, represent the largest single programmes and initiatives and provide the best statistical material. Currently, the Leonardo da Vinci programme is much in evidence in discussions on mobility in VET for exactly these reasons. The practice goes well beyond these programmes, however and encompasses also programmes and initiatives at binational, national and regional level, as well as the activities of organisations and individuals, which are undertaken without any recourse to programme funding.

Benefits

Placements abroad can be a pedagogical exercise. Mobility in a context of education and training differs substantially from other types of mobility in that it is primarily a pedagogical exercise: it is a tool used to produce certain kinds of learning of an affective and cognitive nature in the participant.

Placements abroad can be a means for achieving intercultural understanding, learning how to live peacefully together in Europe and in the world and develop a sense of "European Citizenship" as opposed to a strictly nationalist outlook (corresponding to the initial thoughts of Jean Monnet when forging the European Coal and Steel Union in 1951 - as a means to promote peace and understanding in a war-torn Europe). Latterly, this discourse has also been used in connection with the fight against racism and xenophobia. An example refers the activities of the Franco-German Youth Office.

Placements abroad can be a method for acquiring 'new basic skills' and developing 'employability'. The world has changed fundamentally in the last decade. The world is flattening. We can focus on the many differences between apprentices and placements in Europe. And we can continue to question the importance of experience abroad for apprentices and other young people in IVET, who often work in small and medium-sized enterprises with a regional focus. However. the reality is that experience of mobility provides apprentices and IVET students with particular competences over and above those obtained from the vocational curriculum including communicative, social, meaning-related and change-related skills. These critical competences benefit the individual apprentice and IVET student personally and they are also likely to make them more employable.

Within this discourse, the rationale for the activity lies in the use of placements abroad as a didactic tool to equip participants with so called "key skills" that enable them to cope with the constant changes in occupational profiles, work organisation and career paths arising as a consequence of globalisation and technological change. This corresponds to a focus on education and training as a motor for economic growth and the aims of the Lisbon-declaration concerning the creation of a 'Europe of knowledge'.

Placements abroad can be an activity linked to internationalisation of education and training in Europe. In this case they are the response of national educational systems to the perceived negative effects of globalisation. At the level of the individual, it enables the future workforce to acquire foreign language skills and intercultural skills so that they can deal with increased foreign contacts at the workplace. At systemic level, it allows national educational systems to fill in temporary gaps in training provision by sending trainees abroad to where such opportunities exist.

Increasingly, employees from all levels need to be able to operate in an environment that deals with international customers and suppliers. Those companies and sectors who earn their money abroad, or work with foreign suppliers, are more likely to be engaged in mobility. Although right now less than 50% of small and medium enterprises (SMEs) are internationalised, figures by the World Trade Organization, show that more and more economies are dependent on external and foreign trade. It is likely that this will increase the pressure on employers to hire people with a 'worldly mindset'. In the best tradition of 'Master craftsmen' who only got their credentials after having been abroad, sectors can use this changing environment to train their future employees. To facilitate knowledge-transfer between sectors, economies and generations, education should continue to play its role here.

Placements abroad can be a method for promoting the free movement of workers in Europe. In this case they are concerned with learning how to live and work in another country, how to become a 'migrant worker' willing and able to move across borders and thereby allay skills shortages in other Member States (corresponding to the thoughts in the Treaty of Rome from 1957 creating the European Economic Communities, where the free circulation of labour across borders was seen as an essential element in the economic development of Europe).

The rationales for mobility may differ for each actor. At EU level, several reasons for stimulating mobility are mentioned, i.e. more mobility between regions and jobs represents an essential part of the Lisbon Agenda, mobility is a tool for acquiring language skills and mobility contributes to increasing stability and peace of the EU. More exposure to other countries leads to increased intercultural awareness and good feelings about host nation/culture. Mobility implies acquiring international skills, which become increasingly important with the liberalization of trade and commerce. For individuals, mobility implies developing personal skills and competencies

For vocational schools and training centres hosting students and apprentices and other young people in IVET from abroad creates an international atmosphere that brings benefits for the whole institution (e.g. inspiration of other students, learning language). Transnational mobility projects can serve as a launch pad for transnational partnerships and for a proactive internationalisation strategy and policy. For employers, reasons for engaging in mobility can be a faster diffusion and acquisition of knowledge and skills.

Benefits for Employers

- Mobility is a means to address both short-term and long-term shortages in skills.
- Greater use of mobile workers and trainees is an important measure to cope with recruitment difficulties. In the long run, companies can include recruitment for young people in their human resource policies.
- While time for adaptation to key technologies is becoming shorter, the mobility of employees can facilitate a fast diffusion of knowledge.
- Hiring of trainees implies low costs. The risk of hiring trainees for the sole purpose of lowering the labour costs needs to be mitigated by some forms of control and accreditation by the education system.

Benefits for the Individual

- Mobility implies acquiring of international skills, what becomes increasingly important with the liberalization of trade and commerce.
- Mobility implies developing of personal skills and competencies such as change-related, relational, learning-related and meaning-related skills.

Benefits for Vocational Schools and Training Centres

- Hosting students and apprentices from abroad creates an international atmosphere that brings benefit for the whole institution (e.g. inspiration of other students, learning language).
- VET-institutions have the possibility to benchmark their course contents and pedagogic practices.
- Involvement of a VET-institution in mobility activities makes it attractive for students in comparison with other 'not-towards-mobility-oriented' institutions.
- Transnational mobility projects can serve as a launch pad for transnational partnerships and for a proactive internationalization strategy and policy.

- The role of VET-institutions is gradually changing from a traditional 'school' towards a regional knowledge centre. There is a need to reflect internationalization in their array of competences and skills.
- Mobility projects might imply income-generating activities.

Take-up Statistics

Initially, we should distinguish between placements abroad organised within the framework of programmes and spontaneous placement activities happening outside of these. We have only very limited ability to measure the placements abroad that are undertaken outside of dedicated programmes, or in programmes or initiatives that deal with wider issues and where placements abroad are only a possibility and not a distinct programme activity. Anything concerning this must thus be based on guesswork.

Even when concentrating on dedicated mobility programmes (or programmes where mobility is a distinct activity) are we faced with problems. First, problems of definition can make comparability difficult. Second (and partly as a consequence of this), the way in which information is gathered (and what is gathered) may differ from programme to programme, which makes it yet more difficult to come up with robust and comparable information. It is not possible to see from the statistical material available whether some activities were undertaken as placements or as another form of mobility. Moreover, mobility programmes (or programmes incorporating mobility activities) are undertaken in many different contexts and there is virtually no national level overview of all mobility activities. The annual Dutch BISON monitoring report of international mobility within education and training remains an isolated initiative, but it includes only mobility taking place within the framework of educational establishments. In addition, all the information available is concerned with outgoing mobility (the sending aspect) and there is no indication of incoming mobility (hosting). This lack of quantitative data makes it very difficult to arrive at any figures concerning both the participation rates and financing involved. For the Leonardo da Vinci programme, we can give very precise indications on participation rates and the amount of funding in the programme, but we do not have figures on funding that also involves national cofinancing. Given the different ways of calculating this from project to project and the varying percentage of Commission funding, a conservative estimate would put this at a level equal to the Commission's contribution (e.g. for the second phase of the Leonardo da Vinci programme, approximately EUR 600 million).

Take-up through Programmes

The Leonardo da Vinci programme remains the biggest single funding mechanism for transnational mobility in VET in Europe and in some countries it is more or less the only programme within VET that can be used for funding placements abroad on any significant scale. In other countries there are more funding opportunities.

In the Netherlands 1 230 people benefited from a Leonardo mobility grant in the year 1999-2000.

The total number of people participating in transnational mobility activities in VET in the same period, however, is registered by the BISON monitoring report as close to 7000. Of these, 204 come from the Lingua programme (i.e. another EU programme), but 5158 were financed through the national Onbegrensd talent programme.

Unfortunately we cannot assess the exact amount spent on placements abroad from this programme, since the funds are allocated as lump sums to educational establishments for broad 'internationalisation' purposes. Also, we cannot compare factors like length of stay and target countries. Even without information on mobility financed through other sources than the established programmes, it would seem that Leonardo accounts for less than one fifth of the total figure for mobility within VET in the Netherlands. It is problematic, however, to transpose this figure to the rest of Europe for want of a reliable yardstick for measurement and comparison. In many instances, grant allocations and numbers involved are used as indicators. Another complication is that a mere headcount will not give a correct picture of the scope of mobility in VET.

In the Danish PIU programme, the participants (apprentices) stay abroad for eight to nine months on average, which has greater effect than, for example, a two-week stay financed under Lingua/Socrates. Similarly, Danish apprentices are paid the appropriate apprentice wage by their employer in the host country, which means that programme costs measured by grant allocation only will not give a real picture of the total costs involved. However, some countries have only the Leonardo programme to finance mobility, which tips the scales in the other direction when trying to figure out a European average for participation and funding of mobility.

Take-up through Spontaneous Mobility

Quantifiable information on spontaneous mobility is virtually non-existent, even though we have anecdotal evidence of its existence as a factor. We might have got an indication of sorts from the German Sprungbrett programme; a national-level mobility programme which started in 2003, which gave grants to individuals within initial VET undertaking placement periods in other European countries. Unfortunately this programme was discontinued at the end of 2003 due to budget cuts.

Measuring the factors such as the numbers of applications received may give us a rough estimate of this activity in at least one Member State, but only in initial vocational training, where spontaneous mobility is likely to be low for reasons of age. Almost equally impossible to assess are the activities that are undertaken as pilot projects within programmes that on the surface have nothing to do with the issue of placements abroad. An example of this is the Eurojoker project, which was financed out of funds from the EU Konver II initiative. In this project young unemployed persons from the

Brandenburg region in Germany were sent on one year placements in other European countries with a view to increasing their employability.

Locating such projects mainly relies on the unofficial network of the person collecting the data, or happens by chance. It follows that any estimate of the numbers and amounts involved will doubtless be inaccurate. The scarcity of data is equally pronounced for the qualitative aspects of the phenomenon. Given the scope of activities, it is strange to note that studies on the qualitative aspects of placements abroad as a didactic tool in the context of VET are sparse.

Evaluations of Programmes

Very few evaluations of mobility programmes and projects have been undertaken at European or national level and even fewer of these concentrate on the learning aspects. Most of the evaluations undertaken are summative evaluations carried out by or for programme administrators with a view to justifying expenses and administrative practices and have little to say about learning. After the conclusion of the first phase of the Leonardo da Vinci programme, a 'valorisation' exercise was carried out on selected aspects of the programme, both at national and at European level.

Valorisation is not the same as traditional evaluation or impact assessment, but focuses mainly on the achievements of the programme with a view to formulating recommendations for improvements and future priorities. It is not a very well defined methodology and valorisation exercises consequently vary greatly from country to country, as well as in quality. Each country was given the possibility to choose between certain themes and mobility was an issue in several countries covered by this study as well as an element in European-level valorisation. Other than these evaluations, research-based treatment of the theme of placements abroad is virtually non-existent. Some work, however, has been done on organisational matters, notably on legal and administrative barriers, culminating with the Commission's Green Paper on obstacles to mobility from 1996. The main source of funding for development activities (in the majority of countries the only source) is the strand for pilot-projects under the Leonardo da Vinci programme. The recognition of qualifications acquired abroad is a major issue here. However, only 57 projects dealing with mobility-related subjects could be identified (out of a total project number of over 3000) in the first phase of the programme. Prominent themes were placement finding, preparation and quality assurance.

Engineering Apprentice

Engineering apprenticeships are a great way to get into engineering without a university degree. However, many people are apprehensive because they don't know what is involved in an apprenticeship. Of course, every engineering apprenticeship is tailored to the business you'll be working in, so no two are alike. However, there are some commonalities between all apprenticeships.

An apprenticeship is a training programme based upon learning the skills required for a job. Whilst training towards gaining a nationally recognised qualification. Engineering apprenticeships are available to new and existing employees. Normally with funding available for the business who is training the apprentice. It can take between one and four years to complete the course depending on previous knowledge and experience.

An apprenticeship will generally consist of the following components:

- A minimum of 30 hours per week paid employment.
- A knowledge based element.
- A competency based element.
- Transferable or functional skills.
- A module on employment rights and responsibilities.

Shadowing

The advantage of engineer training on an apprenticeship. Is that it's conducted on real work being done by a real company. So you'll spend a lot of time shadowing the existing engineers in the firm. They will talk you through different aspects of their work. And wherever possible you'll gradually join in, performing some of the work yourself.

Supervised Work

You will gradually start conducting some work on your own and taking responsibility for your own part in various projects. You will work closely with the other engineers. Who will give you all the instruction you need to do your work. There will always be someone close by in case you have any questions or need feedback.

Studying during Engineering Apprenticeships

As well as practical work, engineering apprenticeships involve some desk or classroom-based study. Depending on where you do your apprenticeship, you may do this in-house alongside other apprentices and trainees. Or, you may spend one or two days each week at a local college or university. Alternatively, you might study in blocks of one or two weeks at a time.

Assessment

Throughout your apprenticeship, you'll have regular meetings with a buddy or supervisor to make sure you are up to speed on everything you need to know. Your skills and knowledge will be assessed. Which will usually be through a combination of coursework, written essays, written exams and practical exams.

Key Benefits of an Engineering Apprenticeship

Creative

An engineering career allows you to utilise your creative flair on a daily basis. Whether this is designing new pieces or parts utilising computer-aided design or through more traditional engineering drawings and ranging through to following drawings to create tangible parts and pieces for equipment which will perform a crucial function, the ability to make a real impact is clear.

Collaborating with other professionals across a huge range of industries is often called for, meaning those who love to create, learn and experience new things will feel at home as an engineer.

Earning Potential

There is fantastic scope to earn a good wage working as an engineer – across a variety of specialisms which it is possible to move into as your career progresses.

From electronic and mechanical engineering to operations management and research and development, the options are endless and what is true across the board is that wages for engineers hold up extremely well against other career options.

An engineering apprenticeship offers a supportive network which will work with you to learn and grow – with on-the-job support combining with the key skills you will gain via training.

Building relationships both in work and within training provides a good atmosphere and opportunity to share ideas and increase skills via colleagues and fellow learners.

Earn while you Learn

Building your engineering career through an apprenticeship as opposed to studying at College – you'll get experience in a work environment day-to-day whilst also gaining the benefits from experienced trainers who can help you build your skills and take them straight into the workplace.

An apprenticeship also can allow you to build a career and avoid the high levels of student debt incurred when studying for a degree.

Make an Impact

As an engineer you'll have the opportunity to make a real impact and a difference and benefit from the opportunities that it provides.

With some job roles offering travel opportunities thanks to engineering's global role, the ability to make your mark in a job which inspires you which you love is a real pull for future engineers taking their first steps into the world of work.

Seaman Apprentice

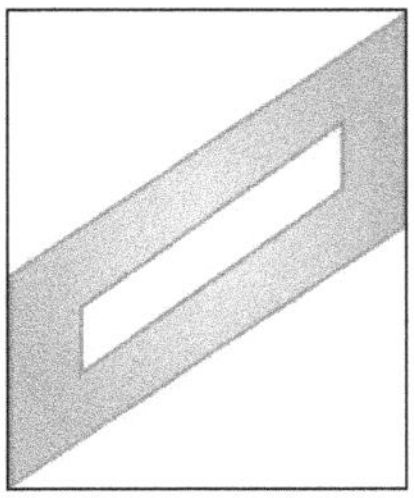

Collar insignia.

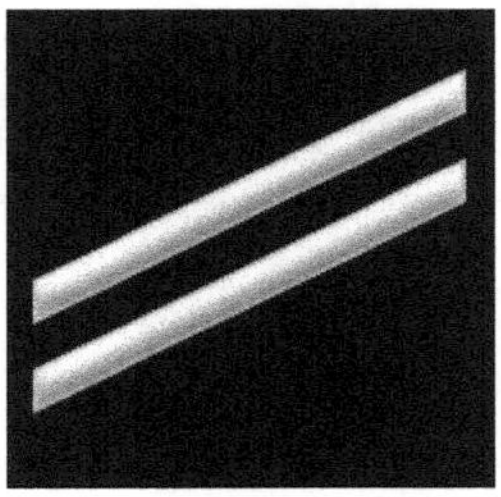

Seaman Apprentice insignia.

Seaman apprentice is the second lowest enlisted rate in the U.S. Navy, U.S. Coast Guard and the U.S. Naval Sea Cadet Corps just above seaman recruit and below seaman; this rank was formerly known as seaman second class.

The actual title for an E-2 in the U.S. Navy varies based on the community to which the sailor belongs. Likewise, the color of their group rate marks also depends on their community.

- Those in the general deck and administrative community are seamen apprentice. They wear white stripes on navy blue uniforms and navy blue (black) stripes on white uniforms.
- Hospital corpsmen are hospitalmen apprentice. They are the only rate in this community. They wear white stripes on navy blue uniforms and navy blue stripes on white uniforms.

- Those in the engineering and hull community are called firemen apprentice and wear red stripes on both navy blue and white uniforms.
- Those in the aviation community are called airmen apprentice and wear green stripes on both navy blue and white uniforms.
- Seabees are called constructionmen apprentice and wear light blue stripes on both navy blue and white uniforms.

No stripes are worn on the working uniforms - coveralls or utilities.

In October 2005, the dental technician rating was merged with the hospital corpsman rating, eliminating the dentalman apprentice title. Those who once held the rank of dentalman apprentice have instead become hospitalman apprentices.

Sailors who have completed the requirements to be assigned a rating and have been accepted by the Bureau of Naval Personnel as holding that rating (a process called "striking") are called designated strikers and are called by their full rate and rating in formal communications (i.e., "machinist's mate fireman apprentice", as opposed to simply "fireman apprentice"), though the rating is often left off in informal communication. Those who have not officially been assigned to a rating are officially referred to as "undesignated" or "non-rates."

Degree Apprenticeship

Degree Apprenticeships are the latest model of apprenticeship to be developed, seeing apprentices achieving a full bachelor's or master's degree (Levels 6 and 7) as a core component of the apprenticeship. Both Higher and Degree Apprenticeships must last a minimum of one year, with Degree Apprenticeships in particular lasting longer, typically up to four years but sometimes five, though there is no fixed maximum duration for a Degree Apprenticeship.

Degree Apprenticeships were announced in 2015 with the roll out of nine new industry designed apprenticeships: a new model bringing together higher and vocational education. Degree Apprenticeships are created and tailored by experts from the industry offering them – groups of businesses work with universities and colleges to develop practical, vocational degree courses that allow people to combine both the academic study from a traditional university degree and the practical experience and wider employment skills vital for career success.

During the programmes, degree apprentices split their time between university study and the workplace and are employed throughout – gaining a full degree while earning a wage and getting real on-the-job experience in their chosen profession.

Higher Apprentices are already able study to degree level as part of their apprenticeship, but sometimes only do the equivalent of a year at university, for example. Degree Apprenticeships go further: they always involve a full degree as an integral part of the apprenticeship, co-designed by employers to make sure it is relevant for the skills industry is looking for.

As with other apprenticeships, the cost of course fees for Degree Apprenticeships are shared between government and employers, meaning that the apprentice can earn a full degree without paying any fees.

As well as being suitable for school leavers as an alternative route to gaining a degree, the new Degree Apprenticeship qualifications are expected to strengthen vocational pathways and be suitable for existing apprentices looking to progress in their career.

Higher Apprenticeships and the new Degree Apprenticeships are part of the same 'apprenticeships family'. However, there are some differences.

'Higher Apprenticeship' refers to all apprenticeships that include the achievement of academic/vocational qualifications from Level 4 up to bachelor's and master's degree at level 6-7. All levels can include vocational qualifications and academic qualifications.

Degree Apprenticeships are the latest model to be developed as part of higher apprenticeship standards, seeing apprentices achieving a full bachelor's or master's degree (Levels 6 and 7) as a core component of the apprenticeship.

Both Higher and Degree Apprenticeships must last a minimum of one year; Degree Apprenticeships in particular will last longer, typically up to four years, though there is no fixed maximum duration. Neither Higher nor Degree Apprentices are eligible for student loans.

Degree Apprenticeships offer the highest academic attainment – bachelor's or master's degrees – without the associated student debt, as well as workplace experience that will set apprentices apart from their peers on standard degree courses.

As with other apprenticeships, the cost of course fees are shared between government and employers, meaning that the apprentice can earn a full bachelors or even master's degree without paying any fees.

Degree Apprentices split their time between university study and the workplace and will be employed throughout – gaining a full bachelor's or master's degree while earning a wage and getting real on-the-job experience in their chosen profession.

Degree Apprenticeships are especially useful as they are designed with the industry's needs in mind. Groups of businesses, universities and colleges develop practical, vocational degree courses that allow students to build up skills and experience relevant to that particular industry, making them very employable in the future.

Another advantage of a Degree Apprenticeship is the working relationships apprentices forge with their employees and colleagues, developing the so-called 'soft skills' – effective teamwork, communications, negotiating skills, ability to work under pressure, problem-solving – that employers so desperately want in young recruits.

These are often what people say standard graduates are missing, despite their academic credentials, so a Degree Apprenticeship can arm you with a desirable and quite rare, skills set alongside a university qualification.

Degree Apprenticeships are relatively new – they were launched in 2015 – but are already being embraced by high profile employers in various industries and new programmes are being announced all the time.

In 2015, Degree Apprenticeships were launched in the digital and software fields, offering the highest academic attainment – bachelor's or master's degrees – without the associated student debt. The first nine Degree Apprenticeships were announced in:

- Chartered surveying,
- Electronic systems engineering,
- Aerospace Engineering,
- Aerospace software development,
- Defence systems engineering,
- Laboratory science,
- Nuclear,
- Power systems,
- Public relations.

Registered Apprenticeship

Registered Apprenticeship is a program of the United States Department of Labor that connects job seekers looking to learn new skills with employers looking for qualified workers. Employers, employer associations and joint labor-management organizations, known collectively as "sponsors", provide apprentices with paid on-the-job learning and academic instruction that reflects industry needs. The goal of such instruction is to provide workers with advanced skillsets that meet the specific needs of their employers.

Following the creation of the first Registered Apprenticeship system in Wisconsin in 1911, the United States Congress passed the National Apprenticeship Act (known as the "Fitzgerald Act") in 1937, establishing federal Registered Apprenticeship. Initially,

Registered Apprenticeship programs consisted mainly of the manufacturing, construction and utilities industries. After World War II, Registered Apprenticeship began to expand into training of health and safety workers, including firefighters, police and emergency medical technicians. Recently, the program guidelines were revised in late 2008 to allow for greater flexibility in serving apprentices and program sponsors in prevailing economic conditions. Currently, Registered Apprenticeship includes 29,000 programs impacting 250,000 employers, involving approximately 450,000 apprentices.

The National Apprenticeship Act authorizes the Federal government, in cooperation with the states, to oversee the nation's apprenticeship system. The U.S. Department of Labor's Office of Apprenticeship works in conjunction with both the Bureau of Apprenticeship and Training states that report directly to the Federal government as well independent State Apprenticeship Agencies to administer the program. These agencies are responsible for:

- Registering apprenticeship programs that meet Federal and State standards.
- Protecting the safety and welfare of apprentices.
- Issuing nationally recognized and portable Certificates of Completion to apprentices.
- Promoting the development of new programs through marketing and technical assistance.
- Assuring that all programs provide high quality training.
- Assuring that all programs produce skilled competent workers.

Program Benefits and Requirements

Registered Apprenticeship provides a wide array of benefits to employers, employees, unions and other stakeholders. For employers, the program provides a pipeline of skilled workers enrolled in customized programs that meet a variety of the employer's needs, e.g., increased competitiveness or higher worker retention rates. For workers, enrolled apprentices receive a paycheck that is guaranteed to increase as their training and skill levels increase. Apprentices also complete a combination of industry-specific classroom education and hands-on career training leading to nationally recognized, portable Certificates of Completion.

Registered Apprenticeship program sponsors identify the minimum qualifications to apply into their apprenticeship program. The eligible starting age can be no less than 16 years of age; however, individuals must usually be 18 to be an apprentice in hazardous occupations. Program sponsors may also identify additional minimum qualifications and credentials to apply, e.g., education, ability to physically perform the essential functions of the occupation, proof of age. Based on the selection method utilized by the sponsor, additional qualification standards, such as fair aptitude tests and interviews, school grades and previous work experience may be identified.

Higher Apprenticeship

When a higher apprentice walks into the room, everybody stops talking. For a moment or two, there is a breathless silence.

A person claps, then another and soon enough, the crowd goes absolutely bananas. The entire room is applauding, cheering and stamping their feet. They demand autographs, selfies and a speech.

A higher apprenticeship, also called level 4 or 5 apprenticeships, are the level above advanced (level 3) and intermediate (level 2) apprenticeships. Higher apprentices work for a company, receiving on-the-job training while the study towards a qualification on the side.

If you complete a higher apprenticeship, you will be awarded with a level 4 (or above) competence qualification and a knowledge based qualification – a higher national diploma or foundation degree.

Higher apprenticeships are designed for students who are aged 18 or over. If you've just finished your GCSEs, an intermediate or advanced apprenticeship are the schemes to be looking at.

Once you have completed an advanced apprenticeship, you will be eligible to apply for a higher apprenticeship. Likewise, if you finish a higher apprenticeship, it can lead onto a degree apprenticeship or a university degree. There are so many pathways – it's like the New Forest.

The entry requirements for higher apprenticeships can vary. However, most employers require applicants to have a minimum of two A-levels, or an advanced apprenticeship under their belt.

Higher apprenticeships are designed to train a candidate for a particular job, or for a specific role within a company. The majority of higher apprenticeships have a permanent job waiting at the end. If the company doesn't employ you after the apprenticeship, or you decide to move on, you will still be a highly employable candidate.

Employers will fight like walruses over you. If that sounds cool and you haven't already, have a look at the vacancies we have for higher apprenticeships. (If you have already looked, look again).

Higher apprenticeships are organised in the same fashion as other types of apprenticeships. You will work full-time for a company, with regular day releases for you to study and attend classes with your training provider. It is combination of work and study.

Each higher apprenticeship will be structured slightly differently. Some companies will send you off to study with the training provider for one day in each week, others could organise a two-week study break intermittently throughout the year.

As a higher apprentice, you will be expected to work for a minimum of thirty hours a week, for a minimum of thirty weeks in a year. The length of your apprenticeship will depend on your employer, but higher apprenticeships can last anywhere between one and four years.

References

- Apprenticeship, human-resources-hr-terms- 15109: mbaskool.com, Retrieved 19 July, 2019
- Types-of-vocational-training: vocationaltraininghq.com, Retrieved 28 August, 2019
- What-is-involved-in-an-engineering-apprenticeship: tteltd.co.uk, Retrieved 26 June, 2019
- 5-key-benefits-of-an-engineering-apprenticeship: training2000.co.uk, Retrieved 14 May, 2019
- What-is-a-degree-apprenticeship- 288: allaboutschoolleavers.co.uk, Retrieved 23 April, 2019
- Higher-apprenticeships: ratemyapprenticeship.co.uk, Retrieved 25 March, 2019

5
Types of Vocational School

Vocational school is an educational institution that provides vocational education and technical skills required by the apprentices. Vocational-technical school, music school, drama school, journalism school, etc. are some of its types. All these types of vocational school have been carefully analyzed in this chapter.

Vocational-technical School

Vocational school is one option for students interested in practical postsecondary education and job training. Vocational schools typically offer relatively short, career-focused programs that quickly prepare graduates for the workforce.

When considering enrollment in postsecondary vocational school, it can be helpful to consider program length, subject offerings and admissions requirements in order to make the best education decision for your career goals.

Vocational schools, sometimes referred to as trade schools or career schools, provide practical training with few unrelated academic course requirements. They are relevant for many kinds of learners, including:

- Individuals who are planning to enter industry for the first time.
- Adults who are looking to reenter the workforce.
- Professionals who wish to pursue a new career field.

The education offered at vocational schools allows adults to focus on the skills to enter a particular industry, with the option of not taking unrelated general education courses required for an associate's degree at a community college. Vocational schools also provide technology training or retraining for workers in their current occupations.

Program Lengths

Vocational schools can offer programs ranging from short-unit classes of ten weeks or less to long-term programs of up to two years in length. Some states offer public vocational schools and career training programs through community colleges, but the majority of vocational schools are private institutions. Vocational school credits don't typically transfer to academic undergraduate programs like an Associate of Arts program, but they may award students with a certificate credential.

Common Programs

Vocational schools generally focus on programs in career fields that can be completed in two years or less. Vocational schools focusing on a single field, such as automotive trades or health services, may offer only one training program or give students a choice of several programs in the same industry, such as hair stylist, barber, nail technician or esthetician programs at a cosmetology school. Other vocational schools offer programs in several unrelated fields, like agriculture, office skills and technical training. The following are some common types of vocational school programs:

- Welding,
- Cosmetology,
- Plumbing,
- Carpentry,
- Locksmithing,
- Electrical installation and maintenance,
- Motorcycle and automotive repair,
- Floral design,
- Medical transcription,
- Hotel and restaurant management.

Vocational University

A vocational university, also known as university of applied sciences (UAS), polytechnic university, technological educational institute, applied technological university, or college of higher vocational studies, is an institution of higher education and sometimes research, which provides both tertiary and sometimes quaternary education and grants academic degrees at all levels (bachelor, master and sometimes doctorate) in a variety of subjects.

Örebro University, Sweden.

In some countries, a vocational university more precisely grants professional degrees like professional bachelor's degree, professional master's degree and professional doctorates. The term is not officially used in many countries and an assignment to a certain type of university in a certain country's educational system is therefore difficult. The UK once had a very extensive vocational university sector with its polytechnic system dating back to the mid-19th century. Vocational universities are often regulated and funded differently (for example, by the local government rather than the state) from research-focused universities and the degrees granted are not necessarily interchangeable.

Education

The education at vocational universities combines teaching of both practical skills and theoretical expertise. It can be contrasted with education in a usually broader scientific field, which may concentrate on theory and abstract conceptual knowledge. There is also the historical background that an educational institution was called a university in the Middle Ages only if a certain classical canon of subjects was taught (typically including philosophy, medicine and theology). In modern times, other subjects, namely natural and engineering sciences, became more important, but institutions of tertiary education focusing on these subjects and not offering the classical canon have until recently or are still denied the prestigious denomination "university" in all countries. They had to use other, more general terms (which in many languages are false friends of the English term "high school", sometimes with modifiers), including *Fachhochschule* in German, *Haute École* in French (Belgium and Switzerland), *Hogeschool* in Dutch, *Høyskole* in Norwegian, *Scuola universitaria professionale* in Italian, etc.

There are different varieties, including vocational universities of applied sciences (also named polytechnics or institutes of technology), vocational universities of liberal arts, etc. In recent years, many vocational universities have received full university status, such as the University of Music and Performing Arts, Vienna, Austria (Universität für Musik und darstellende Kunst Wien, formerly Hochschule für Musik und Darstellende Kunst Wien), or the Örebro University, Sweden (formerly Örebro Högskola). There are also some establishments which now have full university status but continue to use their former names, such as the Royal Institute of Technology in Stockholm, Sweden.

Music School

Graduates of the Rimsky-Korsakov Saint Petersburg Conservatory include Peter Ilyich Tchaikovsky, Sergey Prokofiev, Dmitri Shostakovichand George Balanchine.

A music school is an educational institution specialized in the study, training and research of music. Such an institution can also be known as a school of music, music academy, music faculty, college of music, music department (of a larger institution), conservatory or conservatoire. Instruction consists of training in the performance of musical instruments, singing, musical composition, conducting, musicianship, as well as academic and research fields such as musicology, music history and music theory.

Music instruction can be provided within the compulsory general education system, or within specialized children's music schools such as the Purcell School. Elementary-school children can access music instruction also in after-school institutions such as music academies or music schools. In Venezuela El Sistema of youth orchestras provides free after-school instrumental instruction through music schools called *núcleos*. The term "music school" can also be applied to institutions of higher education under names such as *school of music*, such as the Jacobs School of Music of Indiana University; *music academy*, like the Sibelius Academy or the Royal Academy of Music, London; *music faculty* as the Don Wright Faculty of Music of the University of Western Ontario; *college of music*, characterized by the Royal College of Music and the Berklee College of Music; *music department*, like the Department of Music at the University of California, Santa Cruz; or the term *conservatory*, exemplified by the Conservatoire de Paris and the New England Conservatory. In other parts of Europe, the equivalents of *higher school of music* or *university of music* may be used, such as the Hochschule für Musik und Tanz Köln (Cologne University of Music).

Based around the Notre Dame Cathedral, the Notre Dame School was an important centre of polyphonic music.

Although music and music education may have been in existence for thousands of years, the earliest history is speculative. Even when history starts to be recorded, music is mentioned more frequently than music education. Within the biblical tradition, Hebrew litany was accompanied with rich music, but the Torah or Pentateuch was silent on the practice and instruction of music in the early life of Israel. However, by I Samuel 10, Alfred Sendrey suggests that we find "a sudden and unexplained upsurge of large choirs and orchestras, consisting of thoroughly organized and trained musical groups, which would be virtually inconceivable without lengthy, methodical preparation." This has led some scholars to believe that the prophet Samuel was the patriarch of a school which taught not only prophets and holy men, but also sacred-rite musicians.

The schola cantorum (papal choir) in Rome may be the first recorded music school in history, when Gregory the Great made permanent an existing guild dating from the 4th century (*schola* originally referred more to a guild rather than school). The school consisted of monks, secular clergy and boys. Wells Cathedral School, England founded as a Cathedral School in 909 a.d. to educate choristers, continues today to educate choristers and teaches instrumentalists. However the school appears to have been refounded at least once.

Saint Martial school, 10th to 12th century, was an important school of composition at the Abbey of Saint Martial, Limoges. It is known for the composition of tropes, sequences and early organum. In this respect, it was an important precursor to the Notre Dame School. It was the Notre Dame school (late 12th and early 13th century) which was the earliest repertory of polyphonic (multipart) music to gain international prestige and circulation. The school was a group of composers and singers working under the patronage of the great Cathedral of Notre-Dame in Paris. First records on Escolania de Montserrat, boys' choir linked to a music school, back to 1307 and still continues the musical education.

The Accademia Nazionale di Santa Cecilia (National Academy of St Cecilia) is one of the oldest musical institutions in the world, based in Italy. It is based at the Auditorium

Parco della Musica in Rome and was founded by the papal bull, Ratione congruit, issued by Sixtus V in 1585, which invoked two saints prominent in Western musical history: Gregory the Great, for whom the Gregorian chant is named and Saint Cecilia, the patron saint of music. It was founded as a "congregation" or "confraternity" – a religious guild, so to speak – and over the centuries, has grown from a forum for local musicians and composers to an internationally acclaimed academy active in music scholarship (with 100 prominent music scholars forming the body of the Accademia) to music education (in its role as a conservatory) to performance (with an active choir and symphony orchestra).

The term *conservatory* has its origin in 16th-century Renaissance Italy, where orphanages (*conservatori*) were attached to hospitals. The orphans (*conservati* 'saved') were given a musical education there and the term gradually applied to music schools. These hospitals-conservatories were among the first secular institutions equipped for practical training in music. By the 18th century, Italian conservatories were already playing a major role in the training of artists and composers.

In the city of Naples, a *conservatorio* was strictly a secular place for teaching and learning specializing in music education. There were already four conservatories in Naples active in the 16th and 18th century:

- *I poveri di Gesù Cristo* ('The Paupers of Jesus Christ'), founded in 1599 by Marcello Fossataro, already included in their official record a *magister musicæ* and *magister lyræ* in 1633;
- *Santa Maria di Loreto* was founded in 1535, where the composer Giovan Battista Pergolesi studied;
- *La pietà dei turchini* was founded in 1583 and the earliest findings suggest musical activity around the year 1615;
- *Sant'Onofrio a porta Capuana* was founded in 1578, was the first conservatory in the world. Here the composer Giovanni Paisiello studied and then taught, started teaching music in the mid-1600 and in the following decades will give more priority to the opera buffa;
- plus one only for girls called *dell'Annunziata*.

It is in these very institutions that the so-called *Scuola Musicale Napoletana* was developed, thanks to the work of musicians and educators like Alessandro Scarlatti and Francesco Durante, who was also Pergolesi's and Paisiello's teacher.

It was the example set in Naples, where admission was by competitive examination and tuition was free, that was then copied, with modifications, in many European cities, including Paris, Bologna, Milan, Florence and Prague, Warsaw and Vienna, London, the Hague and Liege. The second half of the 19th century saw the network expanding to the

Americas, Rio de Janeiro, Boston, Baltimore and Chicago, Havana and Buenos Aires. Establishments for advanced training in music were organized in the 1940s in several Asian and African countries, including Iraq, Lebanon and Kenya.

To this extent, projects like El Sistema are more in line with the tradition set in Italy (where tuition at conservatories remains still free) than in an English-speaking country, where students have a very selective access to bursaries.

Primary and Secondary Education

Specialist Music Schools

Musikgymnasium Schloss Belvedere is a specialist music school in Germany.

Specialist music schools exist in many countries and whose purpose is to identify and assist, children with exceptional potential, to benefit from world-class specialist training as part of a broad and balanced education, which will enable them, if they choose, to proceed towards self-sustaining careers in music. These schools may be formally or informally attached to a conservatory. Entry is typically between the ages of ages 8 and 18 and admission is through competitive audition. Schools may be public or independent; where schools are independent, pupils may be in receipt of governmental or private scholarships. Typically as students progress through the school the time spent on music increases and on academic subjects decrease. These schools usually teach only instrumentalists but may also include choristers.

Some schools (like conservatories) are broader and may cover the performing arts: music, drama, dance.

Music Schools within Schools

Many music schools are located within existing schools. The pattern is quite diverse and may include:

Specialist music units in Scotland, where students are drawn from an area wider than the host schools catchment. Students will receive specialist music tuition within the music school but are fully integrated within the host school for other lessons. Entry to the specialist music unit or school is by competitive audition, which also effectively gives entry to the host school.

Many public or independent schools contain *music departments*, some of which achieve high standards. These are sometimes referred to as Music schools. *Music Colleges* in England are schools that get additional private and governmental money to specialise in music. Entry is to the host school and musical ability is not an admission requirement. Schools which perform highly may specialise in an additional area for example sports or technology.

Music schools also frequently operate from church facilities.

300 children attend the Royal College of Music's Junior Department.

Pre-college Divisions

Many conservatories or other tertiary-level institutions have pre-college divisions or junior departments for children of school age. Typically the curriculum includes individual lesson(s), orchestra, chamber music, theory, musicianship, composition and music technology. Classes are usually held on a Saturday and children attend normal schools during the week.

Music Schools outwith the General Education System

Non-governmental or private schools of music offer music education outside the general education system for students aged 4 to 20+ years. In general, students attend these schools weekend or evening. These schools are typically provided by individuals, charitable or commercial organizations.

Tertiary Education

Conservatory

A conservatory of music may also be known in English as *conservatoire* (chiefly in the UK), *conservatorium* (in Australia), *academy* or *college*. Some schools or conservatories are exclusively focused on music. Others have a wider focus, for example covering music, drama and dance. Conservatories are suitable for students who wish to develop their performance, conducting, or composition to a professional standard. Typically, they offer a high percentage of practical training combined with academic study and professional development for those considering a career in the creative arts. Individual teaching is the strength of most components.

Jacobs School of Music, part of Indiana University, has more than 1,600 students.

Students have the opportunity to perform, conduct or have their music played on a regular basis, both informally and in public. This may be solo or as part of an orchestra, ensemble or band. Typically, conservatories focus on Western classical music. However, some schools focus on traditional instruments, such as Chinese instruments. Others may have departments for traditional music which includes both traditional and classical instruments, for example bagpipes alongside the fiddle. Alternatively, students can focus on jazz, world music or pop music.

The time required to complete music degrees is generally not much different from degrees in other fields, i.e. 3–4 years for a Bachelor of Music degree, 1–2 years for a Master of Music degree and 3–5 years for a Doctor of Musical Arts or Doctor of Music Degree. A PhD degree can be gained for areas such as musicology, music theory, music composition, music education, or music therapy. Some schools may offer a non-academic degree that is solely performance based, such as the (United States) A.D. or Artist Diploma; this may be offered at the undergraduate and graduate level.

University Schools of Music

University music departments originally placed more emphasis on academic study of music, rather than performance. However, today, the division may not be so rigid, with many often placing greater emphasis on performance now than they did in the past. The specific balance of vocational training and academic study varies from one institution to another and from one country to another. Some countries separately define their institutions between university status and vocational university status, whilst other countries do not define such a rigid division. In addition to offering degrees similar to those offered at conservatories, some universities offer non-professional music-related degrees such as a Bachelor of Arts in Music or a Bachelor of Arts in Music Education. A number of previously independent conservatories have become affiliated to universities.

The Oberlin Conservatory of Music shares its campus with Oberlin College.

Techskills

TechSkills is a nationally recognized career training school, specializing in skills and certification training for careers in Information Technology, Healthcare Services and Business. It is a private, for-profit provider of career training for adult learners. The company operates 18 campuses in 13 states in the United States.

TechSkills was founded in 1996 as AmeriTrain by John Poland. Its first campus opened in Brookfield, Wisconsin in 1996. In 1999, the company was renamed TechSkills. Five new campuses were opened in 1999, with 12 campuses added in 2000, nine campuses in 2001 and one campus in 2002. TechSkills' corporate headquarters was relocated to Austin, Texas in 2001. Beginning in 2010, TechSkills LLC campuses began to see dramatic decline and began closing multiple campuses and selling other(s) to TechSkills of California (Las Vegas). More campus closures are expected throughout 2011-2012 respectively. More than 40,000 students have graduated from their programs.

Accreditation

The following Tech's kills campuses are nationally accredited by the Accrediting Council for Continuing Education and Training (ACCET): Brookfield, Charlotte, Cincinnati, Columbus, Kansas City, Las Vegas, Sacramento and San Jose.

Courses of Study

TechSkills offers career education programs in Information Technology, Allied Health Services, Accounting and Bookkeeping and Project Management. TechSkills students may pursue industry certification through Information Technology vendors including Microsoft, Cisco, Oracle, Comp TIA, Prosoft and (ISC)2; and through Health Services associations including the National Healthcareer Association and the Pharmacy Technician Certification Board. Information Technology graduates may enter careers in IT engineering, network design, software development, database administration, IT security, web design or computer hardware. Health Services graduates may enter careers in medical coding, medical billing, medical transcription, medical office administration or pharmacy.

Drama School

Drama students performing on stage.

A drama school, stage school or theatre school is an undergraduate and graduate school or department at a college or university; or a free-standing institution (such as the Drama section at the Juilliard School); which specializes in the pre-professional training in drama and theatre arts, such as acting, design and technical theatre, arts administration and related subjects. If the drama school is part of a degree-granting institution, undergraduates typically take an Associate degree, Bachelor of Arts, Bachelor of Fine Arts, or, occasionally, Bachelor of Science or Bachelor of Design. Graduate students may take a Master of Arts, Master of Science, Master of Fine Arts, Doctor of Arts, Doctor of Fine Arts, or Doctor of Philosophy degree.

Entry and Application Process

Romanian students (Drama Club Botosani) in "The Taming of the Shrew".

Entry to drama school is usually through a competitive audition process. Some schools make this a two-stage process. Places on an acting course are limited (usually well below 100) so those who fare best at the audition are selected. Most academies state that applicants must be over 18 years of age. Auditions usually involve the performance of monologues and group workshops and may also include a singing activity. This varies from academy to academy. If this is the case for an acting degree, the school looks more at how an applicant can put character into the song rather than how well they can sing. For a musical theatre degree, the emphasis is on showing one's talent as a singer. Most colleges offer callback auditions, often in several stages, in which students being considered for entry onto a course are brought back to audition again, demonstrating their talents further. It is also possible to get into a drama school by previous grades. Some auditioners may be under 18.

Course Content

The courses offered by drama schools focus on practical courses, rather than theoretical classes. Their aim is to train students as professional actors for stage (theatre or musical theatre) and camera-based work (film and television shows). Students are required to be enthusiastic and motivated in order to meet the demands of the program. At the beginning of the final year (usually the third), most drama schools stage a series of performances throughout the academic year to which agents and casting directors are invited. This helps to build the future of the graduates and serves as a showcase of what the students can do.

Funding

In 1833 the actress Frances Maria Kelly managed the Royal Strand Theatre where she funded and operated a dramatic school, the earliest record of a drama school in

England. In the UK The Conference of Drama Schools comprises Britain's 22 leading Drama Schools. CDS exists in order to strengthen the voice of the member schools, to set and maintain the highest standards of training within the vocational drama sector and to make it easier for prospective students to understand the range of courses on offer and the application process. Founded in 1969, the 22 member schools offer courses in Acting, Musical Theatre, Directing and Technical Theatre training. Graduates of CDS courses are currently working on stage, in front of the camera and behind the scenes in theatres and studios across Britain. In September 2016, Midlands Academy of Musical Theatre opened in Birmingham. Offering West End quality training in Musical Theatre to students aged 18+and with the same or better opportunities as many London drama schools, they offer a regional option for prospective drama school students. In 2012 it was merged with the National Council for Drama Training to create a single national authority Drama UK responsible for both the provision of Drama Training and accreditation of official courses. In 2017 Drama UK was replaced by the Federation of Drama Schools.

In the UK, funding varies from drama school to drama school. Historically drama schools were not part of the mainstream academic system and therefore were not funded on the same basis as universities. Some drama schools are now part of a university, such as Guildhall School of Music and Drama, which is part of the City University of London and Rose Bruford College of Theatre and Performance, which is part of the University of Manchester and these tend to charge similar tuition fees to universities. Student loans, drama awards and scholarships may help to provide students with their funding. The most prominent funding scheme for performing arts education in the UK are the Dance and Drama Awards. This is a government scheme which subsidises the training offered at a selection of the leading performing arts schools in the fields of dance, drama, musical theatre and stage management.

A number of third level institutions provide courses in Drama and Theatre Studies, including Trinity College, Dublin, NUI Maynooth and Dublin City University. A decision by Trinity in Jan 2007 to drop its BA in Acting Studies for cost reasons met with disappointment from the theatre sector. A Forum for Acting Training was convened with leading professionals from the industry who recommended in a report published 27 May 2008, that an Academy for Dramatic Arts, independent of a University, but with third level accreditation should be created. The report was submitted to the Irish Government. On 1 August 2008, The Irish Times reported that a RADA graduate, Danielle Ryan, granddaughter of the late Tony Ryan who founded Ryanair, had announced plans to develop an Irish Academy of Dramatic Arts part-funded from a Trust created by her late father, Captain Cathal Ryan.

This plan went ahead and the academy, known as The Lir Academy, opened in September 2011. The Lir is part of Trinity College and is situated in the Grand Canal Dock area. It is officially associated with RADA.

Journalism School

A journalism school is a school or department, usually part of an established university, where journalists are trained. An increasingly used term for a journalism department, school or college is ‹J-School'. Today, in many parts of the world it is usual for journalists to first complete university-level training which incorporates both technical skills such as research skills, interviewing technique and shorthand and academic studies in media theory, cultural studies and ethics.

Historically, in the United Kingdom entrants used first to complete a non media-studies related degree course, giving maximum educational breadth, prior to taking a specialist postgraduate pre-entry course. However, this has changed in recent years with journalism training and education moving to higher educational institutions.

University of Missouri and the Ecole Supérieure de Journalisme in Paris, France both claim to have established the world's first school of journalism; Missouri in 1908 and the Ecole in 1899. A Diploma of Journalism was established at London University in 1919, but university journalism education in Britain did not become a significant endeavour until the 1970s, with establishment of the University of Wales postgraduate program. Most training from the mid-20th century was run by the National Council for the Training of Journalists.

Top Schools

In 2007 the United Nations Educational, Scientific and Cultural Organization (UNESCO) named what it terms the Potential Centres of Excellence in Journalism Training in Africa. After thorough research there were twelve journalism and media training institutions named on the list and they were not placed in any order.

These twelve UNESCO Potential Centres of Excellence in Journalism Training in Africa are the Department of Journalism at the Tshwane University of Technology in Pretoria in South Africa (TUT), Mass Communication Department at Makerere University in Uganda, School of Journalism and Media Studies at Rhodes University in Grahamstown in South Africa, Department of Mass Communication at the University of Lagos in Nigeria, School of Communication, Legal and Secretarial Studies at the Namibia Polytechnic, Mozambican School of Journalism in Mozambique, Centre d'études des sciences et techniques de l'information in Senegal, The School of Journalism and Mass Communication at the University of Nairobi in Kenya, Department of Journalism at the University of Stellenbosch in South Africa, Institut Supérieur de l'Information et de la Communication in Morocco, School of Communication Studies at Walter Sisulu University in South Africa and Ecole Supérieure de Sciences et Techniques de l'Information et de la Communication in Cameroon.

UNESCo's list is not exhaustive and new schools have been founded since the study was conducted.

With the rise of Internet and social media in the past five years there has been increasing demand for journalism schools offering specialized training in the kinds of modern challenges journalists face in the rapidly changing online-media landscape. E-jicom Graduate School of Journalism and Communication in Dakar, Senegal is one such institution, offering specialized training combining stringent media ethics with the modern technological demands of online media.

In Australia, a ranking of journalism schools has been assembled based on graduating students' assessments of the quality of their courses. The ranking, based on student satisfaction ratings over four years, are Jschool Journalism College in Brisbane, University of the Sunshine Coast in Queensland, University of Western Sydney, Murdoch University in Western Australia and the University of Technology, Sydney. Figures indicated 100 percent satisfaction among students at Bond University and Jschool (both in Queensland)and 85 percent among students at the Universities of Canberra, Newcastle and the Sunshine Coast. Employment rates are mixed, with an estimated 20 percent of university journalism graduates achieving journalism positions in the media, although Jschool has a 63 percent employment rate. A list of journalism graduates in employment shows city-based technological universities with the highest numbers of graduates in media positions, including QUT in Brisbane, RMIT in Melbourne and UTS in Sydney. The biggest employers have been the Australian Broadcasting Corporation, Channel Nine, Channel Seven, *Sydney Morning Herald* and Special Broadcasting Service, although there has been much down-sizing of newsrooms since the figures were assembled.

The New Zealand Training Organisation has published a list of New Zealand's journalism schools recognised by industry.

The New Zealand Institute of Business Studies has been teaching Freelance Journalism and Non-Fiction Writing for more than 20 years. Training is less 'academic-focused' and more 'income-earning' focused. Graduates are given a fortnightly list of journalism job vacancies.

The Department of Journalism Studies at the University of Sheffield is rated Number 1 in the UK by the Guardian for Journalism, Publishing and Public Relations and number 1 in the UK by the Times/Sunday Times for Communication and Media Studies. The National Student Survey results for both 2009 and 2010 placed The University of Sheffield No. 1 in the UK for overall satisfaction with Journalism Studies.

Of City University London's Journalism Department *The Independent* commented that City's postgraduate courses had "rightly accrued legendary status within the media." Former *Guardian* editor Peter Preston wrote: "What's the passport to journalism? The dreaming spires of City University". City's faculty includes Professors George Brock and Roy Greenslade. Alumni include Sophie Raworth of the BBC, Sky's Dermot Murnaghan and Channel 4 News Economics Editor Faisal Islam.

Another well-established course is the highly regarded School of Journalism, Media and Cultural Studies at Cardiff University which was founded in 1970 by Tom Hopkinson. The course was also the UK's top-rated course by the National Council for the Training of Journalists for the academic year 2007/8.

The University of Kent's Centre for Journalism was established with Professor Tim Luckhurst as the first head. The Centre runs both undergraduate and postgraduate degrees that are accredited by the National Council for the Training of Journalists. and the Broadcast Journalism Training Council. The Centre offers guaranteed work placements with the KM Group. It was ranked best for undergraduate study of journalism in *The Guardian*'s University Guide for 2015 and in *The Times Good University Guide 2016* in which it was ranked first for graduate employment prospects in journalism.

One of Europe's longest established centres of journalism education is the department of Journalism, Media and Communication, University of Central Lancashire (also known as UCLan), which launched its first print journalism course in 1962 at the then Harris College, which later became part of the University of Central Lancashire. Of the school, a 2008 article in *The Times* observed that "it is acknowledged as one of the leading centres for the teaching of journalism in Britain". In 2010, the University won the Broadcast Journalism Training Council's award for general excellence.

The School of Journalism at the University of Lincoln was formally opened by the journalist John Pilger in 2004. It provides programmes at all degree levels. Research in the School focuses on media ethics, international human rights, the coverage of US/UK warfare and literary journalism, with 70% of the research output assessed in 2008 as 'internationally excellent' or 'world leading'. Teaching emphasizes the growing focus on the convergence of platforms in the media. Courses are accredited by the BJTC and the Periodicals Training Council (PTC). and the School is ‹Recognised for Excellence' by the European Journalism Training Association (EJTA).

The Press Association offer a fast-track 17-week course in multimedia and print journalism (NCTJ). The short length and intensity of the course makes entry extremely competitive. It was previously owned by *Trinity Mirror* and many national newspapers send trainees to take part in at least some PA training within a graduate scheme.

Liverpool John Moores and Bournemouth have well-respected journalism courses. Kingston University, Bournemouth and Birmingham City have developed fully converged journalism courses without reference to separate production disciplines such as radio, newspaper or magazine journalism. Issues from a European perspective in evaluating journalism schools were discussed by the president of the European Journalism Training Association in an interview with Marianne Peters of this Association.

The London School of Journalism (LSJ) is an independent and highly acclaimed institution with well-recognised Postgraduate programs in Journalism and writing. It was founded in 1920 by Sir Max Pemberton. Kingston University also has a well-respected department of journalism. Founded in 2003 it has courses accredited by the NCTJ and PTC. The campus newspaper and magazine produced by its journalism students have won best student publication in the national Guardian Student Media Awards.

In France, 14 schools are recognized by the profession at the national level. The Centre de Formation des Journalistes (CFJ) was founded in 1946 by two Resistance leaders, although École supérieure de journalisme de Lille had been founded earlier. Other Parisian journalism schools are Ecole de journalisme de Sciences Po, CELSA, Institut français de presse (IFP) and Institut Pratique du Journalisme (IPJ). In the different French regions: Ecole de journalisme de Toulouse (EjT), Institut du Journalisme de Bordeaux-Aquitaine (IJBA), Ecole de journalisme et de communication d'Aix-Marseille (EJCAM), Centre universitaire d'enseigne de journalisme (CUEJ) in Strasburg or Ecole de journalisme de Grenoble (EJDG).

During the Third Reich, the Nazis established the Reichspresseschule (Imperial School of Press), in which journalists were taught to write what the National Socialist German Workers' Party wanted the German public to think.

After the war, the first journalism school in Germany was founded in 1949 as Werner Friedmann Institute. 1961 the school's name was changed into Deutsche Journalistenschule (German school of journalism). In 1979, a new journalism school was created in Hamburg, later renamed after the founder of *Stern* magazine, Henri Nannen.

The International Media Center (Slovenia-Austria-Serbia), offers in cooperation with South East Europe Media Organisation (SEEMO) and South East and Central Europe PR Organisation (SECEPRO) several courses, including master programme.

In Denmark, the University of Southern Denmark established a journalism study programme in 1998 at the then founded Centre for Journalism, as did Roskilde University, following the political decision to break the Danish School of Journalism's monopoly on educating journalists in Denmark. The purpose was and is to increase the diversity of teaching and research within the field of journalism. Since its establishment, the Centre for Journalism has launched several innovative features within the field, including the by now renowned award for journalists, "The Journalistic Fellowship"and the introduction of a journalist's oath similar to the Hippocratic oath. Also, in terms of scientific publications it is the most productive journalism research department in Denmark.

In Russia, the MSU Faculty of Journalism is the leading journalism school and the world's largest school of journalism. The majority of textbooks on journalism in Russian were written by MSU scientists.

In Minsk (Belarus), the Institute of Journalism of BSU is one of the leading scientific and educational centers in the sphere of Mass Media in the territory of the former soviet countries. It possesses a highly respected scientific and pedagogical standard and prepares professionals in mass media for work in Belarus and abroad.

The Hungarian Bálint György Academy of Journalism (previously known as Hungarian School of Journalism) runs under the aegis of the National Association of Hungarian Journalists (MÚOSZ). Before 1989, the Hungarian School of Journalism served as a highly selective post-graduate program for well-trained journalists in Hungary. Since 2003, the Bálint György Academy of Journalism belongs to the accredited professional education system.

The top journalism school in Spain according to *El Mundo* newspaper is the University of Navarra. It is the oldest school of journalism in Spain and among the top 10 world universities of medium size according to the QS ranking. Many reputed and well-known journalists have studied at Universidad Complutense de Madrid, one of Madrid's most prestigious university. Princess Letizia of Spain studied journalism at this university, which is the main public university in the country. Other universities include Carlos III university, Pompeu Fabra University, Autonomous University of Barcelona and Pontifical University of Salamanca.

The most populous continent is also the home to the world's largest democracy and its pace of growth and booming of economies has led to a proliferation of media enterprises. The rise of digital publishing has created newer opportunities for employment and self-employment in the field of journalism and mass communication.

India

Unlike the rest of the world, print media continues to grow and thrive in India with over 1,250 million people. With 892 TV channels and over 1,05,000 daily newspapers, digital publishing has only added to the opportunities. Dozens of regional languages and English being the aspirational language, a large number of Indian media consumers are consuming media in multiple languages. The government of India established the "Indian Institute of Mass Communication (IIMC)" in 1965, which has now 6 campuses across India. Dozens of universities and independent institutes provide education for shaping journalism, media and mass communication professionals.

A listing (unranked) of Canadian journalism schools has been assembled by Canadian-Universities.net. Journalism schools are listed and classified on the "J-Schools and Programs" page of the Canadian Journalism Project.

In the United States the Accrediting Council on Education in Journalism and Mass Communications (ACEJMC) applies nine standards in evaluating university programs: mission, governance and administration; curriculum and instruction; diversity and inclusiveness; full-time and part-time faculty; scholarship: research, creative and professional activity; student services; resources, facilities and equipment; professional and public service; and assessment of learning outcomes. The ACEJMCC has awarded accreditation to 109 university and college programs of study in journalism and mass communications, but does not attempt to rank the courses or programs. It accredits colleges, schools, departments or divisions.

The listing of a unit as accredited indicates that the unit has been judged by ACEJMC to meet its standards. That judgment is rendered after a self-study prepared by the faculty and administration of the unit and an independent evaluation of the unit by educators and practitioners. The listing shows the bachelor's and professional master's degree programs that were examined during the unit's most recent accreditation review. Some units offer degrees in addition to those listed here. ACEJMC does not accredit programs leading to the Ph.D., which is considered a research (and not a professional) degree. The Council does not list sequences or specialties.

There are only four graduate-only journalism programs in North America: Columbia University Graduate School of Journalism, CUNY School of Journalism, UC Berkeley Graduate School of Journalism and University of British Columbia Graduate School of Journalism, although many universities have graduate programs such as the Henry W. Grady College of Journalism and Mass Communication at the University of Georgia that has a Master of Arts in Journalism and Mass Communication (M.A.), a Master of Arts in Health and Medical Journalism (M.A.)and a Doctor of Philosophy in Mass Communication (Ph.D).

Editor and Publisher has presented an unranked list of leading journalism schools, while *U.S. News and World Report* produces annual lists of the top schools in advertising, print and other categories based on responses to questionnaires sent to deans and faculty members. A list based on a variety of resources claims to identify the "ten most popular journalism schools in the United States". One critic has pointed to the anecdotal nature of much j-school ranking in the absence of effective tracking of journalism graduates' career paths.

An evaluation of developments in journalism education in Latin America has been undertaken by Professor Rosental Calmon Alves.

In Colombia, the high court determined in 1998 that journalism was not a career. This court said that journalism is a human right, not a profession.

Because of the ruling there are many schools of communications in Colombia where people study to work in mainly enterprises, but not in mass media.

There are many schools of journalism, at undergraduate level the main ones being: University of Antioquia, a public institution in Medellín, offers Journalism inside the Communications faculty and University of Rosario in Bogotá, a private institution, offers Public Opinion Journalism.and the Externado University, a private institution, offers a degree in Social Communication and Journalism.

Chilean universities with journalism impart the profession as a full five-year degree. With a grade of "bachelor in social communications" and professional title of journalist, there currently exist more than 30 journalism schools in the country. The national system has an accrediting council that independently certifies the universities as a whole and each of the careers. Nevertheless, only a few are accredited.

The top schools in the country are the Faculty of Communications of the Pontifical Catholic University of Chile, accredited by US's ACEJMC and the Institute of Communication and Image of the University of Chile, accredited by the National Accrediting Council (CNA). Outside Santiago, the top school is the School of Journalism of the Pontifical Catholic University of Valparaiso, also accredited by the CNA.

Debate about Role

One of the most cited critiques of a journalism school was Michael Lewis's article in *The New Republic*, "J-school ate my brain", which was strongly criticized by University of Maryland College of Journalism dean Reese Cleghorn in *American Journalism Review*. Discussion of the issues raised by Lewis was evident a decade later in the *Chronicle of Higher Education* colloquy on journalism education, *Columbia Journalism Review*'s "Searching for the perfect j-school"and "The j-school debate" in the Christian Science Monitor. Alternative approaches to journalism education were suggested in Jack Shafer's *Slate* article "Can J-school be saved? Professional advice for Columbia University". An article in *The Australian* discusses "What makes a good school of journalism".

On the internet, a range of weblogs have been set up by journalism students to chronicle or to criticize their journalism colleges. Examples are: "jschoolyear", "jschool05", "the pod" blogspot, "jschool" blog, Australia. An example of a weblog criticising university journalism education in Australia is "What's wrong with the school". One journalism school in the UK, at the University of Westminster, has established a clearing house where all students are expected to contribute to the development and content of their own education and training using blogs.

Various commentaries on journalism education are related to criticisms of contemporary news media standards and values. One example is a paper by Jan Schaffer, executive director of J-Lab: the Institute for Interactive Journalism. A controversial paper to Australia's peak newspaper industry body PANPA (Pacific Area Newspaper Publishers Association) by Professor John Henningham ("Journalism sold short in media courses") blamed industry lack of interest and university cost-cutting for falling standards in journalism education. In Canada, Mark Anderson of the *Ottawa Citizen* has argued the case for teaching business journalism in college rather than on the job. Canadian journalism professor Rick MacLean has rejected criticism by Robert Fulford ("Just what is the point of j-school") that the best potential journalists will find their way into the media, while many existing j-school students show no interest in news or the media. MacLean argues that education in journalism helps empower members of the public to understand how media work.

6

Various Professions under Vocational Education

Various professions that fall under vocational education are dental laboratory technician, carpentry, technical trainer, electrician, fashion design, photographer, wiremen, welding, embroidery, etc. This chapter has been carefully written to provide an easy understanding of these professions of vocational education.

Dental Laboratory Technician

Dental laboratory technology is the art, science and technology of designing and manufacturing corrective devices for and replacements of natural teeth. A dental laboratory technician communicates and collaborates with the dentist to plan, design and fabricate dental prostheses for individual patients.

The dentist is responsible for providing dental laboratory with a prescription detailing final treatment choice and for placement of restoration or corrective device in the patient's mouth. The dental technician aids the dentist in material choices and case design and is responsible for fabrication of the final prostheses or corrective devices.

By fabricating esthetic dental prostheses that work well and by improving the patient's smile, the dental laboratory technician influences not only patient's physical and dental health but also improves his or her confidence and self-esteem.

Two types of dental specialties rely heavily on the skills of a dental laboratory technician:

- Restorative dentistry or prosthodontics is used when the patient loses a part or the entire tooth/teeth due to the decay, disease, illness or accident and the tooth/teeth must be replaced to maintain normal fit, form and function.
- Orthodontics is provided when the tooth/teeth must be moved or stabilized to optimize function, esthetics or to prevent painful dysfunction.

Dental laboratory technology specialties include:

- Crown and bridge,
- Ceramics,
- Dentures,
- Partial dentures,
- Implants,
- Orthodontics.

The profession of dental laboratory technology is:

- An art because each restoration is unique to each patient: The restoration must imitate or improve the beauty and the function of the patient's natural dentition and be in harmony with the rest of the system. The technician's greatest challenge is to create a restoration that looks and feels completely natural in the patient's mouth.
- A science that is advancing rapidly: In order to fabricate the fixed or removable dental prostheses, dental technicians must have a keen knowledge and understanding of tooth anatomy, masticatory functions and the materials and processes utilized in the creation of such devices. A variety of high-tech materials, such as zirconia, ceramics (i.e. lithium disilicate, feldspatic porcelains), plastics (i.e. PMMA, acrylics, composite resins) and metal alloys (i.e. metal substructures, implants, attachments, wires) are utilized in dental laboratories.
- Driven by technology today more than ever: In the past decade, technology has taken over dentistry. In fact, the biggest dental advancements came from the field of dental laboratory technology in the form of computer-aided design/computer-aided manufacturing (CAD/CAM) technologies. Today, CAD/CAM is utilized as an integral part of the laboratory's everyday practice. With these technological advances and those to come, there is a very high demand for dental designers who can design and assist in manufacturing of CAD/CAM restorations. Because of these advances, aspiring dental lab technicians should take courses in computer skills and programming.

Ideal candidates for this career possess excellent eye-hand coordination, attention to minute details, ability to recognize the differences in color and shape, manual dexterity and interest in material sciences and emerging technologies. Dental laboratory technology is ideal for those who are artistic as well as for those who are business and technology savvy. In fact, this is the only allied dental field that offers practitioners the chance to become entrepreneurs by opening their own dental laboratory business.

The changes that affect modern dental laboratory technology are:

- Advancements in material sciences, technologies and manufacturing systems.
- New legislations and regulations.
- Health care and education.
- Aging populations.
- Changing practice models and emerging team-based care systems.
- Global economies and market adjustments.

Due to a shortage of technicians that is already affecting the field, it is certain that there is and will be a high demand for experienced dental technicians who can handle the needs of an ever-increasing number of dentists and their patients.

Most dental laboratory technicians learn their craft on the job. They begin with simple tasks, such as pouring gypsum material into an impression and progress to more complex procedures, such as making dentures, crowns and bridges or bending wires.

Becoming a fully trained technician requires an average of three to four years of experience on the job, depending upon the individual's aptitude and ambition, but it may take a few years more to become an accomplished technician.

With technology becoming an ever-increasing part of the dental laboratory technician's job, it would be useful for aspiring technicians to take courses in computer skills and programming.

Formal training in dental laboratory technology is available through community and junior colleges, vocational-technical institutes and the military. Training programs vary greatly both in length and in the level of training they provide. The most advanced training in dental laboratory technology is offered through two-year accredited associate degree programs followed by continuing education programs offered across the country.

Carpentry

Carpentry is a skilled trade and a craft in which the primary work performed is the cutting, shaping and installation of building materials during the construction of buildings, ships, timber bridges, concrete formwork, etc. Carpenters traditionally worked with natural wood and did the rougher work such as framing, but today many other materials are also used and sometimes the finer trades of cabinetmaking and furniture building are considered carpentry. In the United States, 98.5% of carpenters are male and it was the fourth most male-dominated occupation in the country in 1999. In 2006 in the United States, there were about 1.5 million carpentry positions. Carpenters are usually the first tradesmen on a job and the last to leave. Carpenters normally framed post-and-beam buildings until the end of the 19th century; now this old fashioned carpentry is called timber framing. Carpenters learn this trade by being employed through an apprenticeship training—normally 4 years—and qualify by successfully completing that country's competence test in places such as the United Kingdom, the United States, Canada, Switzerland, Australia and South Africa. It is also common that the skill can be learned by gaining work experience other than a formal training program, which may be the case in many places.

Carpenters at work.

Wood is one of mankind's oldest building materials. The ability to shape wood improved with technological advances from the stone age to the bronze age to the iron age. Some of the oldest archaeological evidence of carpentry are water well casings built using split oak timbers with mortise and tenon and notched corners excavated in eastern Germany dating from about 7,000 years ago in the early neolithic period.

Relatively little information about carpentry is available from pre-history (before written language) or even recent centuries because the knowledge and skills were passed down person to person, rarely in writing, until the printing press was invented in the 15th century and builders began regularly publishing guides and pattern books in the 18th and 19th centuries. The oldest surviving complete architectural text is Vitruvius' ten books collectively titled De architectura, which discuss some carpentry.

Some of the oldest surviving wooden buildings in the world are temples in China such as the Nanchan Temple built in 782, the Greensted Church, parts of which are from the 11th century and the stave churches in Norway from the 12th and 13th centuries.

Log church building in Russia reached spectacular heights such as this example from the 17th century.

Carpenters in Ming China

By the beginning of the Ming dynasty, emperor Taizu categorized people into different occupations. At this time, all the carpenters throughout the state were registered by the imperial court and the occupation remained strictly hereditary, according to the notes from historian Klaas Ruitenbeek. In later times of the Ming dynasty, roughly in the 1560s, however, people broke such restrictions and the path into the occupation in the case of the carpentry became less fixed. Although the restriction regarding the path into the occupation dissolved in later times of the Ming dynasty, approximately starting from 1450s. The Lu Ban Jing was named after the Chinese patriarch of carpenter, Lu Ban. Lu Ban lived in the Zhou dynasty, 2,500 years from modern day and nearly 2,000 years from the beginning of the Ming dynasty. Although the Lu Ban Jing was entitled as the classic of Lu Ban, it was compiled during the Ming dynasty. One interesting fact about the Lu Ban Jing is that it included a detailed biography of Lu Ban and his wife Lady Yun. According to the biography, Lady Yun was "blessed with heavenly skills" and she could produce products with higher quality than those produced by Lu Ban.

Being a carpenter requires a set of techniques, especially for the household carpenters. From the first to the last day of the construction, sometimes even long before the beginning of construction, carpenters must treat their work with a lot of care. With their meticulousness and perseverance, their products were so sophisticated that it appeals to the untrained peoples as impossible. Moreover, in Ming times, people believed that certain behaviors bring good or bad fortunes and the carpenters were responsible for helping their customer to make decisions. Questions like when to build the house and which direction should the house face toward were among some of the most frequently asked. As a result, the techniques were both practical and metaphysical, include accurate calculation, using proper tools, avoiding ominous actions, singing for good fortunes and choosing ideal locations for houses. Interestingly is that the carpenters in China will sing prayer songs for their customer to pray for good fortune. The good fortunes involve a series of good things, including wealth, reputation, social ranking and the sustainability of families. Historian Ronald Knapp recorded one of them in his book China's Living Houses: The Phoenix does not light where there are no treasures. Today it perches at the end of the ridgepole. With one swing of my axe, the house will be solid forever. Ten thousand years solid, then thousand years prosperous, riches and position, a Number One family.

The carpenters in Ming China and particularly the first century of Ming China, experienced the division of labor process. Ruitenbeek emphasizes that the carpenters were divided into two categories, the "resident artisans" and the "shift artisans." The resident artisans, according to Ruitenbeek, lived in the capital of Ming China (first Nanjing, then Beijing) because of the forced immigration launched by Ming Taizu. They were required to do ten days for each month in the imperial palace. According to the difference of their household register, these resident artisans were further categorized as military carpenters and civil carpenters. The military carpenters belong to the division of defense and were required to produce the military arm forces like bows and cannon supports. The civil carpenters belong to the Board of Work. The shift artisans, on the other hand, did not need to reside in capital regions, but they were required to complete service on behalf of the Board of Work. Meanwhile, carpenters in Ming China also avoided intrinsic competitions by establishing guilds. Guilds were long-lasting in premodern China and by the late Ming times, it developed into institutions with complete regulations seek to minimize intrinsic competitions. Ruitenbeek provides a framework for the guilds of carpentry in Ming times: There was a system of apprentice, jourjourneyman andter. Welfare was an important task of the guilds; it ensured for example a decent burial for its poorer members.

Speaking of the codes among the carpenters in the Ming dynasty, it includes a set of rituals or taboos generated by people within the occupation. In the case of carpenter, the Lu Ban Jing regulates carpenter's behavior as it provides a thorough, "from-cradle-to-tomb-style" of guidelines for the carpenters. The Lu Ban Jing also set the rituals for the carpenters when they were given magical spells. Those magical spells, according to Lu Ban Jing, requires a complicated process of preparing the materials and praying for its effectiveness. For instance, carpenters can deliver a curse that forced people to die in river or in water wells. Such curse needs a wooden boat and the carpenters have to turn the boats upside and bury the wooden boat at the northern corner of the house. The mythical traditions for carpenters to deliver blessings and curses are various and such mysterious rituals negatively influenced people's impression of carpenters in Ming times.

By the 16th century sawmills were coming into use in Europe. The founding of America was partly based on a desire to extract resources from the new continent including wood for use in ships and buildings in Europe. In the 18th century part of the Industrial Revolution was the invention of the steam engine and cut nails. These technologies combined with the invention of the circular saw led to the development of balloon framing which was the beginning of the decline of traditional timber framing.

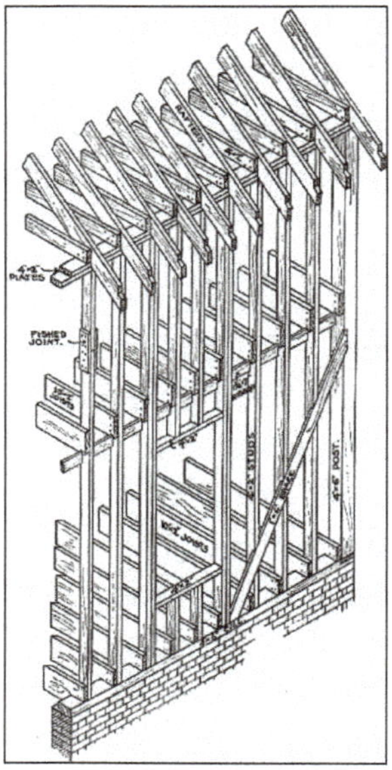

Axonometric diagram of balloon framing.

The 19th century saw the development of electrical engineering and distribution which allowed the development of hand-held power tools, wire nails and machines to mass-produce screws. In the 20th century, portland cement came into common use and concrete foundations allowed carpenters to do away with heavy timber sills. Also, drywall (plasterboard) came into common use replacing lime plaster on wooden lath. Plywood, engineered lumber and chemically treated lumber also came into use.

Training

The Centre Pompidou-Metz museum under construction in Metz, France in 2009. The building possesses one of the most complex examples of carpentry built to date and is composed of 16 kilometers of glued laminated timber for a surface area of 8,000 m^2.

Carpentry requires training which involves both acquiring knowledge and physical practice. In formal training a carpenter begins as an *apprentice*, then becomes a *journeyman* and with enough experience and competency can eventually attain the status of a *master* carpenter. Today pre-apprenticeship training may be gained through non-union vocational programs such as high school shop classes and community colleges.

Informally a laborer may simply work alongside carpenters for years learning skills by observation and peripheral assistance. While such an individual may obtain journeyman status by paying the union entry fee and obtaining a journeyman's card (which provides the right to work on a union carpentry crew) the carpenter foreman will, by necessity, dismiss any worker who presents the card but does not demonstrate the expected skill level.

Carpenters may work for an employer or be self-employed. No matter what kind of training a carpenter has had, some U.S. states require contractors to be licensed which requires passing a written test and having minimum levels of insurance.

Carpentry Schools and Programs

Formal training in the carpentry trade is available in seminars, certificate programs, high-school programs, online classes, in the new construction, restoration and preservation carpentry fields. Sometimes these programs are called pre-apprenticeship training.

In the modern British construction industry, carpenters are trained through apprenticeship schemes where general certificates of secondary education (GCSE) in Mathematics, English and Technology help but are not essential. However, this is deemed the preferred route, as young people can earn and gain field experience whilst training towards a nationally recognized qualification.

There are two main divisions of training: construction-carpentry and cabinetmaking. During pre-apprenticeship, trainees in each of these divisions spend 30 hours a week for 12 weeks in classrooms and indoor workshops learning mathematics, trade terminology and skill in the use of hand and power tools. Construction-carpentry trainees also participate in calisthenics to prepare for the physical aspect of the work.

Upon completion of pre-apprenticeship, trainees who have successfully passed the graded curriculum (taught by highly experienced journeyman carpenters) are assigned to a local union and to union carpentry crews at work on construction sites or in cabinet shops as First Year Apprentices. Over the next four years, as they progress in status to Second Year, Third Year and Fourth Year Apprentice, apprentices periodically return to the training facility every three months for a week of more detailed training in specific aspects of the trade.

Apprenticeships and Journeymen Carpenters

Tradesmen in countries such as Germany and Australia are required to fulfill a formal apprenticeship (usually three to four years) to work as a professional carpenter. Upon graduation from the apprenticeship, he or she is known as a journeyman carpenter.

Up through the 19th and even the early 20th century, the journeyman traveled to another region of the country to learn the building styles and techniques of that area before (usually) returning home. In modern times, journeymen are not required to travel and the term now refers to a level of proficiency and skill. Union carpenters in the United States, that is, members of the United Brotherhood of Carpenters and Joiners of America, are required to pass a skills test to be granted official journeyman status, but uncertified professional carpenters may also be known as journeymen based on their skill level, years of experience, or simply because they support themselves in the trade and not due to any certification or formal woodworking education.

Professional status as a journeyman carpenter in the United States may be obtained in a number of ways. Formal training is acquired in a four-year apprenticeship program administered by the United Brotherhood of Carpenters and Joiners of America, in which journeyman status is obtained after successful completion of twelve weeks of pre-apprenticeship training, followed by four years of on-the-job field training working alongside journeyman carpenters. The Timber Framers Guild also has a formal apprenticeship program for traditional timber framing. Training is also available in groups like the Kim Bong woodworking village in Vietnam where apprentices live and work to learn woodworking and carpentry skills.

In Canada, each province sets its own standards for apprenticeship. The average length of time is four years and includes a minimum number of hours of both on-the-job training and technical instruction at a college or other institution. Depending on the number of hours of instruction an apprentice receives, he or she can earn a Certificate of Proficiency, making him or her a journeyman, or a Certificate of Qualification, which allows him or her to practice a more limited amount of carpentry. Canadian carpenters also have the option of acquiring an additional Interprovincial Red Seal that allows them to practice anywhere in Canada. The Red Seal requires the completion of an apprenticeship and an additional examination.

Master Carpenter

After working as a journeyman for a while, a carpenter may go on to study or test as a master carpenter. In some countries, such as Germany, Iceland and Japan, this is an arduous and expensive process, requiring extensive knowledge (including economic and legal knowledge) and skill to achieve master certification; these countries generally require master status for anyone employing and teaching apprentices in the craft. In others, 'master carpenter' can be a loosely used term to describe any skilled carpenter.

Fully trained carpenters and joiners will often move into related trades such as shop fitting, scaffolding, bench joinery, maintenance and system installation.

Materials Used

Carpenters traditionally worked with natural wood which has been prepared by splitting (riving), hewing, or sawing with a pit saw or sawmill called lumber (American English) or timber (British English). Today natural and engineered lumber and many other building materials carpenters may use are typically prepared by others and delivered to the job site. In 2013 the carpenters union in America used the term carpenter for a catch-all position. Tasks performed by union carpenters include installing "flooring, windows, doors, interior trim, cabinetry, solid surface, roofing, framing, siding, flooring, insulation, acoustical ceilings, computer-access flooring, metal framing, wall partitions, office furniture systems and both custom or factory-produced materials, trim and molding, ceiling treatments, exposed columns and beams, displays, mantels, staircases metal studs, metal lath and drywall".

Health and Safety

Carpentry is often hazardous work. Types of woodworking and carpentry hazards include Machine hazards, flying materials, tool projection, fire and explosion, electrocution, noise, vibration, dust and chemicals. In the United States the Occupational Safety and Health Administration (OSHA) tries to prevent illness, injury and fire through regulations. However, self-employed workers are not covered by the OSHA act. OSHA claims that "Since 1970, workplace fatalities have been reduced by more than 65 percent and occupational injury and illness rates have declined by 67 percent. At the same time, U.S. employment has almost doubled." The leading cause of overall fatalities, called the "fatal four," are falls, followed by struck by object, electrocution and caught-in/between. In general construction "employers must provide working conditions that are free of known dangers. Keep floors in work areas in a clean and, so far as possible, a dry condition. Select and provide required personal protective equipment at no cost to workers. Train workers about job hazards in a language that they can understand." Examples of how to prevent falls includes placing railings and toe-boards at any floor opening which cannot be well covered and elevated platforms and safety harness and lines, safety nets, stair railings and hand rails.

Safety is not just about the workers on the job site. Carpenters work needs to meet the requirements in the Life Safety Code such as in stair building and building codes to promote long term quality and safety for the building occupants.

Types and Occupations

A finish carpenter (North America), also called a joiner (a traditional name now rare in North America), is one who does finish carpentry, that is, cabinetry, furniture making, fine woodworking, model building, instrument making, parquetry, joinery, or other carpentry where exact joints and minimal margins of error are important. Some large-scale construction may be of an exactitude and artistry that it is classed as finish carpentry.

- A carpenter and joiner has much broader skill sets ranging from joinery, finishing carpentry, building construction and form work.
- A trim carpenter specializes in molding and trim, such as door and window casings, mantels, baseboards and other types of ornamental work. Cabinet installers may also be referred to as trim carpenters.
- A cabinetmaker is a carpenter who does fine and detailed work specializing in the making of cabinets made from wood, wardrobes, dressers, storage chests and other furniture designed for storage.
- A ship's carpenter specializes in shipbuilding, maintenance, repair techniques and carpentry specific to nautical needs in addition to many other on-board tasks; usually the term refers to a carpenter who has a post on a specific ship. Steel warships as well as wooden ones need ship's carpenters, especially for making emergency repairs in the case of battle or storm damage.
- A shipwright builds wooden ships on land.
- A cooper is someone who makes barrels: wooden staved vessels of a conical form, of greater length than breadth.
- A scenic carpenter builds and dismantles temporary scenery and sets in filmmaking, television and the theater.
- A framer is a carpenter who builds the skeletal structure or wooden framework of buildings, most often in the platform framing method. Historically, balloon framing was used until the 1950s when fire safety concerns made platform framing inherently better. A carpenter who specializes in building with timbers rather than studs is known as a timber framer and does traditional timber framing with wooden joints, including mortise-and-tenon joinery, post and beam work with metal connectors, or pole building framing.
- A luthier is someone who makes or repairs stringed instruments. The word luthier comes from the French word for lute, "luth".
- A log builder builds structures of stacked, horizontal logs including houses, barns, churches, fortifications and more.
- A formwork carpenter creates the shuttering and falsework used in concrete construction.
- In Japanese carpentry, *daiku* is the simple term for carpenter, a *miya-daiku* (temple carpenter) performs the work of both architect and builder of shrines

and temples and a *sukiya-daiku* works on teahouse construction and houses. *Sashimono-shi* build furniture and *tateguya* do interior finishing work.

- A restoration carpenter is a carpenter who works in historic building restoration, someone who restores a structure to a former state.
- A conservation carpenter works in architectural conservation, known in the U.S. as a "preservation carpenter" who works in historic preservation, someone who keeps structures from changing.
- Green carpentry specializes in the use of environmentally friendly, energy-efficient and sustainable sources of building materials for use in construction projects. They also practice building methods that require using less material and material that has the same structural soundness.
- Recycled (reclaimed, repurposed) carpentry is carpentry that uses scrap wood and parts of discarded or broken furniture to build new wood products.

Driver's Education

Driver's education, driver education, driving education, driver's ed, or driving tuition or driving lessons is a formal class or program that prepares a new driver to obtain a learner's permit or driver's license. The formal class program may also prepare existing license holders for an overseas license conversion or medical assessment driving test or refresher course. It may take place in a classroom, in a vehicle, online, or a combination of the above. Topics of instruction include traffic code or laws and vehicle operation. Typically, instruction will warn of dangerous conditions in driving such as road conditions, driver impairments and hazardous weather. Instructional videos may also be shown, demonstrating proper driving strategies and the consequences for not observing the rules.

Education is intended to supplement the knowledge obtained from government-printed driving handbooks or manuals and prepares students for tests to obtain a driver's license or learner's permit. In-car instruction places a student in a vehicle with an instructor. A car fitted with dual controls, which has pedals or other controls on the passenger side, may be used.

Driver training began as a business in the United Kingdom in 1909-1910. The British School of Motoring (BSM) was founded in 1910 in South London by Hugh Stanley Roberts. It offered hands-on training and courses in driving skills (managing the controls and road aptitude) and repair. It also offered vehicles to drivers who wished to practice.

In the United States, Amos Neyhart, a professor at Penn State University, started the first high school driver's ed course in 1934 at a high school in State College, Pennsylvania.

The more correct and original designation is driver education, without the possessive, as with teacher education, or driving education as with nursing education. However over time the possessive version has become dominant.

Instruction

Royal Automobile Club of Tasmania training vehicle.

Driver's education (or driver education) is intended to supplement the knowledge obtained from government-printed driving handbooks or manuals and prepares students for tests to obtain a driver's license or learner's permit. In-car instruction places a student in a vehicle with an instructor. A car fitted with dual controls, which has pedals or other controls on the passenger side, may be used. In the United States, driver's education is typically offered to students who are sixteen years old or will be by the end of the course. Each state has its own laws regarding the licensing of teenagers. With the growing US population, traffic accidents are becoming more common than ever before. In Germany, space is at a premium while traffic is able to flow very efficiently and with less accidents. The way in which people are taught driving fundamentals plays a huge role in the safety and efficiency of traffic. Within the United States, students may have access to online training, classroom training, or parent-taught courses. While these classes may provide a lot of information to the student, their effectivity may only be limited to one area of knowledge. In Germany, students are given a hybrid of these classes. They have much more exposure throughout their school to real-world scenarios and classroom curriculum. Fundamentals of driving are reinforced in these classes, including the importance of turn-signal usage, keeping a safe distance behind others and maintaining situational awareness. It is argued that more efficient and safer traffic flow can be achieved by increasing the length of driver's education classes in the United States, to involve more hands-on training and a strengthening of driving principles.

Online Courses

An online driving education is one of the most affordable and convenient ways to acquire driving education. Many driver's education courses are available online. It is up to the relevant government authority to accept any such programs as meeting their requirements. Online drivers ed may be taken as a substitute for classroom courses in 13 states. Some car insurance agencies offer discounts to those students who have completed a driver's education program. Online programs allow parents to administer the behind the wheel driving instruction. Many studies have also started looking at the relationship between online activity, especially among the young adults and driving licence holding.

Obtaining a License

Successful completion of a driver education course is required by many agencies before young drivers receive their driver license or learner's permit. In some countries students taking driver's education have the opportunity to receive a waiver for successful course completion which allows them to receive a learner's permit or driver's license without taking some of the tests.

On Track

Some car clubs conduct driver education programs focused on how to handle a car under high-speed driving conditions rather than on learning the rules of the road. These programs take place at road racing courses and include both classroom instruction and vehicle-based instruction.

Students drive with an experienced instructor until they are "signed off". At this point they can continue practicing and improving their skills without an instructor. Driver education programs involve multiple cars together on a racetrack, but they are not considered racing because they are not timed, winners are not declared and drivers must wait to pass until the driver being passed gives permission with a hand signal. These programs require approved racing helmets and rollover protection for convertibles. Some require long-sleeved shirts and long pants for fire safety. However, they do not require full roll cages, five or six-point seat belts, fire extinguishers, fire-resistant racing suits, or other safety features seen in racing and more.

Journeyman

A journeyman is a worker, skilled in a given building trade or craft, who has successfully completed an official apprenticeship qualification. Journeymen are considered competent and authorized to work in that field as a fully qualified employee. They earn their license by education, supervised experience and examination. Although journeymen have completed a trade certificate and are allowed to work as employees, they may not yet work as self-employed master craftsmen.

The term "journeyman" was originally used in the medieval trade guilds. Journeymen were paid daily. Each individual guild generally recognised three ranks of workers: apprentices, journeymen and masters. A journeyman, as a qualified tradesman could become a master and run their own business, but most continued working as employees.

Guidelines were put in place to promote responsible tradesmen, who were held accountable for their own work and to protect the individual trade and the general public from unskilled workers. To become a master, a journeyman has to submit a master piece of work to a guild for evaluation. Only after evaluation can a journeyman be admitted to the guild as a master. Sometimes, a journeyman was required to accomplish a three-year working trip, which may be called the journeyman years.

German journeymen in traditional uniform during journeyman years.

The title "journeyman" refers to the right to charge a fee for each day's work. A journeyman has completed an apprenticeship but is employed by another such as a master craftsman, but they would live apart and might have a family of their own. A journeyman could not employ others. In contrast, an apprentice would be bound to a master, usually for a fixed term of seven years and lived with the master as a member of the household, receiving most or all compensation in the form of food, lodging and training.

In parts of Europe, as in Late Medieval Germany, spending time as a wandering journeyman (*Wandergeselle*), moving from one town to another to gain experience of different workshops, was an important part of the training of an aspirant master. Carpenters and other artisans in German speaking countries have retained the tradition of traveling journeymen even today, but only a few still practice it. In France, wandering journeymen were known as compagnons.

Modern Era

In modern apprenticeship systems, a journeyman has a trades certificate to show the required completion of an apprenticeship. In many countries, it is the highest formal rank, as that of master has been eliminated and they may perform all tasks of the trade in the area certified as well as supervise apprentices and become self-employed.

The modern apprenticeship system aims to build skills by on-the-job training. An apprentice is able to earn a living while learning new skills. The working environment is closely linked to the employer giving the individual company the opportunity to shape the apprentice, within the guidelines, to suit particular requirements. Quite often, a strong working relationship is built between employee and employer.

In Germany, however, master craftsmen, after they complete their apprenticeships, are required to take part-time courses that last three to four years or full-time courses that last one year.

United States

In the United States, employment in some building trades, such as an electrician, carpenter, plumber, machinist and HVAC contractor, usually requires holding state or local (city or county) license as a journeyman or master. The license certifies that the craftsman has met the requirements of time in the field (usually a minimum of 8,000 hours) and time in an approved classroom setting (usually 700 hours). A journeyman has the responsibility of supervising workers of lesser experience and training them and has the qualifications (knowledge and skills) to work unsupervised himself. A journeyman is commonly expected to have a wide range of experience, covering most fields of their trade. For example, a non-journeyman worker of some 20 or 30 years' experience may have most or all of their experience in only residential, commercial, or industrial applications. A journeyman, however, has a broad field of experience in residential, commercial and industrial applications.

Australia

In Australia, a journeyman registration allows the permit holder to work under the general direction of an advanced tradesman. A journeyman may oversee the work of apprentices and trades assistants but may not contract for work using that particular registration. A journeyman level qualification is obtained by completing a formal apprenticeship. An apprenticeship is learning a skilled trade under the supervision of an advanced tradesperson. An apprentice is a trainee who is becoming formally trained and qualified in a particular type of trade. The duration of an apprenticeship is usually three to four years, depending on the individual trade. On completion of the training the apprentice will receive a nationally recognised qualification, a trade certificate. Practical on-the-job learning makes up the majority of an apprenticeship, but it also incorporates some classroom learning. Apprenticeships offer real-life experience in the workplace, a regular income and new skills. Examples of licensed trades are plumbers and gas-fitters, electricians, air-conditioning and refrigeration mechanics and carpenters and joiners.

Canada

In Canada, in addition to completion of Apprenticeship in a Skilled Trade, the worker may also choose to write an exam to be recognized throughout the country via the Interprovincial Standards Red Seal program.

Modern Journeyman

The *modern journeyman* is a term for the many paths of adult education and can be used to describe life's process of continual learning. Although the term *journeyman* is typically traditional, *modern journeyman* is used to refer to current concepts of adult education: *life-long learning*, *up-skilling*, *the knowledge wave* and *modern apprenticeships*.

Technical Trainer

A technical trainer is an educator or teacher who trains or coaches others in some field of technology. The task requires a certain set of competencies, but many technical trainers do not hold specific technical-training qualifications. Although there are professional organizations and publications of relevance to technical trainers, few of these are specifically focused on that profession.

The need for technical training existed before computers or even electronics, but the term "technical trainer" has only been in the common lexicon since the mid-20th century. For example, RAF Technical Training Command was a distinct unit between 1940 and 1968, providing training in aircraft maintenance and other non-flying activities to British forces.

Currently, competence frameworks for technical trainers are not well developed. Among those technical trainers who have university degrees, the most frequent degree is in education; but many technical trainers are not formally qualified in the field.

Several organizations do provide certification for teachers and other educators in technology. For example, the American trade association CompTIA provides the CTT+ (Certified Technical Trainer) qualification, which is internationally recognized for trainers in the information technology field.

The Association for Talent Development, formerly American Society for Training and Development, is a non-profit association for workplace learning and performance professionals. It organizes two regular international conferences relevant to technical trainers: its national convention and the Techknowledge Conference on e-learning. Up to the mid-1990s it published a magazine and hosted a conference specifically for technical trainers.

The International Society for Performance Improvement (ISPI) organizes an annual conference and other educational events, publishes books and periodicals and supports research in performance improvement in the workplace.

Although a generic professional description can be applied to all technical trainers, as is true of any profession, many specializations exist. These include information technology topics such as Computer applications and Computer Architecture and

Design; biomedical technology; educational technology; Aerospace technology; and topics in the field of engineering.

It is often pointed out that effective technical trainers need qualities over and above technical mastery. They need to have skills in working with people and knowledge of a range of training techniques. The former National Skill Standards Board in the United States developed a set of skill standards for technical trainers.

Electrician

An electrician is a tradesman specializing in electrical wiring of buildings, transmission lines, stationary machines and related equipment. Electricians may be employed in the installation of new electrical components or the maintenance and repair of existing electrical infrastructure. Electricians may also specialize in wiring ships, airplanes and other mobile platforms, as well as data and cable lines.

A Navy electrician's mate rewiring the stator of an induction motor.

Electricians were originally people who demonstrated or studied the principles of electricity, often electrostatic generators of one form or another.

In the United States, electricians are divided into two primary categories: linemen, who work on electric utility company distribution systems at higher voltages and wiremen, who work with the lower voltages utilized inside buildings. Wiremen are generally trained in one of five primary specialties: commercial, residential, light industrial, industrial and low-voltage wiring, more commonly known as Voice-Data-Video, or VDV. Other sub-specialties such as control wiring and fire-alarm may be performed by specialists trained in the devices being installed, or by inside wiremen.

Electricians are trained to one of three levels: Apprentice, Journeyman and Master Electrician. In the US and Canada, apprentices work and receive a reduced compensation while learning their trade. They generally take several hundred hours of classroom instruction and are contracted to follow apprenticeship standards for a period of between three and six years, during which time they are paid as a percentage of the Journeyman's pay. Journeymen are electricians who have completed their Apprenticeship and who have been found by the local, State, or National licensing body to be competent in the electrical trade. Master Electricians have performed well in the trade for a period of time, often seven to ten years and have passed an exam to demonstrate superior knowledge of the National Electrical Code, or NEC.

Service electricians are tasked to respond to requests for isolated repairs and upgrades. They have skills troubleshooting wiring problems, installing wiring in existing buildings and making repairs. Construction electricians primarily focus on larger projects, such as installing all new electrical system for an entire building, or upgrading an entire floor of an office building as part of a remodeling process. Other specialty areas are marine electricians, research electricians and hospital electricians. "Electrician" is also used as the name of a role in stagecraft, where electricians are tasked primarily with hanging, focusing and operating stage lighting. In this context, the Master Electrician is the show's chief electrician. Although theater electricians routinely perform electrical work on stage lighting instruments and equipment, they are not part of the electrical trade and have a different set of skills and qualifications from the electricians that work on building wiring.

In the film industry and on a television crew the head electrician is referred to as a *Gaffer*.

Electrical contractors are businesses that employ electricians to design, install and maintain electrical systems. Contractors are responsible for generating bids for new jobs, hiring tradespeople for the job, providing material to electricians in a timely manner and communicating with architects, electrical and building engineers and the customer to plan and complete the finished product.

Training and Regulation of Trade

Many jurisdictions have regulatory restrictions concerning electrical work for safety reasons due to the many hazards of working with electricity. Such requirements may be testing, registration or licensing. Licensing requirements vary between jurisdictions.

An electrician's license entitles the holder to carry out all types of electrical installation work in Australia without supervision. However, to contract, or offer to contract, to carry out electrical installation work, a licensed electrician must also be registered as an electrical contractor. Under Australian law, electrical work that involves fixed wiring is strictly regulated and must almost always be performed by a licensed electrician or electrical contractor. A local electrician can handle a range of work including air conditioning, light fittings and installation, safety switches, smoke alarm installation, inspection and certification and testing and tagging of electrical appliances.

Electrician installing new meter socket on the side of a house.

To provide data, structured cabling systems, home automation and theatre, LAN, WAN and VPN data solutions or phone points, an installer must be licensed as a Telecommunications Cable Provider under a scheme controlled by Australian Communications and Media Authority.

Electrical licensing in Australia is regulated by the individual states. In Western Australia, the Department of Commerce tracks licensee's and allows the public to search for individually named/licensed Electricians.

Currently in Victoria the apprenticeship last for four years, during three of those years the apprentice attends trade school in either a block release of one week each month or one day each week. At the end of the apprenticeship the apprentice is required to pass three examinations, one of which is theory based with the other two practically based. Upon successful completion of these exams, providing all other components of the apprenticeship are satisfactory, the apprentice is granted an A Class licence on application to Energy Safe Victoria (ESV).

An A Class electrician may perform work unsupervised but is unable to work for profit or gain without having the further qualifications necessary to become a Registered Electrical Contractor (REC) or being in the employment of a person holding REC status. However, some exemptions do exist.

In most cases a certificate of electrical safety must be submitted to the relevant body after any electrical works are performed.

Safety equipment used and worn by electricians in Australia (including insulated rubber gloves and mats) needs to be tested regularly to ensure it is still protecting the worker. Because of the high risk involved in this trade, this testing needs performed regularly and regulations vary according to state. Industry best practice is the Queensland Electrical Safety Act 2002 and requires six-monthly testing.

A utility electrician/lineman does maintenance on a utility pole.

Training of electricians follows an apprenticeship model, taking four or five years to progress to fully qualified journeyman level. Typical apprenticeship programs consists of 80-90% hands-on work under the supervision of journeymen and 10-20% classroom training. Training and licensing of electricians is regulated by each province, however professional licenses are valid throughout Canada under Agreement on Internal Trade. An endorsement under the Red Seal Program provides additional competency assurance to industry standards. In order for individuals to become a licensed electricians, they need to have 9000 hours of practical, on the job training. They also need to attend school for 4 terms and pass a provincial exam. This training enables them to become journeyman electricians. Furthermore, in British Columbia, an individual can go a step beyond that and become a "FSR", or field safety representative. This credential gives the ability to become a licensed electrical contractor and to pull permits. Notwithstanding this, some Canadian provinces only grant "permit pulling privileges" to current Master Electricians, that is, a journeyman who has been engaged in the industry for three (3) years AND has passed the Master's examination (i.e. Alberta). The various levels of field safety representatives are A,B and C. The only difference between each class is that they are able to do increasingly higher voltage and current work.

Competency standards in the UK are defined by the Sector Skills council Summit Skills. Qualifications certificated by awarding organisations such as City and Guilds and EAL are based on these National Occupational Standards. Once qualified and demonstrating the required level of competence an Electrician can register with the JIB (Joint industry Board) for an Electrotechnical Certification Scheme (ECS) card. Electrical competence is required at Level 3 to practice as an electrician in the UK. The electrical industry is one of the few that require a trade test to be achieved prior to being fully qualified. This is known as the AM2.

Electricians can demonstrate further competence by studying further qualifications in Design and Verification of Electrical Installations or in the Test and Inspection of Electrical Installations. These qualifications can be listed on the reverse of the JIB card.

The Electricity at Work Regulations are the statutory document that covers electrical installations. Further information is provided in the non-statutory document BS7671 - Requirements for Electrical Installations otherwise known as the Wiring Regulations currently in their 17th Edition. Installations that comply with BS7671 are deemed to have met the EAWR. Electrical Installation in domestic properties is governed by Part P of the Building Regulations and electricians have to register certain aspects of their work in domestic properties with the local building control authority.

With the exception of the work described in Part P of the Building Regulations there are no laws that prevent anyone from carrying out electrical work in the UK. A possible result of this is that during 2010/11 and in 2011/12 there were 3,822 domestic electrical fires in Great Britain, resulting in 14 deaths. Organisations such as the Electrical Safety Council are working hard to educate the public not to use electricians who are not fully qualified or competent and to check the ElectricSafe register to ensure an Electrician has been deemed competent.

Although many electricians work for private contractors, many electricians get their start in the military.

The United States does not offer nationwide licensing and electrical licenses are issued by individual states. There are variations in licensing requirements, however, all states recognize three basic skill categories: level electricians. Journeyman electricians can work unsupervised provided that they work according to a master's direction. Generally, states do not offer journeyman permits and journeyman electricians and other apprentices can only work under permits issued to a master electrician. Apprentices may not work without direct supervision.

Before electricians can work unsupervised, they are usually required to serve an apprenticeship lasting from 3 to 5 years under the general supervision of a Master Electrician and usually the direct supervision of a Journeyman Electrician. Schooling in electrical theory and electrical building codes is required to complete the apprenticeship program. Many apprenticeship programs provide a salary to the apprentice during training. A Journeyman electrician is a classification of licensing granted to those who have met the experience requirements for on the job training (usually 4000 to 6000 hours) and classroom hours (about 144 hours). Requirements include completion of two to six years of apprenticeship training and passing a licensing exam.

Reciprocity

An electrician's license is valid for work in the state where the license was issued. In addition, many states recognize licenses from other states, sometimes called interstate reciprocity participation, although there can be conditions imposed. For example, California reciprocates with Arizona, Nevada and Utah on the condition that licenses are in good standing and have been held at the other state for five years. Nevada reciprocates with Arizona, California and Utah. Maine reciprocates with New Hampshire and Vermont at the master level and the state reciprocates with New Hampshire, North Dakota, Idaho, Oregon, Vermont and Wyoming at the journeyman level.

Tools

Electricians use a range of hand and power tools and instruments.

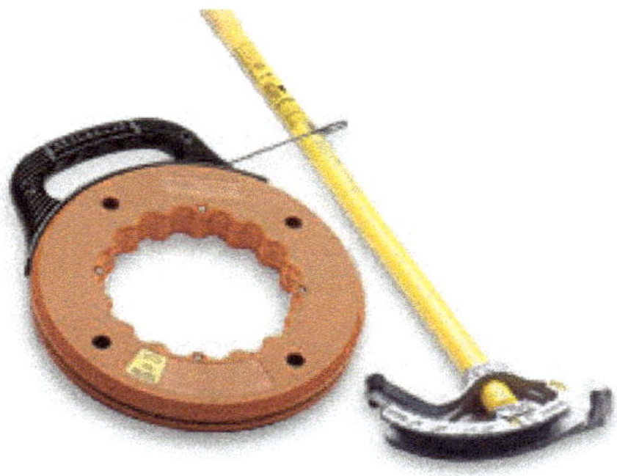

Two of the tools commonly used by electricians. The fish tape is used to pull conductors through conduits, or sometimes to pull conductors through hollow walls. The conduit bender is used to make accurate bends and offsets in electrical conduit.

Some of the more common tools are:

- Conduit Bender: Bender used to bend various types of Electrical Conduit. These come in many variations including hand, electrical and hydraulic powered.
- Non-Contact Voltage Testers.
- Lineman's Pliers: Heavy-duty pliers for general use in cutting, bending, crimping and pulling wire.
- Diagonal Pliers (also known as side cutters or Dikes): Pliers consisting of cutting blades for use on smaller gauge wires, but sometimes also used as a gripping tool for removal of nails and staples.

- Needle-Nose Pliers: Pliers with a long, tapered gripping nose of various size, with or without cutters, generally smaller and for finer work (including very small tools used in electronics wiring).
- Wire Strippers: Plier-like tool available in many sizes and designs featuring special blades to cut and strip wire insulation while leaving the conductor wire intact and without nicks. Some wire strippers include cable strippers among their multiple functions, for removing the outer cable jacket.
- Cable Cutters: Highly leveraged pliers for cutting larger cable.
- Armored Cable Cutters: Commonly referred to by the trademark 'Roto-Split' , is a tool used to cut the metal sleeve on MC (Metal Clad) cable.
- Multimeter: An instrument for electrical measurement with multiple functions. It is available as analog or digital display. Common features include: voltage, resistance and current. Some models offer additional functions.
- Unibit or Step-Bit: A metal-cutting drill bit with stepped-diameter cutting edges to enable convenient drilling holes in preset increments in stamped/rolled metal up to about 1.6mm (1/16 inch) thick. Commonly used to create custom knock-outs in a breaker panel or junction box.
- Cord, Rope or Fish Tape: Used to manipulate cables and wires through cavities. The fishing tool is pushed, dropped, or shot into the installed raceway, stud-bay or joist-bay of a finished wall or in a floor or ceiling. Then the wire or cable is attached and pulled back.
- Crimping Tools: Used to apply terminals or splices. These may be hand or hydraulic powered. Some hand tools have ratchets to insure proper pressure. Hydraulic units achieve cold welding, even for aluminum cable.
- Insulation Resistance Tester: Commonly referred to as a Megger, these testers apply several hundred to several thousand volts to cables and equipment to determine the insulation resistance value.
- Knockout Punch: For punching holes into boxes, panels, switchgear, etc. for inserting cable and pipe connectors.
- GFI/GFCI Testers: Used to test the functionality of Ground-Fault Interrupting receptacles.
- Voltmeter: An electrician's tool used to measure electrical potential difference between two points in an electric circuit.
- Other general-use tools include screwdrivers, hammers, reciprocating saws, drywall saws, flashlights, chisels, tongue and groove pliers and drills.

Safety

In addition to the workplace hazards generally faced by industrial workers, electricians are also particularly exposed to injury by electricity. An electrician may experience electric shock due to direct contact with energized circuit conductors or due to stray voltage caused by faults in a system. An electric arc exposes eyes and skin to hazardous amounts of heat and light. Faulty switchgear may cause an arc flash incident with a resultant blast. Electricians are trained to work safely and take many measures to minimize the danger of injury. Lockout and tagout procedures are used to make sure that circuits are proven to be de-energized before work is done. Limits of approach to energized equipment protect against arc flash exposure; specially designed flash-resistant clothing provides additional protection; grounding (earthing) clamps and chains are used on line conductors to provide a visible assurance that a conductor is de-energized. Personal protective equipment provides electrical insulation as well as protection from mechanical impact; gloves have insulating rubber liners and work boots and hard hats are specially rated to provide protection from shock. If a system cannot be de-energized, insulated tools are used; even high-voltage transmission lines can be repaired while energized, when necessary.

Electrical workers, which includes electricians, accounted for 34% of total electrocutions of construction trades workers in the United States between 1992–2003.

Working Conditions

Working conditions for electricians vary by specialization. Generally an electrician's work is physically demanding such as climbing ladders and lifting tools and supplies. Occasionally an electrician must work in a cramped space or on scaffolding and may frequently be bending, squatting or kneeling, to make connections in awkward locations. Construction electricians may spend much of their days in outdoor or semi-outdoor loud and dirty work sites. Industrial electricians may be exposed to the heat, dust and noise of an industrial plant. Power systems electricians may be called to work in all kinds of adverse weather to make emergency repairs.

Auto Electrician

An auto electrician is a tradesman specializing in electrical wiring of motor vehicles. Auto electricians may be employed in the installation of new electrical components or the maintenance and repair of existing electrical components. Auto electricians specialize in cars and commercial vehicles. The auto electrical trade is generally more difficult than the electrical trade due to the confined spaces, engineering complexity of modern automotive electrical systems and working conditions (often roadside breakdowns or on construction sites, mines, quarries to repair machinery etc.) Also the presence of high-current DC electricity makes injury from burns and arc-flash injury possible.

Electronics Technician

Electronics technicians help design, develop, test, manufacture, install and repair electrical and electronic equipment such as communication equipment, medical monitoring devices, navigational equipment and computers. They may be employed in product evaluation and testing, using measuring and diagnostic devices to adjust, test and repair equipment. Electronics technicians may also work as sales workers or field representatives for manufacturers, wholesalers, or retailers giving advice on the installation, operation and maintenance of complex equipment and may write specifications and technical manuals. Electronics technicians represent over 33% of all engineering technicians in the U.S. In 2009, there were over 160,000 electronics technicians employed in the U.S. Electronics technicians are accredited by organizations such as the Electronics Technicians Association (ETA), or International Society of Certified Electronics Technicians (ISCET).

Most employers prefer to hire electronics technicians with an associate degree or other post-secondary training in engineering technology. Training is available at technical institutes, at community colleges, at extension divisions of colleges and universities, at public and private vocational-technical schools and in the Armed Forces. Naval electronics technicians are the largest group of engineering technicians in the military. Many 2-year associate degree programs accredited by the Technology Accreditation Commission of the Accreditation Board for Engineering and Technology (ABET) include at least college algebra and trigonometry and one or two basic science courses. Depending on the specialty, more math or science may be required. About 200 ABET-accredited programs are offered in engineering technology specialities. ABET-accredited electronics technician programs usually require at least two mathematics courses and two physics courses in addition to the core competencies.

Electronics technician curriculum generally consists of courses in basic electricity and electronics, including Ohm's Law, Parallel and Series Circuits, Magnetism, AC/DC Circuits, Capacitance, Inductance, Transformers, Resonance, Filters, Semiconductors, Transistors, Amplifiers, Integrated Circuits and Digital electronics. In addition to vocational learning outcomes associated with the study of electronics and control systems, graduates of electronics technician programs are also expected to have essential employability skills and meet certain general education learning outcomes. Individual schools largely determine the specific program structure, delivery methods and other curriculum components to be used to assist students in achieving the required program outcomes.

A significant component of course material includes laboratory experimentation. These lab courses and projects often represent up to 50% of the course material and are used to reinforce theoretical concepts associated with the study of electronics. Schools offering electronics technician programs will have electronics laboratories to support the delivery of course curriculum. Historically, these laboratories have been traditional "hands on" learning environments, although in recent years the trend is moving towards electronics simulation software such as Multisim and CircuitLogix. Electronics software simulation is also used in conjunction with traditional labs to provide greater opportunities for students to complete laboratory projects as part of their studies.

Career Prospects

The demand for jobs in the electronics engineering and service fields is the result of a recent proliferation of both consumer and industrial electronics products. The design, installation, servicing and maintenance of this equipment has created significant employment opportunities in the electronics industry.

Typical job-related activities may involve:

- Design,
- Assembly,
- Installation,
- maintenance,
- Testing,
- troubleshooting,
- Repair,
- Upgrading of associated electronic equipment and systems.

Job opportunities for electrical and electronics technologists and technicians are increasing because many industries use electronic products and systems. Key sectors are telecommunications, audio/video, computers, robotics, energy conversion and efficiency, power generation, transmission and distribution and electrical equipment manufacturing. Employment opportunities for electronics technicians vary and are largely based on their areas of expertise. For example, employment growth for Electronics technicians in areas such as robotics, energy conversion and power generation is expected to grow by 5%/yr from 2010 through 2020.

Fashion Design

Fashion design is the art of applying design, aesthetics and natural beauty to clothing and its accessories. It is influenced by cultural and social attitudes and has varied over time and place. Fashion designers work in a number of ways in designing clothing and accessories such as bracelets and necklaces. Because of the time required to bring a garment onto the market, designers must at times anticipate changes to consumer tastes.

Designers conduct research on fashion trends and interpret them for their audience. Their specific designs are used by manufacturers. This is the essence of a designer's role; however, there is variation within this that is determined by the buying and merchandising approach and product quality; for example, budget retailers will use inexpensive fabrics to interpret trends, but high-end retailers will ensure that the best available fabrics are used.

Fashion designers attempt to design clothes which are functional as well as aesthetically pleasing. They consider who is likely to wear a garment and the situations in which it will be worn and they work within a wide range of materials, colors, patterns and styles. Though most clothing worn for everyday wear falls within a narrow range of conventional styles, unusual garments are usually sought for special occasions such as evening wear or party dresses.

Some clothes are made specifically for an individual, as in the case of haute couture or bespoke tailoring. Today, most clothing is designed for the mass market, especially casual and every-day wear are called ready to wear.

Structure

Fashion designers may work full-time for one fashion house, as 'in-house designers', which owns the designs, or they work alone or as part of a team. Freelance designers work for themselves, selling their designs to fashion houses, directly to shops, or to clothing manufacturers. The garments bear the buyer's label. Some fashion designers set up their own labels, under which their designs are marketed. Some fashion designers are self-employed and design for individual clients. Other high-end fashion designers cater to specialty stores or high-end fashion department stores. These designers create original garments, as well as those that follow established fashion trends. Most fashion designers, however, work for apparel manufacturers, creating designs of men's, women's and children's fashions for the mass market. Large designer brands which have a ‹name' as their brand such as Abercrombie and Fitch, Justice, or Juicy are likely to be designed by a team of individual designers under the direction of a design director.

Designing a Garment

Fashion designers work in different ways. Some sketch their ideas on paper, while others drape fabric on a dress form. When a designer is completely satisfied with the fit of the *toile* (or muslin), he or she will consult a professional pattern maker who then makes the finished, working version of the pattern out of card or via a computerized system. Finally, a sample garment is made up and tested on a model to make sure it is an operational outfit.

Types of Fashion

The garments produced by clothing manufacturers fall into three main categories, although these may be split up into additional, more specific categories

Haute Couture

Until the 1950s, fashion clothing was predominately designed and manufactured on a made-to-measure or haute couture basis (French for high-sewing), with each garment being created for a specific client. A couture garment is made to order for an individual customer and is usually made from high-quality, expensive fabric, sewn with extreme attention to detail and finish, often using time-consuming, hand-executed techniques. Look and fit take priority over the cost of materials and the time it takes to make. Due to the high cost of each garment, haute couture makes little direct profit for the fashion houses, but is important for prestige and publicity.

Ready-to-wear (prêt-à-porter)

Left: An Indian woman wearing a ready-to-wear little black dress. *Right:* A German man wearing a bow tie and black blazer.

Ready-to-wear, or prêt-à-porter, clothes are a cross between haute couture and mass market. They are not made for individual customers, but great care is taken in the choice and cut of the fabric. Clothes are made in small quantities to guarantee exclusivity, so they are rather expensive. Ready-to-wear collections are usually presented by fashion houses each season during a period known as Fashion Week. This takes place on a citywide basis and occurs twice a year. The main seasons of Fashion Week include: spring/summer, fall/winter, resort, swim and bridal.

Half-way garments are an alternative to ready-to-wear, "off-the-peg", or prêt-à-porter fashion. Half-way garments are intentionally unfinished pieces of clothing that encourages co-design between the "primary designer" of the garment and what would usually be considered, the passive "consumer". This differs from ready-to-wear fashion, as the consumer is able to participate in the process of making and co-designing their clothing. During the Makeable workshop, Hirscher and Niinimaki found that personal involvement in the garment-making process created a meaningful "narrative" for the user, which established a person-product attachment and increased the sentimental value of the final product.

Otto von Busch also explores half-way garments and fashion co-design in his thesis, "Fashion-able, Hacktivism and engaged Fashion Design".

Mass Market

Left: A student poses at a fashion show in University of Texas at Austin, USA. *Right:* A couple in casual wear at an event.

Currently the fashion industry relies more on mass market sales. The mass market caters for a wide range of customers, producing ready-to-wear garments using trends set by the famous names in fashion. They often wait around a season to make sure a style is going to catch on before producing their own versions of the original look. To save money and time, they use cheaper fabrics and simpler production techniques which can easily be done by machine. The end product can therefore be sold much more cheaply.

There is a type of design called "kutch" design originated from the German word *kitschig*, meaning "ugly" or "not aesthetically pleasing". *Kitsch* can also refer to "wearing or displaying something that is therefore no longer in fashion".

Clothing Types

Clothing type	Characteristics	Market segment
Women's day wear: Practical, comfortable, fashionable		Haute couture, ready-to wear, mass market
Women's evening wear	Glamorous, sophisticated, suited for the occasion	Haute couture, ready-to-wear, mass market
Women's lingerie	Glamorous, comfortable, washable	Haute couture, ready-to-wear, mass market
Men's day wear	Casual, practical, comfortable	Tailoring, ready-to-wear, mass market
Men's evening wear	Smart, elegant, formal, apt for the occasion	Tailoring, ready-to-wear, mass market
Kids' wear	Trendy or classy, practical, washable, functional	Ready-to-wear, mass market
Girls' wear	Pretty, colorful, practical, washable, inexpensive	Ready-to-wear, mass market
Teenager girl wear	Colorful, comfortable, glamorous, pretty, cute	Ready-to-wear, mass market
Jeans wear	Unisex, democratic, comfortable, practical, functional	Ready-to-wear, mass market
Swimwear	Trendy, stylish, practical, functional, colorful	Haute couture, ready to-wear, mass market
Sports wear	Comfortable, practical, well-ventilated, washable, functional	Ready-to-wear, mass market
Knitwear	Right weight and color for the season	Ready-to-wear, mass market
Outerwear	Stylish, warm, right weight and color for the season	Ready-to-wear, mass market
Bridal wear	Sumptuous, glamorous, classic	Haute couture, ready-to-wear, mass market
Accessories	Striking, fashionable	Haute couture, ready to-wear, mass market
Performance wear	Sporty, dependent on the sport	Ready-to-wear, mass market

World Fashion Industry

Fashion today is a global industry and most major countries have a fashion industry. Seven countries have established an international reputation in fashion: France, Italy, United Kingdom, United States, Japan, Germany and Belgium. The "big four" centers of the fashion industry are Paris, Milan, New York City and London. The biggest manufacturers of clothing are China, Bangladesh and India and other notable clothing manufacturing countries are Germany, Indonesia, Malaysia, India, Philippines, South Korea, Spain and Brazil.

Fashion show at a fashion designing college.

Most fashion houses in the United States are based in New York City, with a high concentration centered in the Garment District neighborhood. On the US west coast, there is also a significant number of fashion houses in Los Angeles, where a substantial percentage of high fashion clothing manufactured in the United States is actually made. Beverly Hills, particularly on Rodeo Drive, is globally renowned for its fashion design and prestigious shopping. Burgeoning industries in Miami, Chicago, Dallas and especially San Francisco have developed as well. A semi-annual event held every February and September, New York Fashion Week, is the oldest of the four major fashion weeks held throughout the world. Parsons The New School for Design, located in the Greenwich Village neighborhood of Lower Manhattan in New York City, is considered one of the top fashion schools in the world. There are numerous fashion magazines published in the United States and distributed to a global readership. Examples include Vogue, Harper's Bazaar and Cosmopolitan.

American fashion design is highly diverse, reflecting the enormous ethnic diversity of the population, but is largely dominated by a clean-cut, urban, hip aesthetic and often favors a more casual style, reflecting the athletic, health-conscious lifestyles of the suburban and urban middle class. Many American fashion trends are defined by teenagers, a generational distinction first named in the US in the 1950s. American fashion is also often influenced by popular sports and activities, namely skateboarding, baseball, basketball, surfing and even motorcycle riding. A designer who helped to set the trend in the United States for sport-influenced day wear throughout the 1940s and 50s was Claire McCardell. Many of her designs have been revived in recent decades. American fashion takes influence from and is promoted by, the United States' prominent musical and cinematic culture. Hollywood, as well as musical movements and subcultures such as Hip-Hop, Disco, Rock, Punk, Grunge, Jazz and Country have all had a profound effect on American fashion and the way it is envisioned around the globe.

In the late 1980s and early 1990s, Belgian fashion designers brought a new fashion image that mixed East and West and brought a highly individualised, personal vision on fashion.

Models at an event in UK, wearing (from left to right)- shorts, trousers, mini skirt.

London has long been the capital of the United Kingdom fashion industry and has a wide range of foreign designs which have integrated with modern British styles. Typical, British design is smart but innovative yet recently has become more and more unconventional, fusing traditional styles with modern techniques. Vintage styles play an important role in the British fashion and styling industry. Stylists regularly ‹mix and match' the old with the new, which gives British style that unique, bohemian aesthetic that many of the other fashion capitals try to imitate. Irish fashion (both design and styling) is also heavily influenced by fashion trends from Britain.

Most French fashion houses are in Paris, which is the capital of French fashion. Traditionally, French fashion is chic and stylish, defined by its sophistication, cut and smart accessories. French fashion is internationally acclaimed.

Berlin is the centre of fashion in Germany (prominently displayed at Berlin Fashion Week), while Düsseldorf holds Europe's largest fashion trade fairs with *Igedo*. Other important centres of the scene are Munich, Hamburg and Cologne. German fashion is famed for its elegant lines as well as unconventional young designs and the great variety of styles.

Globally renowned fashion designers from Germany are Karl Lagerfeld, Hugo Boss, Wolfgang Joop, Jil Sander, Michael Michalsky, Etienne Aigner, Rudolph Moshammer, Torsten Amft, Willy Bogner and Philipp Plein.

Milan is Italy's fashion capital. Most of the older Italian couturiers are in Rome. However, Milan and Florence are the Italian fashion capitals and it is the exhibition venue for their collections. Italian fashion features casual and glamorous elegance.

Most Japanese fashion houses are in Tokyo. The Japanese look is loose and unstructured (often resulting from complicated cutting), colours tend to the sombre and subtle and richly textured fabrics.

Hong Kong clothing brand Shanghai Tang's design concept is inspired by Chinese clothing and set out to rejuvenate Chinese fashion of the 1920s and 30s, with a modern twist of the 21st century and its usage of bright colours.

Fashion in the Soviet Union largely followed general trends of the Western world. However, the state's socialist ideology consistently moderated and influenced these trends. In addition, shortages of consumer goods meant that the general public did not have ready access to pre-made fashion.

Most of the Swiss fashion houses are in Zürich. The Swiss look is casual elegant and luxurious with a slight touch of quirkiness. Additionally, it has been greatly influenced by the dance club scene.

In the development of Mexican indigenous dress, the fabrication was determined by the materials and resources that are available in specific regions, impacting the "fabric, shape and construction of a people's clothing". Textiles were created from plant fibers including cotton and agave. Class status differentiated what fabric was worn. Mexican dress was influenced by geometric shapes to create the silhouettes. Huipil a blouse characterized by a "loose, sleeveless tunic made of two or three joined webs of cloth sewn lengthwise" is an important historical garment, often seen today. After the Spanish Conquest, traditional Mexican clothing shifted to take a Spanish resemblance.

Mexican indigenous groups rely on specific embroidery and colors to differentiate themselves from each other.

Mexican Pink is a significant color to the identity of Mexican art and design and general spirit. The term "Rosa Mexicano" as described by Ramón Valdiosera was established by prominent figures such as Dolores del Río and designer Ramón Val in New York.

When newspapers and magazines such as El Imparcial and El Mundo Ilustrado circulated in Mexico, became a significant movement, as it informed the large cities, such as Mexico City, of European fashions. This encouraged the founding of department stores, changing the existent pace of fashion. With access to European fashion and dress, those with high social status relied on adopting those elements to distinguish themselves from the rest. Juana Catarina Romero was a successful entrepreneur and pioneer in this movement.

Mexico holds a Mercedes Benz fashion week in Mexico City once (or twice) a year showcasing about 25 designers.This takes place at about 6 different venues.

Fashion Design Services

Fashion design services provide services like trend and color forecasting, market analysis, design concepts and design documentation for manufacturers. This way the manufacturer can contract out the design requirements rather than maintaining an in-house design team. Fashion design services providers can either sell the designs outright or license them out on a royalty basis.

If someone is interested in launching a line in footwear, handbags, bedding etc. and are looking to outsource the design work, then a fashion design services provider can help. When initially launching the business, it might be expensive to launch with many new designs and thus a licensing option from such a company might save startup cost.

Instrument Mechanic

Instrument mechanics in engineering are tradesmen who specialize in installing, troubleshooting and repairing instrumentation, automation and control systems. The term instrument mechanic came about because it was a combination of light mechanical and specialised instrumentation skills. The term is still is used in certain industries; predominantly in industrial process control.

Pneumatic PID (Three term) controller. This type of controller was completely mechanical; hence the expression "instrument mechanic" for someone repair or calibrating it.

Instrumentation has existed for hundreds of years in one form or another; the oldest manometer was invented by Evangelista Torricelli in 1643 and the thermometer has been credited to many scientists of about the same period. Over that time, small and large scale industrial plants and manufacturing processes have always needed accurate and reliable process measurements. Originally the demand would only be for measurement instruments, but as process complexity grew, automatic control became more common.

The huge growth in process control instrumentation was boosted by the use of pneumatic controllers, which were used widely after 1930 when Clesson E Mason of the Foxboro Company invented a wide-band pneumatic controller by combining the nozzle and flapper high-gain pneumatic amplifier with negative feedback in a completely mechanical device. The repair and calibration of these devices required both fine mechanical skills and an understanding of the control operation. Likewise the use of control valves with positioners appeared, which required a similar combination of skills.

World War II also brought about a revolution in the use of instrumentation. Further advanced processes requires tighter control than people could provide and advanced instruments were required to provide measurements in modern processes. Also, the war left industry with a substantially reduced workforce. Industrial instrumentation solved both problems, leading to a rise in its use. Pipe fitters had to learn more about instrumentation and control theory and a new trade was born.

Today, instrument mechanics combine the skills of repair and calibration with the theoretical understand of how the instrumentation and control works, which is a specialised combination of electronic and mechanical disciplines. Now, almost all new instrumentation is electronic, using either 4-20mA control signals or digital signalling standards, the term instrument mechanic is still used colloquially in some cases.

Air-actuated control valves each with a valve positioner to control valve travel. The skills to repair/calibrate require understanding of electronic, control, pneumatic and light mechanical engineering.

In Canada, journeyman tradesmen who work with instrumentation are called "Instrument Mechanics". In the United States, Australia and elsewhere, they can be called "Instrument fitters". The term may have originated from earlier instrument-qualified people being originally mechanically trained Machinists (also known as a fitter and turner) rather than electricians or "pure" instrument fitters (No secondary trade) as is now the norm.

In the United Kingdom a particular trend has been to call them Electrical/instrument (E/I) craftsmen, with progression to technician level.

Training and Regulation of Trade

In most countries, the job of an instrument mechanic is a regulated trade for safety reasons due to the many hazards of working with electricity, as well as the dangers posed by incorrectly installed or calibrated instrumentation. The training requires testing, registration, or licensing. Licensing of instrument mechanics is usually controlled through government or educational bodies, and professional societies.

The apprenticeship period has been reduced in some cases for Instrumentation Engineering Technologists, who can get their apprenticeship in 2 years rather than

4, depending on the college. In the United Kingdom, the "modern apprenticeship" is 42 months and requires theory training to National Vocational Qualification (NVQ) level 3.

In Canada, the trade of Instrumentation and Control technician is included in the Red Seal inter-provincial journeyman program.

The trade itself is called different things in different provinces. The two most popular names are "Industrial Instrument Mechanic" and "Instrumentation and Control Technician", though Alberta and the Northwest Territories call the certification "Instrument Technician" and Saskatchewan and Nunavut call their certification "Industrial Instrument Technician".

The 1995 Agreement on Internal Trade, agreed upon by all provinces except Nunavut, states that each party to the agreement will provide automatic recognition and free access to all workers holding an inter-provincial standards (Red Seal) program qualification.

Although there is a federal agreement, each province implements the program with its own legislation:

- Prince Edward Island's Journeyman program is regulated by the Apprenticeship and Trades Qualification Act.
- Nova Scotia's Journeyman program is regulated by the Apprenticeship and Trades Qualification Act.
- Newfoundland's Journeyman program is regulated by the Apprenticeship and Certification Act.
- New Brunswick's Journeyman program is regulated by the Apprenticeship and Occupational Certification Act.
- Quebec's Journeyman program is regulated by the Manpower Vocational Training and Qualification Act.
- Ontario 's Journeyman program is regulated by the Ontario College of Trades act.
- Manitoba's Journeyman program is regulated by the Apprenticeship and Certification act.
- Saskatchewan's Journeyman program is regulated by the Apprenticeship and Trade Certification Act.
- Alberta's Journeyman program is regulated by the Apprenticeship and Industry Training Act.
- British Columbia's Journeyman program is regulated by the Industry Training and Apprenticeship Act.

- Nunavut's Journeyman program is regulated by the Trade and Occupations Certification Act.
- The Yukon Territories' Journeyman program is regulated by the Apprenticeship Training Act.
- The Northwest Territories' Journeyman program is regulated by the Apprenticeship, Trade and Occupation Certification Act.

Recipients receive a "Certificate of Qualification".

Different provincial jurisdictions may have different regulations.In Ontario, the Instrumentation and Control apprenticeship program does not contain any restricted skill sets as per Ontario Regulation 565/99, Restricted skill sets. This means that a worker does not need a certificate of apprenticeship or a certificate of qualification to practice the trade.

Training of instrument mechanics follows an apprenticeship model, taking four or five years to progress to fully qualified journeyman level. Typical apprenticeship programs emphasize hands-on work under the supervision of journeymen, but also include a substantial component of classroom training and testing. Training and licensing of instrument mechanics is by province and some provinces don't have an instrument mechanic licensing program, but provinces recognize qualifications received in others.

Different provincial jurisdictions may have different regulations regarding certification. In Ontario, the On-The-Job training duration for apprentices is 8000 hours and the in-school training duration is generally 720 hours. One person of journeyman or equivalent status must be working for every apprentice.

Prior to receiving their Journeyman designation, candidates seeking their certificate of qualification must complete a trade exam, testing knowledge of a number of essential skill sets:

- Safe Working Practices and Procedures.
- Occupational Skills.
- Process Measurement and Indicating Devices.
- Process Analyzers, Quality Control Analyzers and Environmental Emission Analyzers.
- Safety Systems and Security Systems.
- Energy Development Systems.
- Communication Systems and Devices.
- Final Control Devices.
- Process Control Systems.

The trade exam consists of a number of questions in each of these skill sets.

Australian instrument fitters are usually re-qualified electricians who complete a 2-year conversion course at an accredited technical college, such as a TAFE, or start as new apprentices with no prior qualifications and complete a 3 year course and a 4 year apprenticeship, in combination with workplace experience of material studied. The first year of the 3 is a basic electrical module, covering AC and DC principals, plus some workshop practicals. The 4th year generally consists of an apprentice choosing a post-trade qualification to study for.

As there is no journeyman accreditation in Australia, at the completion of their trade course and collection of the required workplace experience, aspirant instrument fitters must pass a "capstone" test, which involves theoretical testing and practical exercises to determine competency. Qualification is recognised with a craft certificate, but not a license in any form.

Other Names

Instrument mechanics are sometimes known as:

- Instrument artificers.
- Instrument fitters.
- Instrumentation Techs.
- Instrument technicians.
- E/I craftsmen (United Kingdom).

Fields of Study

Instrument mechanics are required to study a large body of knowledge. This includes information on:

- Process Control,
- Measurement Instrumentation,
- Final Control Elements,
- Motors,
- Electronics,
- Industrial networks,
- Signalling standards,

- Chemistry,
- Fluid Dynamics.

Photographer

A photographer is a person who makes photographs.

Duties and Types of Photographers

An English photographer in his studio.

As in other arts, the definitions of amateur and professional are not entirely categorical.

An amateur photographer takes snapshots for pleasure to remember events, places or friends with no intention of selling the images to others.

A professional photographer is likely to take photographs for a session and image purchase fee, by salary or through the display, resale or use of those photographs.

A professional photographer may be an employee, for example of a newspaper, or may contract to cover a particular planned event such as a wedding or graduation, or to illustrate an advertisement. Others, like fine art photographers, are freelancers, first making an image and then licensing or making printed copies of it for sale or display. Some workers, such as crime scene photographers, estate agents, journalists and scientists, make photographs as part of other work. Photographers who produce moving rather than still pictures are often called cinematographers, videographers or camera operators, depending on the commercial context.

The term professional may also imply preparation, for example, by academic study or apprenticeship by the photographer in pursuit of photographic skills. A hallmark of a professional is often that they invest in continuing education through associations. Many associations offer the opportunity to test and exhibit acumen in order to attain credentials such as Certified Professional Photographer (CPP) or Master Photographer. While there is no compulsory registration requirement for professional photographer status, operating a business requires having a business license in most cities and counties. Similarly, having commercial insurance is required by most venues if photographing a wedding or a public event. Photographers who operate a legitimate business can provide these items.

Photographers can be categorized based on the subjects they photograph.

Some photographers explore subjects typical of paintings such as landscape, still life and portraiture. Other photographers specialize in subjects unique to photography, including sports photography, street photography, documentary photography, fashion photography, wedding photography, war photography, photojournalism, aviation photography and commercial photography. It is worth noting that the type of work commissioned will have pricing associated with the image's usage.

Selling Photographs

A Navy photographer.

The exclusive right of photographers to copy and use their products is protected by copyright. Countless industries purchase photographs for use in publications and on products. The photographs seen on magazine covers, in television advertising, on greeting cards or calendars, on websites, or on products and packages, have generally been purchased for this use, either directly from the photographer or through an agency that represents the photographer. A photographer uses a contract to sell the "license" or use of his or her photograph with exact controls regarding how often the photograph will be used, in what territory it will be used (for example U.S. or U.K. or other) and exactly for which products. This is usually referred to as usage fee and is used to distinguish from production fees (payment for the actual creation of a photograph or photographs). An additional contract and royalty would apply for each additional use of the photograph.

The contract may be for only one year, or other duration. The photographer usually charges a royalty as well as a one-time fee, depending on the terms of the contract. The contract may be for non-exclusive use of the photograph (meaning the photographer can sell the same photograph for more than one use during the same year) or for exclusive use of the photograph (i.e. only that company may use the photograph during the term). The contract can also stipulate that the photographer is entitled to audit the company for determination of royalty payments. Royalties vary depending on the industry buying the photograph and the use, for example, royalties for a photograph used on a poster or in television advertising may be higher than for use on a limited run of brochures. A royalty is also often based on the size at which the photo will be used in a magazine or book and cover photos usually command higher fees than photos used elsewhere in a book or magazine.

Photos taken by a photographer while working on assignment are often work for hire belonging to the company or publication unless stipulated otherwise by contract. Professional portrait and wedding photographers often stipulate by contract that they retain the copyright of their photos, so that only they can sell further prints of the photographs to the consumer, rather than the customer reproducing the photos by other means. If the customer wishes to be able to reproduce the photos themselves, they may discuss an alternative contract with the photographer in advance before the pictures are taken, in which a larger upfront fee may be paid in exchange for reprint rights passing to the customer.

There are major companies who have maintained catalogues of stock photography and images for decades, such as Getty Images and others. Since the turn of the 21st century many online stock photography catalogues have appeared that invite photographers to sell their photos online easily and quickly, but often for very little money, without a royalty and without control over the use of the photo, the market it will be used in, the products it will be used on, time duration, etc.

Commercial photographers may also promote their work to advertising and editorial art buyers via printed and online marketing vehicles.

Wireman

A wireman is an electrician who installs and repairs electrical wiring and components in homes and other facilities. Wiremen are distinct from power linemen. Both are electricians, but a lineman mainly works outdoors on power transmission lines and equipment. Wireman generally works inside buildings. A wireman is a highly trained technician who must spend several years as a helper or apprentice in order to advance to journeyman status. The pay and job market for wiremen are good, although a college degree is not required. This is a good occupation for the person who is technically oriented and who enjoys a hands-on work environment.

Wireman duties and responsibilities include installing, maintaining and repairing wiring and related electrical devices in homes, businesses, factories and construction sites The job often begins with reading technical diagrams and blueprints. Wiremen also inspect existing wiring and electrical systems to identify and correct problems or replace worn-out or defective components. Wiremen use a wide range of tools, including testing devices, soldering irons, wire cutters and standard tools such as hammers and screwdrivers. They also use power tools to cut conduit pipes, drill holes and perform other tasks.

A wireman is responsible for the safety of electrical systems so she must know and adhere to government regulations, building codes and safety rules. Because the occupation is based on the apprenticeship system, a wireman may also be responsible for training and supervising apprentices and electrician's helpers.

As electricians, wiremen must have a high school diploma or the equivalent. Some learn on the job or by attending technical programs at vocational schools or community colleges. Most learn the wireman trade through an apprenticeship sponsored by a contractors' association or trade union. Apprenticeships take four to five years and require 144 hours of classes ad 2,000 hours work annually. Upon completion, the wireman is considered a journeyman electrician. Most states require electricians to be licensed. A new wireman must pass a test to prove his knowledge ad skills, including familiarity with the National Electrical Code and state codes.

Wireman Work Environment

Although electrical wiremen work mostly indoors, they usually don't have a fixed work location. They must travel to where their services are required. Some do have a single work venue such as a school or factory. 65 percent of wiremen were employed by electrical or wiring installation contractors in 2017. Another 8 percent were self-employed. Manufacturing companies employed another 8 percent. About 4 percent worked for government agencies and 2 percent were employed by employment services.

A wireman does a lot of standing and kneeling and may have to work in confined spaces. Those who work outside on jobs such as installing solar panels have to deal with temperature and weather extremes. Safety precautions are a priority due to the risk of electric shock, burns and falls. Most electricians work regular hours on a full time basis. However, emergencies or tight construction schedules may necessitate evening, weekend and overtime work at times.

Welding

Gas Metal Arc Welding (GMAW welding) on pipe.

Welding is a fabrication or sculptural process that joins materials, usually metals or thermoplastics, by using high heat to melt the parts together and allowing them to cool causing fusion. Welding is distinct from lower temperature metal-joining techniques such as brazing and soldering, which do not melt the base metal.

In addition to melting the base metal, a filler material is typically added to the joint to form a pool of molten material (the weld pool) that cools to form a joint that, based on weld configuration (butt, full penetration, fillet, etc.), can be stronger than the base material (parent metal). Pressure may also be used in conjunction with heat, or by itself, to produce a weld. Welding also requires a form of shield to protect the filler metals or melted metals from being contaminated or oxidized.

Many different energy sources can be used for welding, including a gas flame (chemical), an electric arc (electrical), a laser, an electron beam, friction and ultrasound. While often an industrial process, welding may be performed in many different environments, including in open air, under water and in outer space. Welding is a hazardous undertaking and precautions are required to avoid burns, electric shock, vision damage, inhalation of poisonous gases and fumes and exposure to intense ultraviolet radiation.

Until the end of the 19th century, the only welding process was forge welding, which blacksmiths had used for millennia to join iron and steel by heating and hammering. Arc welding and oxy-fuel welding were among the first processes to develop late in the century and electric resistance welding followed soon after. Welding technology advanced quickly during the early 20th century as the world wars drove the demand for reliable and inexpensive joining methods. Following the wars, several modern welding techniques were developed, including manual methods like shielded metal arc welding, now one of the most popular welding methods, as well as semi-automatic and automatic processes such as gas metal arc welding, submerged arc welding, flux-cored arc welding and electroslag welding. Developments continued with the invention of laser beam welding, electron beam welding, magnetic pulse welding and friction stir welding in the latter half of the century. Today, the science continues to advance. Robot welding is commonplace in industrial settings and researchers continue to develop new welding methods and gain greater understanding of weld quality.

The iron pillar of Delhi, India.

The history of joining metals goes back several millennia. The earliest examples of this come from the Bronze and Iron Ages in Europe and the Middle East. The ancient Greek historian Herodotus states in *The Histories* of the 5th century BC that Glaucus of Chios "was the man who single-handedly invented iron welding". Welding was used in the construction of the Iron pillar of Delhi, erected in Delhi, India about 310 AD and weighing 5.4 metric tons.

The Middle Ages brought advances in forge welding, in which blacksmiths pounded heated metal repeatedly until bonding occurred. In 1540, Vannoccio Biringuccio published *De la pirotechnia*, which includes descriptions of the forging operation. Renaissance craftsmen were skilled in the process and the industry continued to grow during the following centuries.

In 1800, Sir Humphry Davy discovered the "short-pulse" electrical arc and presented his results in 1801. In 1802, Russian scientist Vasily Petrov created the continuous electric arc and subsequently published "News of Galvanic-Voltaic Experiments" in 1803, in which he described experiments carried out in 1802. Of great importance in this work was the description of a stable arc discharge and the indication of its possible use for many applications, one being melting metals. In 1808, Davy, who was unaware of Petrov's work, rediscovered the continuous electric arc. In 1881–82 inventors Nikolai Benardos (Russian) and Stanisław Olszewski (Polish) created the first electric arc welding method known as carbon arc welding using carbon electrodes. The advances in arc welding continued with the invention of metal electrodes in the late 1800s by a Russian, Nikolai Slavyanov and an American, C. L. Coffin . Around 1900, A. P. Strohmenger released a coated metal electrode in Britain, which gave a more stable arc. In 1905, Russian scientist Vladimir Mitkevich proposed using a three-phase electric arc for welding. Alternating current welding was invented by C. J. Holslag in 1919, but did not become popular for another decade.

Resistance welding was also developed during the final decades of the 19th century, with the first patents going to Elihu Thomson in 1885, who produced further advances over the next 15 years. Thermite welding was invented in 1893 and around that time another process, oxyfuel welding, became well established. Acetylene was discovered in 1836 by Edmund Davy, but its use was not practical in welding until about 1900, when a suitable torch was developed. At first, oxyfuel welding was one of the more popular welding methods due to its portability and relatively low cost. As the 20th century progressed, however, it fell out of favor for industrial applications. It was largely replaced with arc welding, as advances in metal coverings (known as flux) were made. Flux covering the electrode primarily shields the base material from impurities, but also stabilizes the arc and can add alloying components to the weld metal.

Bridge of Maurzyce.

World War I caused a major surge in the use of welding, with the various military powers attempting to determine which of the several new welding processes would be best. The British primarily used arc welding, even constructing a ship, the "Fullagar" with an entirely welded hull. Arc welding was first applied to aircraft during the war as well, as some German airplane fuselages were constructed using the process. Also noteworthy is the first welded road bridge in the world, the Maurzyce Bridge designed by Stefan Bryła of the Lwów University of Technology in 1927 and built across the river Słudwia near Łowicz, Poland in 1928.

Acetylene welding on cylinder water jacket.

During the 1920s, major advances were made in welding technology, including the introduction of automatic welding in 1920, in which electrode wire was fed continuously. Shielding gas became a subject receiving much attention, as scientists attempted to protect welds from the effects of oxygen and nitrogen in the atmosphere. Porosity and brittleness were the primary problems and the solutions that developed included the use of hydrogen, argon and helium as welding atmospheres. During the following decade, further advances allowed for the welding of reactive metals like aluminum and magnesium. This in conjunction with developments in automatic welding, alternating current and fluxes fed a major expansion of arc welding during the 1930s and then during World War II. In 1930, the first all-welded merchant vessel, M/S *Carolinian*, was launched.

During the middle of the century, many new welding methods were invented. In 1930, Kyle Taylor was responsible for the release of stud welding, which soon became popular in shipbuilding and construction. Submerged arc welding was invented the same year and continues to be popular today. In 1932 a Russian, Konstantin Khrenov eventually implemented the first underwater electric arc welding. Gas tungsten arc welding, after decades of development, was finally perfected in 1941 and gas metal arc welding followed in 1948, allowing for fast welding of non-ferrous materials but requiring expensive shielding gases. Shielded metal arc welding was developed during the 1950s, using a flux-coated consumable electrode and it quickly became the most popular metal arc welding process. In 1957, the flux-cored arc welding process debuted, in which the self-shielded wire electrode could be used with automatic equipment, resulting in greatly increased welding speeds and that same year, plasma arc welding was invented. Electroslag welding was introduced in 1958 and it was followed by its cousin, electrogas welding, in 1961. In 1953, the Soviet scientist N. F. Kazakov proposed the diffusion bonding method.

Other recent developments in welding include the 1958 breakthrough of electron beam welding, making deep and narrow welding possible through the concentrated heat source. Following the invention of the laser in 1960, laser beam welding debuted several decades later and has proved to be especially useful in high-speed, automated welding. Magnetic pulse welding (MPW) is industrially used since 1967. Friction stir welding was invented in 1991 by Wayne Thomas at The Welding Institute (TWI, UK) and found high-quality applications all over the world. All of these four new processes continue to be quite expensive due to the high cost of the necessary equipment and this has limited their applications.

Methods

Some of the most common current welding methods are:

- Shielded metal arc welding (SMAW), also known as "stick welding."
- Gas tungsten arc welding (GTAW), also known as TIG (tungsten, inert gas).
- Gas metal arc welding (GMAW), also known as MIG (metal, inert gas).
- Flux-cored arc welding (FCAW), very similar to MIG.
- Submerged arc welding (SAW), usually called Sub Arc.
- Electroslag welding (ESW), a highly productive process for thicker materials.

Processes

Arc

Man welding a metal structure in a newly constructed house in Bengaluru, India.

These processes use a welding power supply to create and maintain an electric arc between an electrode and the base material to melt metals at the welding point. They can use either direct current (DC) or alternating current (AC) and consumable or non-consumable electrodes. The welding region is sometimes protected by some type of inert or semi-inert gas, known as a shielding gas and filler material is sometimes used as well.

Power Supplies

To supply the electrical power necessary for arc welding processes, a variety of different power supplies can be used. The most common welding power supplies are constant current power supplies and constant voltage power supplies. In arc welding, the length of the arc is directly related to the voltage and the amount of heat input is related to the current. Constant current power supplies are most often used for manual welding processes such as gas tungsten arc welding and shielded metal arc welding, because they maintain a relatively constant current even as the voltage varies. This is important because in manual welding, it can be difficult to hold the electrode perfectly steady and as a result, the arc length and thus voltage tend to fluctuate. Constant voltage power supplies hold the voltage constant and vary the current and as a result, are most often used for automated welding processes such as gas metal arc welding, flux cored arc welding and submerged arc welding. In these processes, arc length is kept constant, since any fluctuation in the distance between the wire and the base material is quickly rectified by a large change in current. For example, if the wire and the base material get too close, the current will rapidly increase, which in turn causes the heat to increase and the tip of the wire to melt, returning it to its original separation distance.

The type of current used plays an important role in arc welding. Consumable electrode processes such as shielded metal arc welding and gas metal arc welding generally use direct current, but the electrode can be charged either positively or negatively. In welding, the positively charged anode will have a greater heat concentration and as a result, changing the polarity of the electrode affects weld properties. If the electrode is positively charged, the base metal will be hotter, increasing weld penetration and welding speed. Alternatively, a negatively charged electrode results in more shallow welds. Nonconsumable electrode processes, such as gas tungsten arc welding, can use either type of direct current, as well as alternating current. However, with direct current, because the electrode only creates the arc and does not provide filler material, a positively charged electrode causes shallow welds, while a negatively charged electrode makes deeper welds. Alternating current rapidly moves between these two, resulting in medium-penetration welds. One disadvantage of AC, the fact that the arc must be re-ignited after every zero crossing, has been addressed with the invention of special power units that produce a square wave pattern instead of the normal sine wave, making rapid zero crossings possible and minimizing the effects of the problem.

Processes

One of the most common types of arc welding is shielded metal arc welding (SMAW); it is also known as manual metal arc welding (MMAW) or stick welding. Electric current is used to strike an arc between the base material and consumable electrode rod, which is made of filler material (typically steel) and is covered with a flux that protects the weld area from oxidation and contamination by producing carbon dioxide (CO_2) gas during the welding process. The electrode core itself acts as filler material, making a separate filler unnecessary.

Shielded metal arc welding.

The process is versatile and can be performed with relatively inexpensive equipment, making it well suited to shop jobs and field work. An operator can become reasonably proficient with a modest amount of training and can achieve mastery with experience. Weld times are rather slow, since the consumable electrodes must be frequently replaced and because slag, the residue from the flux, must be chipped away after welding. Furthermore, the process is generally limited to welding ferrous materials, though special electrodes have made possible the welding of cast iron, nickel, aluminum, copper and other metals.

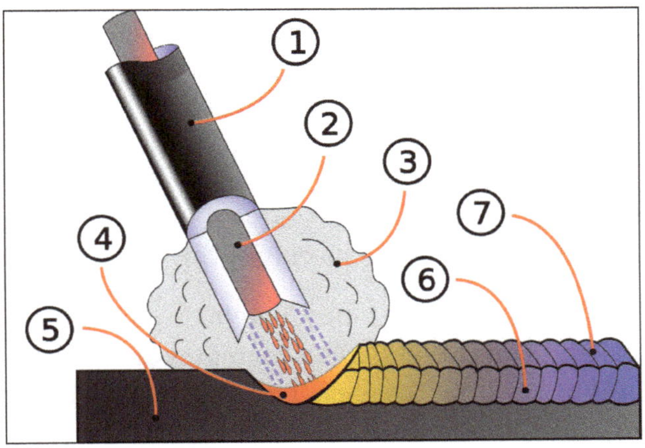

Diagram of arc and weld area, in shielded metal arc welding.

- Coating Flow,
- Rod,
- Shield Gas,
- Fusion,
- Base metal,
- Weld metal,
- Solidified Slag.

Gas metal arc welding (GMAW), also known as metal inert gas or MIG welding, is a semi-automatic or automatic process that uses a continuous wire feed as an electrode and an inert or semi-inert gas mixture to protect the weld from contamination. Since the electrode is continuous, welding speeds are greater for GMAW than for SMAW.

A related process, flux-cored arc welding (FCAW), uses similar equipment but uses wire consisting of a steel electrode surrounding a powder fill material. This cored wire is more expensive than the standard solid wire and can generate fumes and slag, but it permits even higher welding speed and greater metal penetration.

Gas tungsten arc welding (GTAW), or tungsten inert gas (TIG) welding, is a manual welding process that uses a nonconsumable tungsten electrode, an inert or semi-inert gas mixture and a separate filler material. Especially useful for welding thin materials, this method is characterized by a stable arc and high quality welds, but it requires significant operator skill and can only be accomplished at relatively low speeds.

GTAW can be used on nearly all weldable metals, though it is most often applied to stainless steel and light metals. It is often used when quality welds are extremely important, such as in bicycle, aircraft and naval applications. A related process, plasma arc welding, also uses a tungsten electrode but uses plasma gas to make the arc. The arc is more concentrated than the GTAW arc, making transverse control more critical and thus generally restricting the technique to a mechanized process. Because of its stable current, the method can be used on a wider range of material thicknesses than can the GTAW process and it is much faster. It can be applied to all of the same materials as GTAW except magnesium and automated welding of stainless steel is one important application of the process. A variation of the process is plasma cutting, an efficient steel cutting process.

Submerged arc welding (SAW) is a high-productivity welding method in which the arc is struck beneath a covering layer of flux. This increases arc quality, since contaminants in the atmosphere are blocked by the flux. The slag that forms on the weld generally comes off by itself and combined with the use of a continuous wire feed, the weld deposition rate is high. Working conditions are much improved over other arc welding processes, since the flux hides the arc and almost no smoke is produced. The process is commonly used in industry, especially for large products and in the manufacture of welded pressure vessels. Other arc welding processes include atomic hydrogen welding, electroslag welding (ESW), electrogas welding and stud arc welding. ESW is a highly productive, single pass welding process for thicker materials between 1 inch (25 mm) and 12 inches (300 mm) in a vertical or close to vertical position.

Gas Welding

The most common gas welding process is oxyfuel welding, also known as oxyacetylene welding. It is one of the oldest and most versatile welding processes, but in recent years it has become less popular in industrial applications. It is still widely used for welding pipes and tubes, as well as repair work.

The equipment is relatively inexpensive and simple, generally employing the combustion of acetylene in oxygen to produce a welding flame temperature of about 3100 °C (5600 °F). The flame, since it is less concentrated than an electric arc, causes slower weld cooling, which can lead to greater residual stresses and weld distortion, though it eases the welding of high alloy steels. A similar process, generally called oxyfuel cutting, is used to cut metals.

Resistance

Resistance welding involves the generation of heat by passing current through the resistance caused by the contact between two or more metal surfaces. Small pools of molten metal are formed at the weld area as high current (1000–100,000 A) is passed through the metal. In general, resistance welding methods are efficient and cause little pollution, but their applications are somewhat limited and the equipment cost can be high.

Spot welder.

Spot welding is a popular resistance welding method used to join overlapping metal sheets of up to 3 mm thick. Two electrodes are simultaneously used to clamp the metal sheets together and to pass current through the sheets. The advantages of the method include efficient energy use, limited workpiece deformation, high production rates, easy automation and no required filler materials. Weld strength is significantly lower than with other welding methods, making the process suitable for only certain applications. It is used extensively in the automotive industry—ordinary cars can have several thousand spot welds made by industrial robots. A specialized process, called shot welding, can be used to spot weld stainless steel.

Like spot welding, seam welding relies on two electrodes to apply pressure and current to join metal sheets. However, instead of pointed electrodes, wheel-shaped electrodes roll along and often feed the workpiece, making it possible to make long continuous welds. In the past, this process was used in the manufacture of beverage cans, but now its uses are more limited. Other resistance welding methods include butt welding, flash welding, projection welding and upset welding.

Energy Beam

Energy beam welding methods, namely laser beam welding and electron beam welding, are relatively new processes that have become quite popular in high production applications. The two processes are quite similar, differing most notably in their source of power. Laser beam welding employs a highly focused laser beam, while electron beam welding is done in a vacuum and uses an electron beam. Both have a very high energy density, making deep weld penetration possible and minimizing the size of the weld area. Both processes are extremely fast and are easily automated, making them highly productive. The primary disadvantages are their very high equipment costs (though these are decreasing) and a susceptibility to thermal cracking. Developments in this area include laser-hybrid welding, which uses principles from both laser beam welding and arc welding for even better weld properties, laser cladding and x-ray welding.

Solid-state

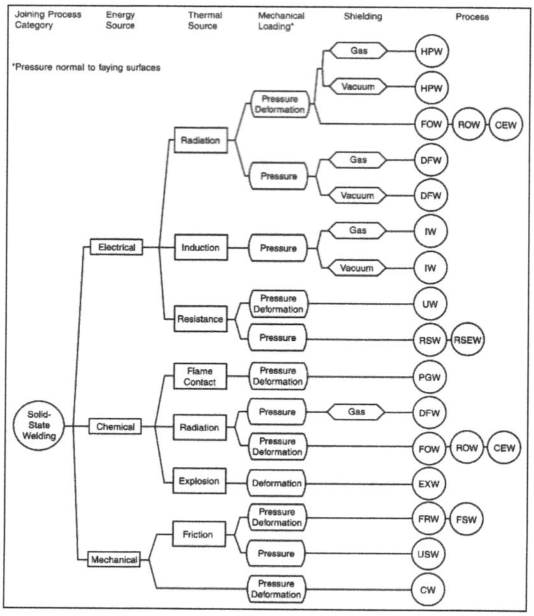

Like the first welding process, forge welding, some modern welding methods do not involve the melting of the materials being joined. One of the most popular, ultrasonic welding, is used to connect thin sheets or wires made of metal or thermoplastic by vibrating them at high frequency and under high pressure. The equipment and methods involved are similar to that of resistance welding, but instead of electric current, vibration provides energy input. Welding metals with this process does not involve melting the materials; instead, the weld is formed by introducing mechanical vibrations horizontally under pressure. When welding plastics, the materials should have similar melting temperatures and the vibrations are introduced vertically. Ultrasonic welding is commonly used for making electrical connections out of aluminum or copper and it is also a very common polymer welding process.

Another common process, explosion welding, involves the joining of materials by pushing them together under extremely high pressure. The energy from the impact plasticizes the materials, forming a weld, even though only a limited amount of heat is generated. The process is commonly used for welding dissimilar materials, including bonding aluminum to carbon steel in ship hulls and stainless steel or titanium to carbon steel in petrochemical pressure vessels.

Other solid-state welding processes include friction welding (including friction stir welding), magnetic pulse welding, co-extrusion welding, cold welding, diffusion bonding, exothermic welding, high frequency welding, hot pressure welding, induction welding and roll welding.

Geometry

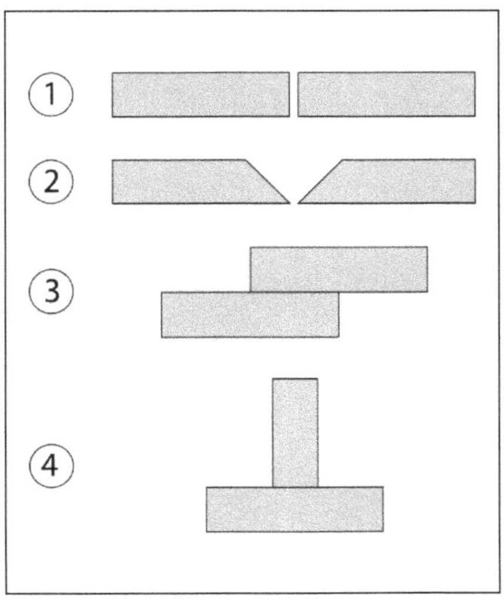

Common welding joint types – (1) Square butt joint, (2) V butt joint, (3) Lap joint, (4) T-joint.

Welds can be geometrically prepared in many different ways. The five basic types of weld joints are the butt joint, lap joint, corner joint, edge joint and T-joint (a variant of this last is the cruciform joint). Other variations exist as well—for example, double-V preparation joints are characterized by the two pieces of material each tapering to a single center point at one-half their height. Single-U and double-U preparation joints are also fairly common—instead of having straight edges like the single-V and double-V preparation joints, they are curved, forming the shape of a U. Lap joints are also commonly more than two pieces thick—depending on the process used and the thickness of the material, many pieces can be welded together in a lap joint geometry.

Many welding processes require the use of a particular joint design; for example, resistance spot welding, laser beam welding and electron beam welding are most frequently performed on lap joints. Other welding methods, like shielded metal arc welding, are extremely versatile and can weld virtually any type of joint. Some processes can also be used to make multipass welds, in which one weld is allowed to cool and then another weld is performed on top of it. This allows for the welding of thick sections arranged in a single-V preparation joint, for example.

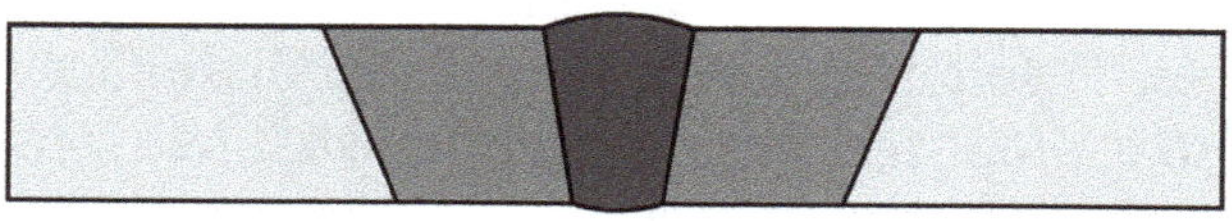

The cross-section of a welded butt joint, with the darkest gray representing the weld or fusion zone, the medium gray the heat-affected zone and the lightest gray the base material.

After welding, a number of distinct regions can be identified in the weld area. The weld itself is called the fusion zone—more specifically, it is where the filler metal was laid during the welding process. The properties of the fusion zone depend primarily on the filler metal used and its compatibility with the base materials. It is surrounded by the heat-affected zone, the area that had its microstructure and properties altered by the weld. These properties depend on the base material's behavior when subjected to heat. The metal in this area is often weaker than both the base material and the fusion zone and is also where residual stresses are found.

Glass and Plastic Welding

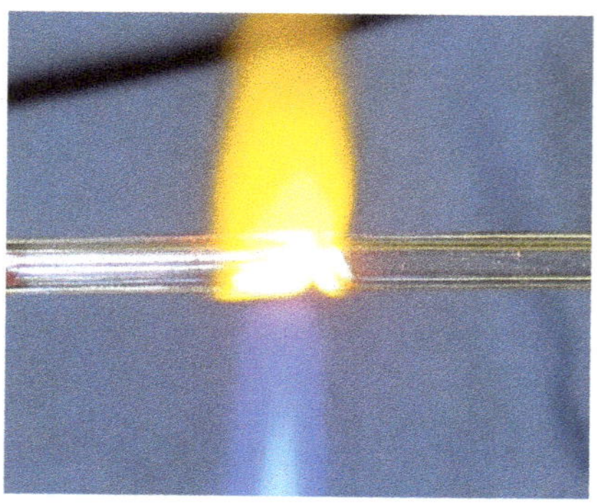

The welding together of two tubes made from lead glass.

A bowl made from cast-glass. The two halves are joined together by the weld seam, running down the middle.

Glasses and certain types of plastics are commonly welded materials. Unlike metals, which have a specific melting point, glasses and plastics have a melting range, called the glass transition. When heating the solid material past the glass-transition temperature (Tg) into this range, it will generally become softer and more pliable. When it crosses through the range, above the glass-melting temperature (Tm), it will become a very thick, sluggish, viscous liquid, slowly decreasing in viscosity as temperature increases. Typically, this viscous liquid will have very little surface tension compared to metals, becoming a sticky, taffy to honey-like consistency, so welding can usually take place by simply pressing two melted surfaces together. The two liquids will generally mix and join at first contact. Upon cooling through the glass transition, the welded piece will solidify as one solid piece of amorphous material.

Glass Welding

Glass welding is a common practice during glassblowing. It is used very often in the construction of lighting, neon signs, flashtubes, scientific equipment and the manufacture of dishes and other glassware. It is also used during glass casting for joining the halves of glass molds, making items such as bottles and jars. Welding glass is accomplished by heating the glass through the glass transition, turning it into a thick, formable, liquid mass. Heating is usually done with a gas or oxy-gas torch, or a furnace, because the temperatures for melting glass are often quite high. This temperature may vary, depending on the type of glass. For example, lead glass becomes a weldable liquid at around 1,600 °F (870 °C) and can be welded with a simple propane torch. On the other hand, quartz glass (fused silica) must be heated to over 3,000 °F (1,650 °C), but quickly loses its viscosity and formability if overheated, so an oxyhydrogen torch must be used. Sometimes a tube may be attached to the glass, allowing it to be blown into various shapes, such as bulbs, bottles, or tubes. When two pieces of liquid glass are pressed together, they will usually weld very readily. Welding a handle onto a pitcher can usually be done with relative ease. However, when welding a tube to another tube, a combination of blowing and suction and pressing and pulling is used to ensure a good seal, to shape the glass and to keep the surface tension from closing the tube in on itself. Sometimes a filler rod may be used, but usually not.

Because glass is very brittle in its solid state, it is often prone to cracking upon heating and cooling, especially if the heating and cooling are uneven. This is because the brittleness of glass does not allow for uneven thermal expansion. Glass that has been welded will usually need to be cooled very slowly and evenly through the glass transition, in a process called annealing, to relieve any internal stresses created by a temperature gradient.

There are many types of glass and it is most common to weld using the same types. Different glasses often have different rates of thermal expansion, which can cause them to crack upon cooling when they contract differently. For instance, quartz has very low thermal expansion, while soda-lime glass has very high thermal expansion. When welding different glasses to each other, it is usually important to closely match their coefficients of thermal expansion, to ensure that cracking does not occur. Also, some glasses will simply not mix with others, so welding between certain types may not be possible.

Glass can also be welded to metals and ceramics, although with metals the process is usually more adhesion to the surface of the metal rather than a commingling of the two materials. However, certain glasses will typically bond only to certain metals. For example, lead glass bonds readily to copper or molybdenum, but not to aluminum. Tungsten electrodes are often used in lighting but will not bond to quartz glass, so the tungsten is often wetted with molten borosilicate glass, which bonds to both tungsten and quartz. However, care must be taken to ensure that all materials have similar coefficients of thermal expansion to prevent cracking both when the object cools and when it is heated again. Special alloys are often used for this purpose, ensuring that the coefficients of expansion match and sometimes thin, metallic coatings may be applied to a metal to create a good bond with the glass.

Plastic Welding

Plastics are generally divided into two categories, which are "thermosets" and "thermoplastics." A thermoset is a plastic in which a chemical reaction sets the molecular bonds after first forming the plastic and then the bonds cannot be broken again without degrading the plastic. Thermosets cannot be melted, therefore, once a thermoset has set it is impossible to weld it. Examples of thermosets include epoxies, silicone, vulcanized rubber, polyester and polyurethane.

Thermoplastics, by contrast, form long molecular chains, which are often coiled or intertwined, forming an amorphous structure without any long-range, crystalline order. Some thermoplastics may be fully amorphous, while others have a partially crystalline/partially amorphous structure. Both amorphous and semicrystalline thermoplastics have a glass transition, above which welding can occur, but semicrystallines also have a specific melting point which is above the glass transition. Above this melting point, the viscous liquid will become a free-flowing liquid. Examples of thermoplastics include polyethylene, polypropylene, polystyrene, polyvinylchloride (PVC) and fluoroplastics like Teflon and Spectralon.

Welding thermoplastic is very similar to welding glass. The plastic first must be cleaned and then heated through the glass transition, turning the weld-interface into a thick, viscous liquid. Two heated interfaces can then be pressed together, allowing the molecules to mix through intermolecular diffusion, joining them as one. Then the plastic is cooled through the glass transition, allowing the weld to solidify. A filler rod may often be used for certain types of joints. The main differences between welding glass and plastic are the types of heating methods, the much lower melting temperatures and the fact that plastics will burn if overheated. Many different methods have been devised for heating plastic to a weldable temperature without burning it. Ovens or electric heating tools can be used to melt the plastic. Ultrasonic, laser, or friction heating are other methods. Resistive metals may be implanted in the plastic, which respond to induction heating. Some plastics will begin to burn at temperatures lower than their glass transition, so welding can be performed by blowing a heated, inert gas onto the plastic, melting it while, at the same time, shielding it from oxygen.

Many thermoplastics can also be welded using chemical solvents. When placed in contact with the plastic, the solvent will begin to soften it, bringing the surface into a thick, liquid solution. When two melted surfaces are pressed together, the molecules in the solution mix, joining them as one. Because the solvent can permeate the plastic, the solvent evaporates out through the surface of the plastic, causing the weld to drop out of solution and solidify. A common use for solvent welding is for joining PVC or ABS (acrylonitrile butadiene styrene) pipes during plumbing, or for welding styrene and polystyrene plastics in the construction of models. Solvent welding is especially effective on plastics like PVC which burn at or below their glass transition, but may be ineffective on plastics like Teflon or polyethylene that are resistant to chemical decomposition.

Embroidery

Gold embroidery on an *gognots* (apron).

Embroidery is the craft of decorating fabric or other materials using a needle to apply thread or yarn. Embroidery may also incorporate other materials such as pearls, beads, quills and sequins. In modern days, embroidery is usually seen on caps, hats, coats, blankets, dress shirts, denim, dresses, stockings and golf shirts. Embroidery is available with a wide variety of thread or yarn color.

Some of the basic techniques or stitches of the earliest embroidery are chain stitch, buttonhole or blanket stitch, running stitch, satin stitch, cross stitch. Those stitches remain the fundamental techniques of hand embroidery today.

Classification

Decorated Easter eggs. Works by Inna Forostyuk, the folk master from the Luhansk region.

Japanese free embroidery in silk and metal threads, contemporary.

Embroidery can be classified according to what degree the design takes into account the nature of the base material and by the relationship of stitch placement to the fabric. The main categories are free or surface embroidery, counted embroidery and needlepoint or canvas work.

In free or surface embroidery, designs are applied without regard to the weave of the underlying fabric. Examples include crewel and traditional Chinese and Japanese embroidery.

Counted-thread embroidery patterns are created by making stitches over a predetermined number of threads in the foundation fabric. Counted-thread embroidery is more easily worked on an even-weave foundation fabric such as embroidery canvas, aida cloth, or specially woven cotton and linen fabrics. Examples include cross-stitch and some forms of blackwork embroidery.

While similar to counted thread in regards to technique, in canvas work or needlepoint, threads are stitched through a fabric mesh to create a dense pattern that completely covers the foundation fabric. Examples of canvas work include bargello and Berlin wool work.

Embroidery can also be classified by the similarity of appearance. In drawn thread work and cutwork, the foundation fabric is deformed or cut away to create holes that are then embellished with embroidery, often with thread in the same color as the foundation fabric. When created with white thread on white linen or cotton, this work is collectively referred to as whitework. However, whitework can either be counted or free. Hardanger embroidery is a counted embroidery and the designs are often geometric. Conversely, styles such as Broderie anglaise are similar to free embroidery, with floral or abstract designs that are not dependent on the weave of the fabric.

Tea-cloth.

Materials

Phulkari from the Punjab region of India. Phulkari embroidery, is traditionally done on hand-spun cotton cloth with simple darning stitches using silk floss.

Laid threads, a surface technique in wool on linen. The Bayeux Tapestry.

The fabrics and yarns used in traditional embroidery vary from place to place. Wool, linen and silk have been in use for thousands of years for both fabric and yarn. Today, embroidery thread is manufactured in cotton, rayon and novelty yarns as well as in traditional wool, linen and silk. Ribbon embroidery uses narrow ribbon in silk or silk/organza blend ribbon, most commonly to create floral motifs.

Surface embroidery techniques such as chain stitch and couching or laid-work are the most economical of expensive yarns; couching is generally used for goldwork. Canvas work techniques, in which large amounts of yarn are buried on the back of the work, use more materials but provide a sturdier and more substantial finished textile.

In both canvas work and surface embroidery an embroidery hoop or frame can be used to stretch the material and ensure even stitching tension that prevents pattern distortion. Modern canvas work tends to follow symmetrical counted stitching patterns with designs emerging from the repetition of one or just a few similar stitches in a variety of hues. In contrast, many forms of surface embroidery make use of a wide range of stitching patterns in a single piece of work.

Machine

Commercial machine embroidery in chain stitch on a voile curtain, China.

Contemporary embroidery is stitched with a computerized embroidery machine using patterns digitized with embroidery software. In machine embroidery, different types of "fills" add texture and design to the finished work. Machine embroidery is used to add logos and monograms to business shirts or jackets, gifts and team apparel as well as to decorate household linens, draperies and decorator fabrics that mimic the elaborate hand embroidery of the past.

Machine embroidery is most typically done with rayon thread, although polyester thread can also be used. Cotton thread, on the other hand, is prone to breaking and should be avoided if under 30 wt.

Traditional Bulgarian Floral embrodery from Sofia and Trun.

There has also been a development in free hand machine embroidery, new machines have been designed that allow for the user to create free-motion embroidery which has its place in textile arts, quilting, dressmaking, home furnishings and more. Users can use the embroidery software to digitize the digital embroidery designs. These digitized design are then transferred to the embroidery machine with the help of a flash drive and then the embroidery machine embroiders the selected design onto the fabric.

Resurgence of Hand Embroidery

In the last couple of years there has been an exponential growth in the popularity of embroidering by hand. As a result of visual media such as Pinterest and Instagram, artists are able to share their work more extensively, which has inspired younger generations to pick up needle and threads.

Contemporary embroidery artists believe hand embroidery has grown in popularity as a result of an increasing need for relaxation and digitally disconnecting practises. Along with technological advancements and social media, people are getting more aware of the need for digital detox and hand embroidery (just like other hand work such as knitting and crocheting) allows for that.

Modern hand embroidery, as opposed to cross-stitching, is characterised by a more "liberal" approach. Where stitches are more freely combined in unconventional ways to create various textures and designs.

Qualifications

City and Guilds qualification in embroidery allows embroiderers to become recognized for their skill. This qualification also gives them the credibility to teach. For example, the notable textiles artist, Kathleen Laurel Sage, began her teaching career by getting the City and Guilds Embroidery 1 and 2 qualifications. She has now gone on to write a book on the subject.

Machine Embroidery

Commercial machine embroidery in chain stitch on a voile curtain.

Machine embroidery is an embroidery process whereby a sewing machine or embroidery machine is used to create patterns on textiles. It is used commercially in product branding, corporate advertising and uniform adornment. It is also used in the fashion industry to decorate garments and apparel. Machine embroidery is used by hobbyists and crafters to decorate gifts, clothing and home decor. Examples include designs on quilts, pillows and wall hangings.

There are multiple types of machine embroidery. Free-motion sewing machine embroidery uses a basic zigzag sewing machine. Designs are done manually. Most commercial embroidery is done with link stitch embroidery. In link stitch embroidery, patterns may be manually or automatically controlled. Link Stitch embroidery is also known as chenille embroidery and was patented by Pulse Microsystems in 1994. More modern computerized machine embroidery uses an embroidery machine or sewing/embroidery machine that is controlled with a computer that embroiders stored patterns. These machines may have multiple heads and threads.

Free-motion Machine Embroidery

In free-motion machine embroidery, embroidered designs are created by using a basic zigzag sewing machine. As this type of machine is used primarily for tailoring, it lacks the automated features of a specialized machine.

To create free-motion machine embroidery, the embroiderer runs the machine and skillfully moves tightly hooped fabric under the needle to create a design. The "feed dogs" or machine teeth are lowered or covered and the embroiderer moves the fabric manually. The embroiderer develops the embroidery manually, using the machine's settings for running stitch and fancier built-in stitches. In this way, the stitches form an image on a piece of fabric. An embroiderer can produce a filled-in effect by sewing many parallel rows of straight stitching. A machine's zigzag stitch can create thicker lines within a design or be used to create a border. Many quilters and fabric artists use a process called thread drawing (or thread painting) to create embellishments on their projects or to create textile art.

Free-motion machine embroidery can be time-consuming. Since a standard sewing machine has only one needle, the operator must pause to re-thread the machine manually for each subsequent color in a multi-color design. He or she must also manually trim and clean up loose or connecting threads after the design is completed.

As this is a manual process rather than a digital reproduction, any pattern created using free-motion machine embroidery is unique and cannot be exactly reproduced, unlike with computerized embroidery.

With the advent of computerized machine embroidery, the main use of manual machine embroidery is in fiber art and quilting projects. Though some manufacturers still use manual embroidery to embellish garments, many prefer computerized embroidery's ease and reduced costs.

Computerized Machine Embroidery

Most modern embroidery machines are computer controlled and specifically engineered for embroidery. Industrial and commercial embroidery machines and combination sewing-embroidery machines have a hooping or framing system that holds the framed area of fabric taut under the sewing needle and moves it automatically to create a design from a pre-programmed digital embroidery pattern.

Depending on its capabilities, the machine will require varying degrees of user input to read and sew embroidery designs. Sewing-embroidery machines generally have only one needle and require the user to change thread colors during the embroidery process. Multi-needle industrial machines are generally threaded prior to running the design and do not require re-threading. These machines require the user to input the correct color change sequence before beginning to embroider. Some can trim and change colors automatically.

A multi-needle machine may consist of multiple sewing heads, each of which can sew the same design onto a separate garment concurrently. Such a machine might have 20 or more heads, each consisting of 15 or more needles. A head is usually capable of producing many special fabric effects, including satin stitch embroidery, chain stitch embroidery, sequins, appliqué and cutwork.

The Computerized Machine Embroidery Process

Machine embroidery is a multi-step process with many variables that impact the quality of the final product, including the type of fabric to be embellished, design size, stabilizer choice and type of thread utilized. The basic steps for creating embroidery with a computerized embroidery machine are as follows:

- Create an embroidery *design* file or purchase a stitchable machine embroidery file. Creation may take hours depending on the complexity of the design and the software can be costly.
- Edit the design and combine with other designs.
- Export the design file to a (proprietary machine) embroidery file that mostly just contains commands for the embroidery machine. If you bought such a file, you may have to convert the file.
- Load the embroidery file into the embroidery machine, making sure it is the correct format for the machine and that the stitched design will fit in the appropriate hoop.
- Determine and mark the location of embroidery placement on the fabric to be embellished.
- Secure the fabric in a hoop with the appropriate stabilizer and place it on the machine.
- Center the needle over the start point of the design.
- Start and monitor the embroidery machine, watching for errors and issues. Troubleshoot any problems as they arise. The operator should have plenty of needles, bobbins, a can of air (or small air compressor), a small brush and scissors.
- Remove the completed design from machine. Separate the fabric from the hoop and trim the stabilizer, loose threads, etc.

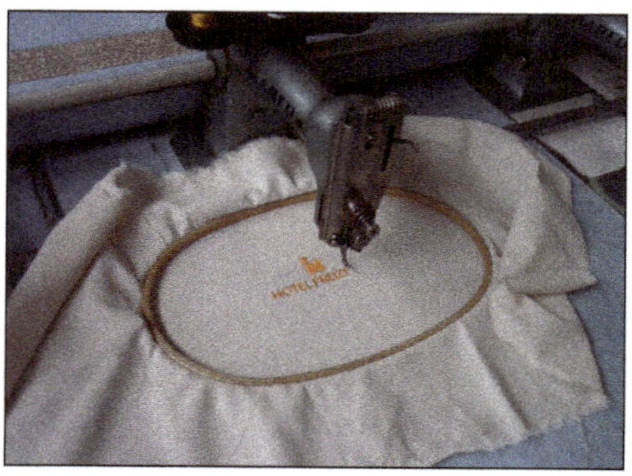

Machine embroidery in progress.

Design Files

Digitized embroidery design files can be either purchased or created with industry-specific embroidery digitizing software. Embroidery file formats broadly fall into two categories. The first, source formats, are specific to the software used to create the design. For these formats, the digitizer keeps the original file for the purposes of editing. The second, machine formats, are specific to a particular brand or model of embroidery machine, they contain primarily stitch data (offsets) and machine functions (stitch, trims, jumps, etc.) and are thus not easily scaled or edited without extensive manual work. However, because these files easy to decode, they serve as easy exchange formats, with some formats such as Tajima's .dst and Melco's .exp being so prevalent that they have effectively become industry standards and are often supported directly by machines built by rival companies, or through provided software to convert them for the machine.

Many embroidery designs can be downloaded in popular machine formats from embroidery websites. However, since not all designs are available for every machine's specific format, some machine embroiderers use conversion programs to convert from one machine's format file to another, with various degrees of reliability.

A person who creates a design is known as an embroidery digitizer or puncher. A digitizer uses software to create an object-based embroidery design, which can be easily reshaped and edited. These files retain important information such as object outlines, thread colors and original artwork used to punch the designs. When the file is converted to a stitch file, it loses much of this information, rendering editing difficult or impossible.

Software vendors often advertise auto-punching or auto-digitizing capabilities. However, if high-quality embroidery is essential, then industry experts highly recommend either purchasing solid designs from reputable digitizers or obtaining training on solid digitization techniques.

Editing Designs

Once a design has been digitized, an embroiderer can use software to edit it or combine it with other designs. Most embroidery programs allow the user to rotate, scale, move, stretch, distort, split, crop, or duplicate the design in an endless pattern. Most software allows the user to add text quickly and easily. Often the colors of the design can be changed, made monochrome, or re-sorted. More sophisticated packages allow the user to edit, add, or remove individual stitches. Some embroidery machines have rudimentary built-in design editing features.

Loading the Design

After editing the final design, the file is loaded into the embroidery machine. Different machines require different formats that are proprietary to that company. Common design file formats for the home and hobby market include .ART, .HUS, .JEF, .PES, .SEW and .VIP. Embroidery patterns can be transferred to the computerized embroidery machines through cables, CDs, floppy disks, USB interfaces, or special cards that resemble flash or compact cards.

Due to some commonality between the controllers and the software manufacturers, some of the formats are headers and additional information surrounding similarly encoded stitches. .TAP is a .DST file without the header. .EXP file stitches are very close to .JEF, .SHV and .SEW but without the surrounding data about thread color and hoop positioning. .100 is encoded in the same manner as .F01, .GT, .DSB, .DAT, .INB and .U01 but with different headers and surrounding information.

Stabilizing the Fabric

To prevent wrinkles and other problems, the fabric must be stabilized. The method of stabilizing depends on the type of machine, the fabric type and the design density. For example, knits and large designs typically require firm stabilization. There are many methods for stabilizing fabric, but most often one or more additional pieces of material called stabilizers or interfacing are added beneath or on top of the fabric, or both. Stabilizer types include cut-away, tear-away, solvy water-soluble, heat-n-gone, filmoplast and open mesh, sometimes in various combinations. Stabilizer helps to keep the embroidered piece from rubbing or irritating the skin like in left chest polo shirt designs or in children's wear.

For embroidered wearable items, the fabric is placed in a hoop. This is then attached to the machine . An X and Y drive mechanism moves the hoop under the needle following the design coordinates created when the design was digitized for embroidery.

Embroidering the Design

Bookmark of black fabric with multicolored Bedouin embroidery and tassel of embroidery floss.

Finally, the embroidery machine is started and monitored. For commercial machines, this process is more automated than for the home machines. Many designs require more than one color and may involve additional processing for appliqués, foam, or other special effects. Since home machines have only one needle, every color change requires the user to cut the thread and change the color manually. In addition, most designs have one or more jumps that need to be cut. Depending on the quality and size of the design, sewing a design file can require anywhere from a few minutes to over half a day.

Embroidery Machines

Not all machines are solely used for embroidery; some are also used for sewing. Some of the more advanced computerized embroidery machines have an array of easy to navigate features. Some of the main ones include LCD touchscreens, a USB connectivity, auto threading, built-in design editing software, embroidery adviser software and design file storage systems. Commercial embroidery machines can be purchased with a set number of needle colors per head(1, 2, 3, 4, 6, 12, 15,18 or more colors). Industrial embroidery machines are available with 1 to 56 heads.

Commercial and Contract Embroidery Factories

Factories can have a few small machines or many large machines, or any combination of machines. Contract embroidery is done on goods that the customer supplies to the embroidery house and is limited to the trade, "ASI" and marketing firms use these services almost exclusively. A company offering contract embroidery sews designs onto wearable items for brokers, other embroiderers, specialty firms and screen printers at a wholesale rates. The customer of a contract embroiderer usually supplies the items to the factory and only pays for the embroidery service.

Commercial embroiderers and some contract embroiderers, offer their services to the public and can supply the wearable items and usually have a vast collection of stock designs and text available, Keeping up with current market trends and offering names and personalization as well as designs for embroidery.

Other Supplies

Almost any type of fabric can be embroidered, given the proper stabilizer. Base materials include paper, fabric and lightweight balsa wood.

Machine embroidery commonly uses polyester, rayon, or metallic embroidery thread, though other thread types are available. 40 wt thread is the most commonly used embroidery thread weight. Bobbin thread is usually either 60 wt or 90 wt. The quality of thread used can greatly affect the number of thread breaks and other embroidery problems. Polyester thread is generally more color-safe and durable.

Other associated costs are thread, stabilizer, purchased designs, needles, bobbins and other miscellaneous tools and supplies.

Sewing Machine Operator

A sewing machine operator is a textile worker who sews fabric with an electronic sewing machine. Although many couture houses employ hand sewers to do delicate beading and embroidery, most clothing manufacturers also keep a legion of sewing machine operators on their payroll because using the machine speeds things up dramatically.

Some sewing machine operators do their work on machines identical or similar to those commonly used in domestic sewing projects; others use larger, more powerful machines that are faster and able to handle thicker fabrics easily.

Work of Sewing Machine Operator

Sewing machine operators operate, inspect and repair sewing machines. A sewing machine operator threads the machine (this is a very intricate process on many machine models), adjusts the tension settings based on the type of thread being used, selects stitch settings and then gets down to sewing. Sewing machine operators must monitor their machines for symptoms of metal fatigue or motor failure and may have to perform minor repairs on the spot. Even experienced operators occasionally make mistakes; one of the most difficult aspects of work as a sewing machine operator is catching and fixing any mistakes made.

Sewing machine operators must understand the limits of their machine. All sewing machines are not created equal; those with weaker motors cannot accommodate heavy fabrics such as denim and canvas and may break if the operator tries to force the fabric through. Needle selection is also relevant here; thicker fabrics require longer, thicker needles because they are stronger and less likely to bend or break. If the proper needle gauge and type of sewing machine are not available, the operator may have to hand-stitch the heaviest fabrics. This is time consuming, but prevents broken equipment and the injuries that may result from flying needle parts.

Sewing machine operator's duties (depending on type of job):

- Assemble pieces of garments by matching patterns and dye lots.

- Operate single, double or multi-needle serging, flat bed felling, banding and other sewing machines, to join sections of garments or other articles into finished products on a piece-work or production basis.
- Operate fur sewing machines to join fur pelt strips to required size and shape and join pelts into garment sections or shells.
- Operate stitching machines to sew leather parts together for leather garments, handbags, shoes and other leather articles.
- Operate serging machines to sew and overcast edges of material simultaneously.
- Operate tackers, pocketsetters, buttonhole makers and fusing, hemmer and other machines to perform various operations in the fabrication of garments and other articles.
- Examine garments and operate sewing machines, sergers and other machines to repair garments and other articles during the manufacturing process.
- Complete production reports.
- May perform minor maintenance and repairs on sewing machine.

Workplace

Most sewing machine operators work in the garment industry, although tough industrial sewing machines are also used to make boat sails, curtains, fabric napkins and upholstery. Sewing machine operators may also work for sewing machine manufacturers. Their experience "out in the trenches" is invaluable for companies that are developing new sewing machine models because the operators know what works, what doesn't and what they'd change if they could.

Those who specialize in altering wedding gowns often do their work in a small, cramped room in the rear of a bridal salon; others offer a broader range of alteration services and handle clothing for both women and men. Sewing machine operators who work for large clothing manufacturers often work in a huge warehouse environment, where the focus is on churning out garments as quickly as possible.

If a sewing machine operator prefers creating and altering theatrical costumes, he or she can expect to set up shop in a long string of temporary locations. These operators must often bring their own sewing machine with them and are given work space in the basement of a theatre or opera house. In this type of environment, the sewing machine operator must be able to think quickly, block out distractions and work under extremely short deadlines. Some sewing machine operators specialize in costumes for dancers and figure skaters; athletic costumes must be durable, comfortable, have an attractive appearance and must also not interfere with the athlete's movements.

Permissions

All chapters in this book are published with permission under the Creative Commons Attribution Share Alike License or equivalent. Every chapter published in this book has been scrutinized by our experts. Their significance has been extensively debated. The topics covered herein carry significant information for a comprehensive understanding. They may even be implemented as practical applications or may be referred to as a beginning point for further studies.

We would like to thank the editorial team for lending their expertise to make the book truly unique. They have played a crucial role in the development of this book. Without their invaluable contributions this book wouldn't have been possible. They have made vital efforts to compile up to date information on the varied aspects of this subject to make this book a valuable addition to the collection of many professionals and students.

This book was conceptualized with the vision of imparting up-to-date and integrated information in this field. To ensure the same, a matchless editorial board was set up. Every individual on the board went through rigorous rounds of assessment to prove their worth. After which they invested a large part of their time researching and compiling the most relevant data for our readers.

The editorial board has been involved in producing this book since its inception. They have spent rigorous hours researching and exploring the diverse topics which have resulted in the successful publishing of this book. They have passed on their knowledge of decades through this book. To expedite this challenging task, the publisher supported the team at every step. A small team of assistant editors was also appointed to further simplify the editing procedure and attain best results for the readers.

Apart from the editorial board, the designing team has also invested a significant amount of their time in understanding the subject and creating the most relevant covers. They scrutinized every image to scout for the most suitable representation of the subject and create an appropriate cover for the book.

The publishing team has been an ardent support to the editorial, designing and production team. Their endless efforts to recruit the best for this project, has resulted in the accomplishment of this book. They are a veteran in the field of academics and their pool of knowledge is as vast as their experience in printing. Their expertise and guidance has proved useful at every step. Their uncompromising quality standards have made this book an exceptional effort. Their encouragement from time to time has been an inspiration for everyone.

The publisher and the editorial board hope that this book will prove to be a valuable piece of knowledge for students, practitioners and scholars across the globe.

Index

CPSIA information can be obtained
at www.ICGtesting.com
Printed in the USA
LVHW062024100122
708212LV00002B/425

9 781641 726504